SOLIDWORKS 2019
Learn by doing

Tutorial Books

SOLIDWORKS 2019 Learn by doing

Copyright@2019

This book may not be duplicated in any way without the express written consent of the publisher, except in the form of brief excerpts or quotations for the purpose of review. The information contained herein is for the personal use of the reader and may not be incorporated in any commercial programs, other books, database, or any kind of software without written consent of the publisher. Making copies of this book or any portion for purpose other than your own is a violation of copyright laws.

Limit of Liability/Disclaimer of Warranty:

The author and publisher make no representations or warranties with respect to the accuracy or completeness of the contents of this work and specifically disclaim all warranties, including without limitation warranties of fitness for a particular purpose. The advice and strategies contained herein may not be suitable for every situation. Neither the publisher nor the author shall be liable for damages arising here from.

Trademarks:

All brand names and product names used in this book are trademarks, registered trademarks, or trade names of their respective holders. The author and publisher are not associated with any product or vendor mentioned in this book.

Download resource files

http://www.tutorialbook.info/solidworks-2019-learn-by-doing/

SOLIDWORKS 2019 Learn by doing

Table of Contents

Chapter 1: Getting Started 1
    Starting SOLIDWORKS 3
    User Interface 5
        Quick Access Toolbar 5
        Menu 5
        CommandManager 6
        Features tab 6
        Evaluate tab 6
        Sketch tab 6
        Assemble tab 6
        Drawing Environment tabs 6
        Sheet Metal tab 7
        FeatureManager Design Tree 7
        Status bar 7
        View (Heads Up) Toolbar 7
        Shortcut Menus 8
        PropertyManager 8
        Breadcrumbs 9
    Mouse Functions 10
    Customizing the CommandManager, Shortcut Bars, and Menus 11
        Customizing the Mouse Gestures 11
    Changing the Background Color 13

Chapter 2: Modeling Basics 15
    TUTORIAL 1 15
        Opening a New Part File 16
        Starting a Sketch 16
        Adding Dimensions 17
        Constructing the Base Feature 18
        Adding an Extruded Feature 18
        Adding another Extruded Feature 21
        Saving the Part 24
    TUTORIAL 2 25
        Opening a New Part File 26
        Sketching a Revolve Profile 26
        Constructing the Revolved Boss 28
        Constructing the Cut feature 29
        Constructing another Cut feature 30
        Adding a Fillet 32
        Viewing Parent and Child relationships between features 33
        Saving the Part 34
    TUTORIAL 3 34
        Opening a New Part File 34
        Constructing the Cylindrical Feature 34

  Constructing Cut feature 35
  Saving and Closing the Part 36
 TUTORIAL 4 36
  Applying Draft 37
  Saving and Closing the Part 37

Chapter 3: Assembly Basics 39
 TUTORIAL 1 39
  Opening a New Assembly File 39
  Inserting the Base Component 39
  Adding the second component 40
  Applying Mates 40
  Adding the Third Component 44
  Checking the Interference 47
  Saving the Assembly 47
  Starting the Main assembly 47
  Adding Disc to the Assembly 47
  Placing the Sub-assembly 48
  Adding Constraints 48
  Placing the second instance of the Sub-assembly 49
  Saving the Assembly 51
 TUTORIAL 2 51
 Creating the Exploded View 51
  Creating Explode lines 52

Chapter 4: Creating Drawings 57
 TUTORIAL 1 57
  Opening a New Drawing File 58
  Generating the Base View 58
  Creating the Section View 59
  Creating the Detailed View 59
  Creating the Centerline 61
  Specifying Dimension Settings 61
  Retrieving Dimensions 62
  Adding additional dimensions 63
  Saving the Drawing 64
 TUTORIAL 2 64
  Creating a Custom Sheet Format 64
  Starting a New drawing 66
  Generating the Drawing Views 67
 TUTORIAL 3 68
  Creating the Isometric View 68
  Generating the Exploded View 68
  Creating the Bill of Materials 69
  Creating Balloons 70
  Adding Comments to the Drawing 70

Chapter 5: Sketching 73

- Creating Rectangles 73
- Creating Polygons 75
- Relations 76
  - Merge 76
  - Horizontal 76
  - Vertical 77
  - Tangent 77
  - Parallel 77
  - Perpendicular 77
  - Midpoint 77
  - Automatic Relations 77
  - Deleting Relations 79
  - Hiding Relations 80
- Sketch Numeric Input 80
- Replace Entity 80
- Make Path 83
- Path Length Dimension 83
- Convert Entities 84
- Midpoint line, Perimeter Circle, and SketchXpert 85
- Ellipses 87
- Partial Ellipse 88
- Conic 89
- Move and Rotate Entities 89
- Rotate Entities 90
- Copy Entities 90
- Scale Entities 91
- Trim Entities 92
- Extend Entities 94
- Offset Entities 95
- TUTORIAL 1 95
- Sketch Fillet 95
- Sketch Chamfer 96
- Mirror Entities 97
- Stretch Entities 98
- Circular Sketch Pattern 98
- 3D Sketch 101
  - Mirroring Entities in a 3D Sketch 102
- The Slicing command 103
- Generic Splines 104

Chapter 6: Additional Modeling Tools 107
- TUTORIAL 1 107
  - Constructing the Helix 108
  - Adding the Reference Plane 108
  - Constructing the Swept feature 109
- TUTORIAL 2 111

SOLIDWORKS 2019 Learn by doing

- Constructing a Revolved Cut 112
- Constructing a Mirror Feature 113
- TUTORIAL 3 114
  - Creating Sections and Guide curves 114
  - Creating another section 115
  - Constructing the swept feature 116
  - Constructing the Extruded feature 117
  - Adding Fillets 117
  - Shelling the Model 118
  - Adding the Indent feature 118
  - Adding Threads 121
- TUTORIAL 4 126
  - Constructing a cylindrical shell 127
  - Adding a Slot 127
  - Constructing the Axis 128
  - Constructing the Linear pattern 128
  - Constructing the Circular pattern 129
- TUTORIAL 5 130
  - Constructing the first feature 130
  - Constructing the Second Feature 130
  - Constructing the third feature 130
  - Inserting Holes 131
  - Adding Chamfers 132
  - Creating Bounding Box 133
- TUTORIAL 6 133
  - Constructing the first feature 134
  - Constructing the Extruded cut 134
  - Making the Curve Driven Pattern 135
- TUTORIAL 7 136
  - Start a new part file 136
  - Creating the second feature 136
  - Adding Cosmetic Threads 137
  - Creating Configurations Table 137
- TUTORIAL 8 139
  - Creating the First Feature 139
  - Creating the Extruded surface 140
  - Replacing the top face of the model with the surface 140
  - Creating a Face fillet 141
  - Creating a Variable Radius fillet 141
  - Shelling the Model 142
  - Creating the Mounting Bosses 143
  - Creating the Vent Feature 145
  - Creating the Wrap Feature 145
- TUTORIAL 9 146
- TUTORIAL 10 149

Chapter 7: Sheet metal Modeling 151
TUTORIAL 1 151
- Opening a New File 152
- Constructing the Base Flange 152
- Adding an Edge flange 152
- Constructing the Miter Flange 153
- Closing the Corners 155
- Adding Corner Reliefs 155
- Adding a Tab feature 156
- Adding a Jog 157
- Unfolding the bends 158
- Creating Cuts across bends 158
- Folding the Unfolded bends 158
- Performing the Forming Operations 159
- Making the Linear Pattern 160
- Adding a Hem 160
- Adding a vent 161
- Adding Sheet Metal Gussets 161
- Making a Fill Pattern 162
- View the Flat Pattern 164
TUTORIAL 2 164
TUTORIAL 3 165
TUTORIAL 4 167
TUTORIAL 5 169
TUTORIAL 6 172
TUTORIAL 7 173
TUTORIAL 8 174

Chapter 8: Top-Down Assembly 179
TUTORIAL 1 179
- Creating a New Assembly File 179
- Creating a component in the Assembly 179
- Creating the Second Component of the Assembly 181
- Creating the third Component of the Assembly 182
- Adding Bolt Connections to the assembly 183
- Patterning components in an assembly 186
- Sectioning an Assembly with Transparency 186
TUTORIAL 2 187
- Creating Smart Mates 188
- Creating the Limit Mate 189
- Creating the Slot Mate 190

Chapter 9: Dimensions and Annotations 193
TUTORIAL 1 193
- Creating a Model View with Center Marks 194
- Creating Centerlines and Center Marks 195

Editing the Hatch Pattern 196
　　Emphasizing the Outline of the Section View 196
　　Applying Dimensions 197
　　Placing the Datum Feature 201
　　Placing the Feature Control Frame 201
　　Placing the Surface Texture Symbols 202

Chapter 10: Surface Design 203
　TUTORIAL 1 (Extruded Surfaces) 203
　TUTORIAL 2 (Revolved Surfaces) 203
　TUTORIAL 3 (Swept Surfaces) 204
　TUTORIAL 4 (Lofted Surfaces) 205
　TUTORIAL 5 (Planar Surfaces) 206
　TUTORIAL 6 (Creating a Ruled Surface using the Tangent to Surface option) 207
　TUTORIAL 7 (Creating a Ruled Surface using the Normal to Surface option) 208
　TUTORIAL 8 (Creating a Ruled Surface using the Tapered to Vector option) 209
　TUTORIAL 9 (Creating a Ruled Surface using the Perpendicular to Vector option) 209
　TUTORIAL 10 (Creating a Ruled Surface using the Sweep option) 210
　TUTORIAL 11 (Offset Surface) 210
　TUTORIAL 12 (Knitting Surfaces) 211
　　Creating a Solid by Knitting Surfaces 212
　TUTORIAL 13 (Trimming Surfaces) 212
　　Trimming a Surface using the Standard option 212
　　Trimming Surfaces using the Mutual option 213
　TUTORIAL 14 (Extending Surfaces) 214
　TUTORIAL 15 (Offset on Surface) 215
　TUTORIAL 16 (Untrimming a Surface) 217
　TUTORIAL 17 (Deleting Holes) 218
　TUTORIAL 18 (Filled Surface) 219
　TUTORIAL 19 220
　TUTORIAL 20 (Converting a Surface to Solid) 221
　TUTORIAL 21 (Thickening the Surface) 222
　TUTORIAL 22 (Deleting Faces) 223
　TUTORIAL 23 (Replacing Faces) 224
　TUTORIAL 24 (Cutting with Surfaces) 225
　TUTORIAL 25 (Thickened Cut) 225
　TUTORIAL 26 (Freeform Surfaces) 226
　TUTORIAL 27 (Boundary Surfaces) 230
　TUTORIAL 28 (Flatten Surface) 232

Chapter 11: Mold Tools 235
　TUTORIAL 1 235
　　Performing Draft Analysis 235
　　Applying Shrinkage allowance 236
　　Inserting Mold Folders 237
　　Creating a Parting Line 237
　　Creating Shut-off Surfaces 238

  Creating Parting Surfaces...239
  Creating the Tooling Split..240
  Performing the Undercut analysis...241
  Creating side cores..242
  Creating your own surfaces...243

Chapter 12: Weldments 247
 TUTORIAL 1..247
 TUTORIAL 2..251
  Adding Structural members 253
  Trimming the Structural Members 255
  Creating Gussets...256
  Creating Base Plates 258
  Mirroring Gussets and Base plates 258
  Creating Fillet Beads 260
  Creating Weld Beads...260
 TUTORIAL 3 (Creating End Caps) 264
 TUTORIAL 4 (Working with Cut lists) 266
  Adding Cut list to the Weldment Drawing 267
  Adding Columns to the Cut list table 269
  Creating Bounding box..269
  Adding a Weld table to the Weldment Drawing 270
  Adding a Weld Symbols..270
  Creating Sub Weldments...271
 TUTORIAL 5 (Creating Custom Profiles for structural members) 272

Chapter 13: MBD Dimensions..275
 Geometric Dimensioning and Tolerancing..275
 TUTORIAL 1 (Auto Dimension Scheme)..276
 TUTORIAL 2 (Adding the GD&T Information Manually) 278
  Adding Size Dimensions 279
  Adding Location Dimensions...280
  Adding Geometric Tolerances...280
  Adding other dimensions to Fully-define the part...282
 TUTORIAL 3 (Using the MBD Dimensions Annotations in drawings) 283
 TUTORIAL 4 (Pattern Feature) 284
 TUTORIAL 5 (DimXpert Options) 285

Chapter 14: Appearances and Rendering..289
 TUTORIAL 1 (Adding Appearances to the Complete Part) 289
 TUTORIAL 2 (Adding Appearances to Faces, Surfaces, and Features) 291
 TUTORIAL 3 (Adding Textures) 293
 TUTORIAL 4 (Texture Mapping options) 294
 TUTORIAL 5 (Surface Finish) 297
 TUTORIAL 6 (Illumination) 297
 Tutorial 7 (Scenes)..297
 TUTORIAL 8 (Rendering using PhotoView 360)..301

SOLIDWORKS 2019 Learn by doing

    Adding Cameras 302
    PhotoView 360 Options 303
TUTORIAL 9 (Lights) 304
    Editing the Ambient Light 305
TUTORIAL 10 (Working with Directional Lights) 305
TUTORIAL 11 (Working with Point Lights) 306
TUTORIAL 12 (Working with Spot Lights) 307
TUTORIAL 13 (Working with Sun Lights) 308
TUTORIAL 14 (Walk-through) 309
TUTORIAL 15 (Decals) 311
    Adding the default Decals to the Model 311
    Creating your own Decals 311

SOLIDWORKS 2019 Learn by doing

INTRODUCTION

SOLIDWORKS is a package adding a great value to enterprises. It offers a set of tools, which are easy-to-use to design, document and simulate 3D models. Using this software, you can speed up the design process and reduce the product development costs.

This book provides a systematic approach for users to learn SOLIDWORKS. It is aimed at new SOLIDWORKS users. However, users of previous versions of SOLIDWORKS may also find this book useful for them to learn the new enhancements. This book guides the user from starting a SOLIDWORKS 2019 session to constructing parts, assemblies, and drawings. Each chapter has components explained with the help of real-world models.

Scope of this book

If you are a student or engineer who is interested to learn SOLIDWORKS 2019 for mechanical design, then this book helps you to do it easily and quickly. You will also enjoy the learning process by creating real world models. In addition, if you are a graphical learner, then you will find this book very interesting.

The topics in this book include Getting Started with SOLIDWORKS 2019, Basic Part Modeling, Creating Assemblies, Creating Drawings, Additional Modeling Tools, and Sheet Metal Modeling.

Chapter 1 introduces SOLIDWORKS. The user interface and terminology are discussed in this chapter.

Chapter 2 takes you through the creation of your first SOLIDWORKS model. You create simple parts.

Chapter 3 teaches you to create assemblies. It explains the Top-down and Bottom-up approaches for designing an assembly. You create an assembly using the Bottom-up approach.

Chapter 4 teaches you to create drawings of the models created in the earlier chapters. You will also learn to place exploded views, and part list of an assembly.

Chapter 5: In this chapter, you will learn sketch tools.

Chapter 6: In this chapter, you will learn additional modeling tools to create complex models.

Chapter 7: introduces you to Sheet Metal modeling. You will create a sheet metal part using the tools available in the Sheet Metal environment.

Chapter 8: In this chapter, you will learn to create assemblies using Top-down approach and apply some advanced mates.

Chapter 9: In this chapter, you will learn to add annotations to drawings.

Chapter 10: In this chapter, you will learn Surface Modeling tools.

Chapter 11: This chapter introduces you Mold design.

Chapter 12: In this chapter, you will learn to create Weldments.

Chapter 13: In this chapter, you will learn Model based dimension tools.

Chapter 14: This chapter introduces you to Appearances and Rendering.

Chapter 1: Getting Started

In this chapter, you will learn some of the most commonly used features of SOLIDWORKS. In addition, you will learn about the user interface.

SOLIDWORKS is a parametric and feature-based system that allows you to create 3D parts, assemblies, and 2D drawings. The following figure shows the design process in SOLIDWORKS.

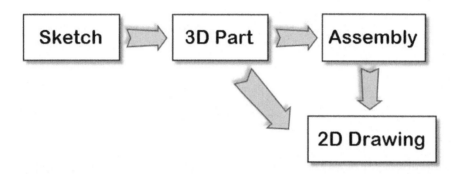

In SOLIDWORKS, you create parts by combining features.

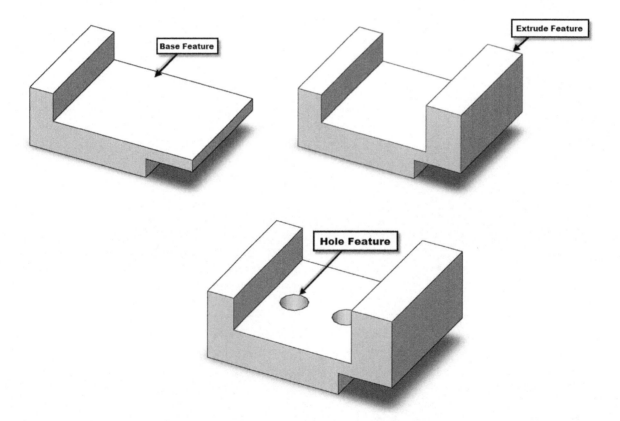

Features are of two types: sketch-based and placed. You create a sketch-based feature by drawing a sketch and extruding, revolving, sweeping along a path, or lofting it.

SOLIDWORKS 2019 Learn by doing

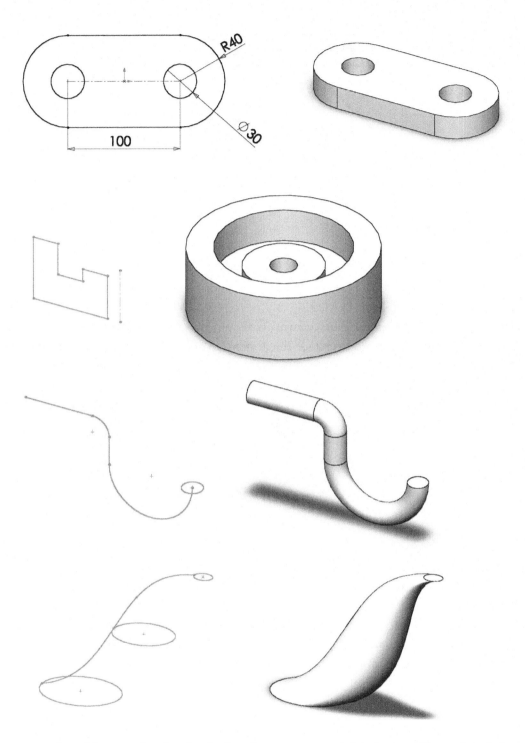

You create placed features by simply placing them onto an existing feature. Examples of placed features are fillets, chamfers, drafts, shells, holes and so on.

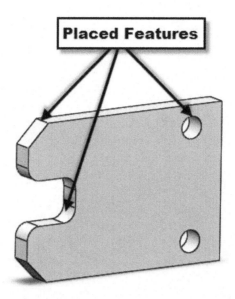

In SOLIDWORKS, parameters, dimensions, or relations control everything. For example, if you want to change the position of the hole shown in figure, you need to change the dimension or relation that controls its position.

 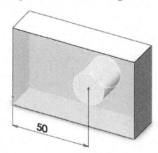 

Starting SOLIDWORKS

- Type Solidworks in the search bar located on the taskbar.
- Select SOLIDWORKS 2019 from the search results; the SOLIDWORKS 2019 application window appears along with the Welcome window.
- Click the **New** button on the Quick Access Toolbar; the **Units and Dimension Standard** dialog appears.
- On the **Units and Dimension Standard** dialog, select **MMGS (millimeter, gram, second)** and **ANSI** from the **Units** and **Dimension Standard** drop-downs, respectively.

SOLIDWORKS 2019 Learn by doing

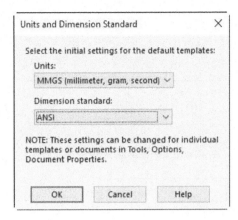

- Click **OK** on the **Units and Dimension Standard** drop-down.
- On the **New SOLIDWORKS Document** dialog, click **Part**.

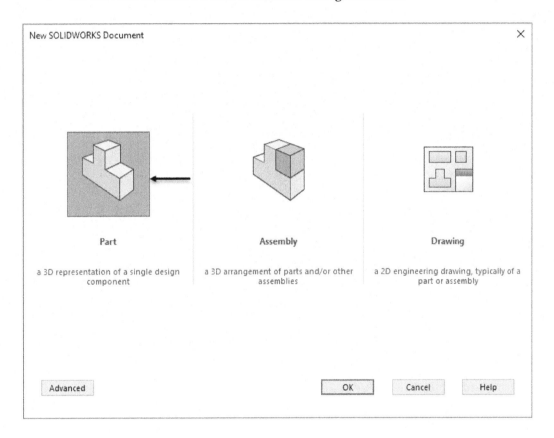

- Click **OK** button.

Notice these important features of the SOLIDWORKS window.

SOLIDWORKS 2019 Learn by doing

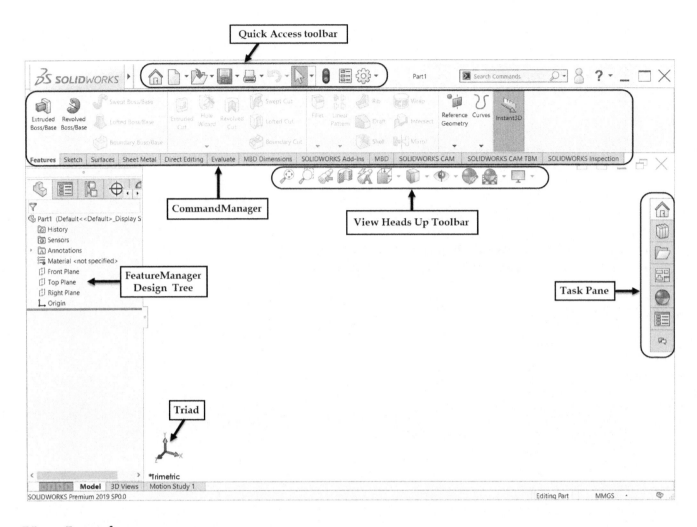

User Interface

The following sections explain various components of the user interface.

Quick Access Toolbar

This is available at the top of the window. It contains the tools such as **New**, **Save**, **Open** and so on.

Menu

Menu is located at the top of the window. You can display it by placing the pointer on the arrow located at the top left corner. It has various options (menu titles). When you click on a menu title, a drop-down appears. Select any option from this drop-down.

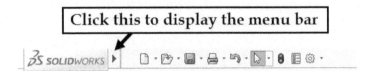

SOLIDWORKS 2019 Learn by doing

CommandManager

CommandManager is located below the menu. It consists of various tabs. When you click on a tab, a set of tools appear. You can select the required tool from the tab. The following sections explain the CommandManager tabs available in SOLIDWORKS.

Features tab

This CommandManager tab contains the tools to create 3D features.

Evaluate tab

This CommandManager tab has the tools to measure the objects. It also has analysis tools to analyze the draft, curvature, surface and so on.

Sketch tab

This tab contains all the sketch tools.

Assemble tab

This CommandManager tab contains the tools to create an assembly. This tab is available in an assembly document.

Drawing Environment tabs

In the Drawing Environment, you can create orthographic views of the 3D model. The CommandManager tabs in this environment contain tools to create 2D drawings.

Sheet Metal tab

Use the tools in this tab to create sheet metal components. Note that this tab is no displayed by default. You can display it by right clicking on anyone of the CommandManager tabs and selecting Sheet Metal from the menu.

FeatureManager Design Tree

This is located on the left pane of the application window. It contains the list of operations carried in a SOLIDWORKS document.

Status bar

This is available below the graphics window. It displays status of the SOLIDWORKS document. For example, if you are drawing a sketch, it displays **Editing sketch**.

View (Heads Up) Toolbar

This is located at the top of the graphics window. It contains the tools to modify the display of the model.

SOLIDWORKS 2019 Learn by doing

Shortcut Menus

When you click the right mouse button, a shortcut menu appears. A shortcut menu contains a list of some important options that can accessed very quickly.

PropertyManager

When you activate any tool in SOLIDWORKS, the PropertyManager related to it appears. It consists of various options that are part of the selected tool. The following figure shows the components of the PropertyManager.

SOLIDWORKS 2019 Learn by doing

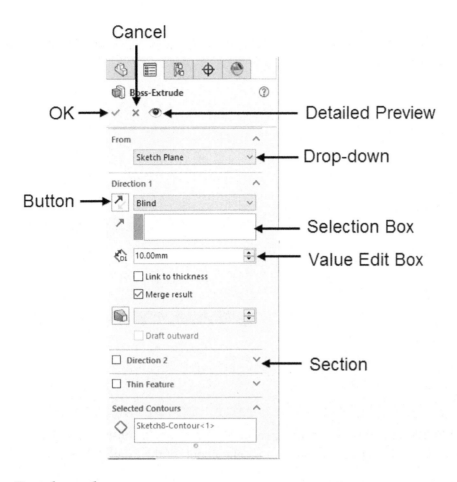

Breadcrumbs

Breadcrumbs is a useful functionality added SOLIDWORKS in recent years. Whenever you click on an item or a feature of the model geometry, the **Breadcrumbs** toolbar appears at the top left corner of the graphics window. For example, click on a face of the part geometry, as shown; the Selection Breadcrumbs toolbar appears, as shown. On the toolbar, you can select the entire part, solid body, feature or sketch related to the feature, or a face.

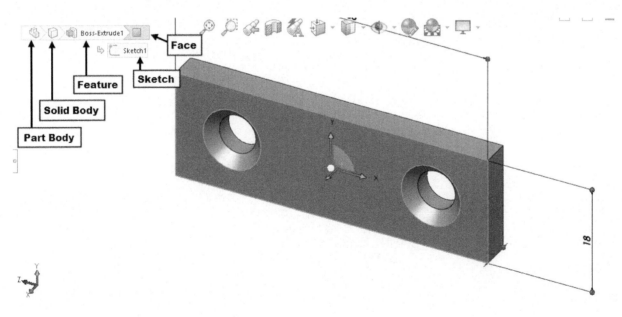

SOLIDWORKS 2019 Learn by doing

Select the feature from the Breadcrumbs toolbar and notice the options to edit the feature, suppress, hide, zoom, and so on. You can hide the left pane and use the Breadcrumbs toolbar to edit model geometry.

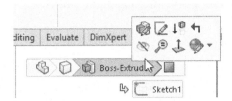

Mouse Functions

Various functions of the mouse buttons are:

Left Mouse button (MB1)

You can select an object, tool, or option using clicking the left mouse button. When you double-click the left mouse button (MB1) on an object, the dimensions related to the object appear. You can then edit the dimensions of the objects.

Middle Mouse button (MB2)

Click and drag this button to rotate the model view.

Right Mouse button (MB3)

Click this button to open a shortcut menu. Click and drag the right mouse button to display the mouse gestures.

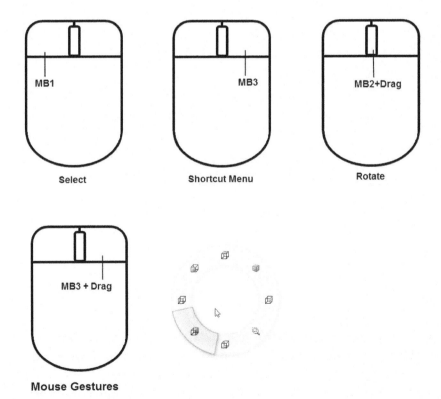

Customizing the CommandManager, Shortcut Bars, and Menus

To customize the CommandManager, shortcut keys, or menus, click **Options > Customize** on the **Quick Access Toolbar**. On the **Customize** dialog, use the tabs to customize the CommandManager or menu, or shortcut bars.

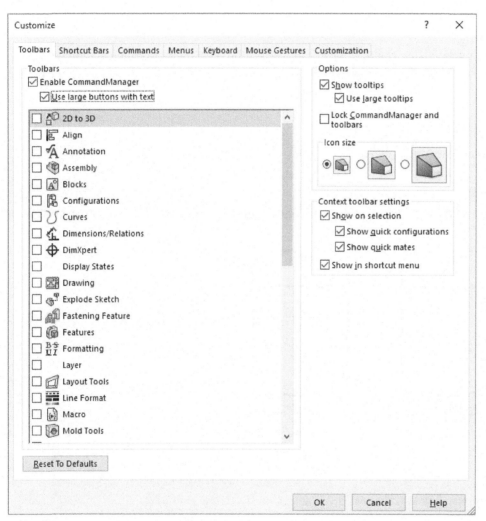

Customizing the Mouse Gestures

To customize the Mouse Gestures, click the right mouse button on the CommandManager, and then select **Customize** from the menu. Next, click the **Mouse Gestures** tab on the **Customize** dialog, and make sure that the **Enable mouse gestures** option is selected. Select the number of commands to be displayed on the gestures from the drop-down available below the **Enable mouse gestures** option. Next, click and drag the required commands from the commands list. Move the pointer and release onto anyone of the mouse gestures (Part, Sketch,

Assembly, or Drawing mouse gestures) available on the **Mouse Gestures Guide** dialog. Click **OK** to close the **Customize** dialog. There four mouse gestures available on the Mouse Gestures Guide dialog: Part, Sketch, Assembly, and Drawing. You can copy a command located on anyone of the mouse gestures onto another mouse gestures. To do this, press the Ctrl key and drag the command onto another mouse gesture.

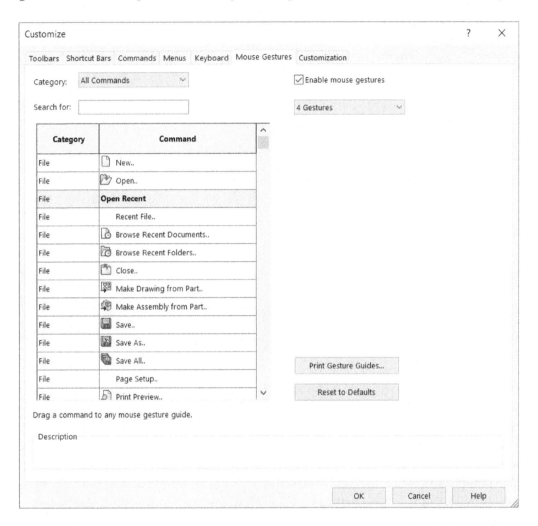

SOLIDWORKS 2019 Learn by doing

Changing the Background Color

To change the background color of the graphics window, click the **Options** icon on the Quick Access Toolbar. On the **System Options** dialog, click the **Colors** option from the tree available on the left side. Now, you can set the icon color, user interface background, and background appearance of the graphics window. By default, the **Background appearance** is set to **Use document scene background(recommended)**. You can also select the **Plain**, **Gradient**, or **Image file options**. If you select the **Plain** option, the viewport background color available in the **Color scheme Settings** section is applied to the background. You can change the viewport background color by clicking the **Edit** button available in the **Color scheme Settings** section. Next, select color from the Color dialog, and click **OK**. If you select the **Image file** option from **Background appearance** section, click the **Browse** button and select an image file from a location on your computer. Next, click **OK** on the **System Options** dialog.

SOLIDWORKS 2019 Learn by doing

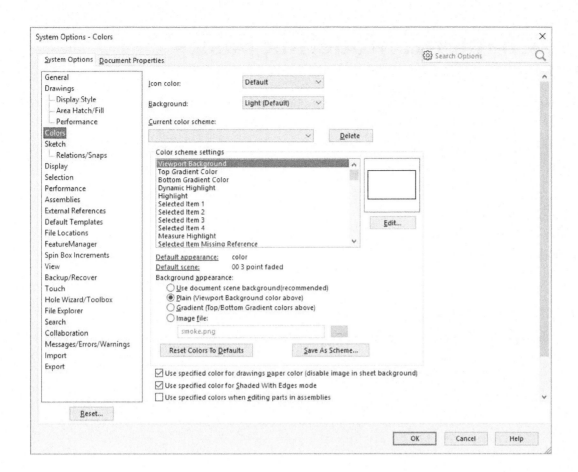

Chapter 2: Modeling Basics

This chapter teaches you to construct your first SOLIDWORKS model. You will construct parts of an Oldham Coupling:

In this chapter, you will:
- Construct Sketches
- Construct a base feature
- Add another feature to it
- Construct revolved features
- Construct cylindrical features and
- Apply draft

TUTORIAL 1

This tutorial takes you through the creation of your first SOLIDWORKS model. You construct the Disc of the Oldham coupling assembly:

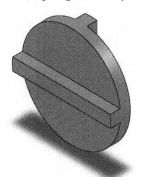

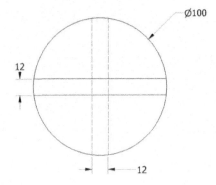
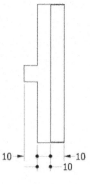

SOLIDWORKS 2019 Learn by doing

Opening a New Part File
1. Start SOLIDWORKS 2019 by clicking the **SOLIDWORKS 2019** icon on the desktop; the Welcome window appears.
2. On the Welcome window, click the **Home** tab, and then click the **Part** icon; a new part file is opened.

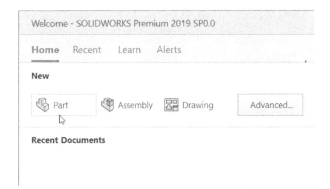

Starting a Sketch
1. In the SOLIDWORKS 2019 window, click the **Unit System** drop-down at the lower right corner.

2. Select **MMGS (millimeter, gram, second)** from the drop-down.

3. To start a new sketch, click **Sketch > Sketch** on the CommandManager.

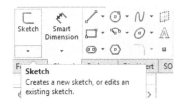

4. Select the front plane.

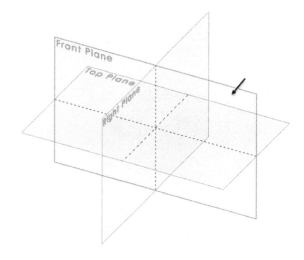

5. Click **Sketch > Circle** on the CommandManager to start creating a circle.

6. Select the origin point of the coordinate system.

7. Move the pointer away from the origin and click to draw the circle.

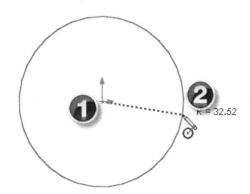

8. Press **ESC** to deactivate the tool.

Notice that the sketch appears shaded. This is the result of the **Shaded Sketch Contours** icon active on the **Sketch** tab of the ribbon. You can hide/show the shade inside the sketch by turning ON/OFF the **Shaded Sketch Contours** icon.

SOLIDWORKS 2019 Learn by doing

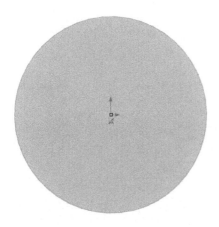

Adding Dimensions

In this section, you will specify the size of the sketched circle by adding dimensions.

As you add dimensions, the sketch can attain any one of the following three states:

Fully Constrained sketch: In a fully constrained sketch, the positions of all the entities are fully described by dimensions, relations, or both. In a fully constrained sketch, all the entities are black color.

Under Constrained sketch: To define the geometry completely, you need additional dimensions, relations, or both. In this state, you can drag the sketch elements to modify the sketch. An under constrained sketch element is in blue color.

Over Constrained sketch: In this state, an object has conflicting dimensions, relations, or both. An over constraining dimension is in yellow color.

1. Click **Sketch > Smart Dimension** 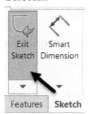 on the CommandManager to start dimensioning the sketch.
2. Select the circle, move the pointer, and click; the **Modify** box appears.
3. Type-in **100** in the box and press **Enter** on the keyboard.
4. Press **Esc** to deactivate the **Smart Dimension** tool.

5. To display the entire circle at full size and to center it in the graphics area, use one of the following methods:

   - On the **View (Heads Up)** toolbar, click **Zoom to Fit**.

   - On the Menu bar, click **View > Modify > Zoom to Fit**.

6. On the CommandManager, click **Sketch > Exit Sketch**.

7. On the **View (Heads Up)** toolbar, click **View Orientation**.
8. Click on the top-right corner of the **View Selector** cube.

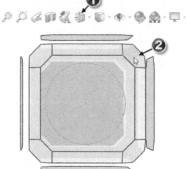

17

SOLIDWORKS 2019 Learn by doing

Constructing the Base Feature

You can call the first feature of any part as a base feature. You now construct this feature by extruding the sketched circle.

1. On the CommandManager, click **Features > Extruded Boss/Base** .
2. Click on the sketched circle, if it not already selected.

3. On the **Boss-Extrude** PropertyManager, type-in 10 in the **Depth** box, and then click **OK** .

Notice the new feature, **Boss-Extrude1**, in the **FeatureManager Design Tree**.

Adding an Extruded Feature

To construct additional features on the part, you must draw sketches on the model faces or planes, and then convert them into features.

1. On the CommandManager, click **Features > Extruded Boss/Base** .
2. Click on the front face of the model.
3. On the CommandManager, click **Sketch > Convert Entities** .
4. Click on the circular edge of the model geometry.

5. On the **Convert Entities** PropertyManager, click **OK** .

SOLIDWORKS 2019 Learn by doing

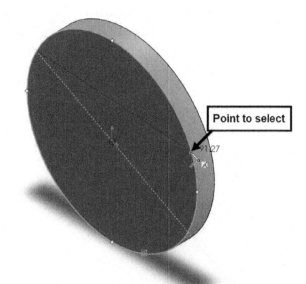

6. On the CommandManager, click **Sketch > Line**.

7. Click on the circular edge to specify the first point of the line, as shown.

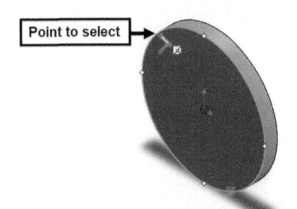

8. Move the pointer towards right.
9. Click on the other side of the circular edge; a line is drawn. In addition, another line is attached to the pointer.

10. Right-click and select **End chain (double-click)** to end the line.

11. Draw another line below the previous line.

9. Press **Esc** to deactivate the **Line** tool.

19

10. On the CommandManager, click **Sketch > Display/Delete Relations > Add Relation**.

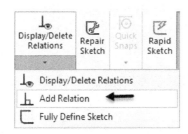

12. Select the two lines.
13. On the **Add Relations** PropertyManager, under the **Add Relations** section, click **Horizontal** to make the two lines horizontal.
14. Under the **Add Relations** section, click **Equal** to make the lines equal in length.

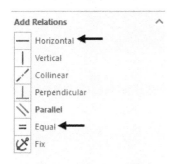

15. Click **OK** on the PropertyManager.
16. On the CommandManager, click **Sketch > Smart Dimension**.
17. Select the two horizontal lines.
18. Move the pointer toward right and click to locate the dimension.
19. Type-in **12** in the Modify box and click **OK**.

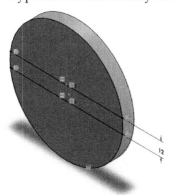

20. On the CommandManager, click **Sketch > Trim Entities**.
21. Click the **Trim to Closest** icon on the PropertyManager.

22. Click on the arc portions of the projected entity.

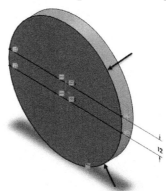

The projected entities are trimmed.

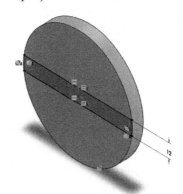

23. Click **OK** on the **Trim** PropertyManager.
24. On the top right corner of the graphics window, select **Exit Sketch**.

SOLIDWORKS 2019 Learn by doing

25. On the **Boss-Extrude** PropertyManager, type-in **10** in the **Depth** box, and then click **OK** ✓.

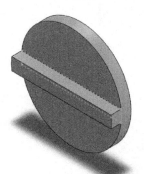

Adding another Extruded Feature

1. Press and hold the Middle Mouse Button and drag the pointer to rotate the part such that the back face of the part is displayed.

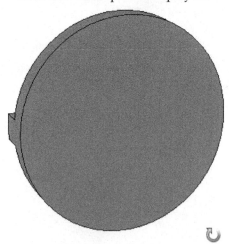

2. On the CommandManager, click **Sketch > Sketch**.

3. Click on the back face of the part.
4. Activate the **Convert Entities** tool and convert the circular edge into a sketch entity.
5. Click **OK** on the Convert Entities PropertyManager.

6. Draw two lines, as shown below (follow the steps, as discussed earlier in this chapter).

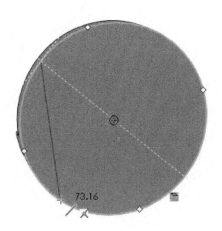

SOLIDWORKS 2019 Learn by doing

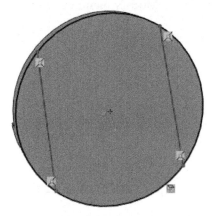

7. Press **Esc** to deactivate the **Line** tool.
8. Press the **Ctrl** key and click on the lines.
9. On the PropertyManager, under the **Add Relations** section, click **Vertical**.
10. Click **Equal**, and then click **OK** on the PropertyManager.

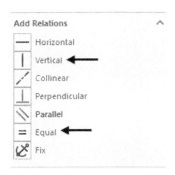

11. Activate the **Smart Dimension** tool and apply a dimension of 12 mm distance between the vertical lines (follow the steps to create dimensions, as discussed earlier).

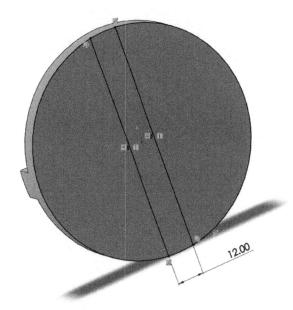

12. Activate the **Trim Entities** tool.
13. Click the **Power Trim** icon on the PropertyManager.

14. Press and hold the left mouse button, and then drag the pointer across the right side arc; the arc is trimmed.

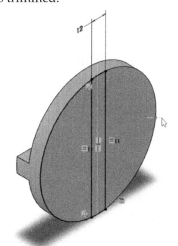

15. Release the left mouse button.
16. Likewise, trim the left side arc by dragging the mouse across it.

SOLIDWORKS 2019 Learn by doing

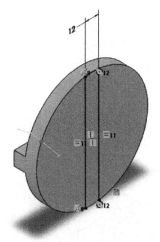

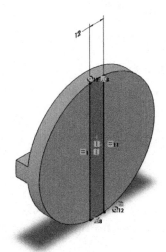

17. Click **Exit Sketch**.
18. Extrude the sketch up to 10 mm depth.
19. Click **OK** on the PropertyManager.

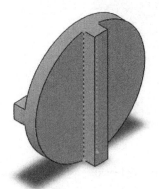

To magnify a model in the graphics area, you can use the zoom tools available on the **View (Heads**

Up) toolbar or **View > Modify** menu or on the Shortcut menu.

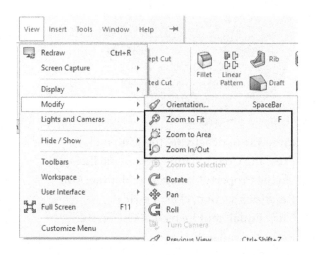

Click **Zoom to Fit** to display the part full size in the current window.

Click **Zoom to Area**, and then drag the pointer to construct a rectangle; the area in the rectangle zooms to fill the window.

Click **Zoom In/Out**, and then drag the pointer. Dragging up zooms in; dragging down zooms out.

Click on a face, edge, vertex or any object, and then click **Zoom to Selection** on the Context Toolbar. You will zoom to the selection.

To move the part view, click the right mouse button and select **Pan**.

Drag the part to move it around in the graphics area.

Select **Rotate About Scene Floor** from the right-click shortcut menu helps you to rotate the view about axis perpendicular to the scene floor. After enabling this option, you can use the **Roll View** option to rotate the view.

Saving the Part
1. Click the **Save** button on the **Quick Access Toolbar**.
2. Enter **Disc** in the **File name** field.
3. Browse to **C:\Users\Username\Documents** folder, and then create a new folder with the name Oldham Coupling.
4. Click **Save** to save the file.
5. Click **File > Close**.

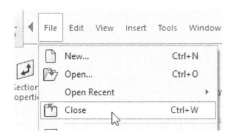

Note:
*.prt or *.sldprt are the file extensions for the files that are created in the Part environment of SOLIDWORKS.

TUTORIAL 2

In this tutorial, you will construct a flange by performing the following operations:

- Constructing revolved feature
- Constructing cut features
- Adding Rounds

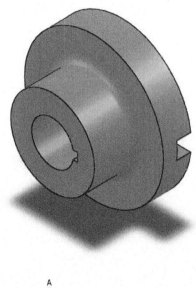

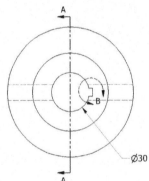

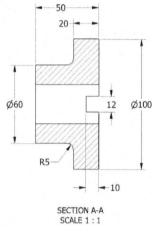

SECTION A-A
SCALE 1 : 1

DETAIL B
SCALE 2 : 1

SOLIDWORKS 2019 Learn by Doing

Opening a New Part File

1. To open a new part, click the **New** button on the **Quick Access Toolbar**.
2. On the **New SOLIDWORKS Document** dialog, click **Part**, and then click **OK**.

Sketching a Revolve Profile

Now, you will construct a sketch for the revolved feature.

1. On the CommandManager, click **Sketch > Sketch**.
2. Click on the right plane.
3. Activate the **Line** tool and place the pointer on the sketch origin.
4. Move the pointer upward and notice a dotted line.
5. Click along the dotted line to specify the start point of the line.

6. Move the pointer upwards. You will notice that the Vertical relation symbol appears.
7. Click to draw a vertical line.

8. Move the pointer toward left. You will notice that the Horizontal relation symbol appears.
9. Click to draw a horizontal line.

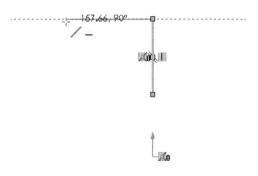

10. Complete the sketch by constructing the other lines.

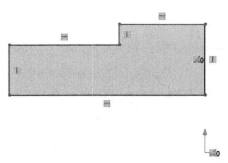

11. On the CommandManager, click **Sketch > Line > Centerline**.

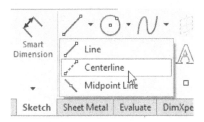

12. Draw a horizontal line passing through the horizontal axis of the coordinate system.

SOLIDWORKS 2019 Learn by Doing

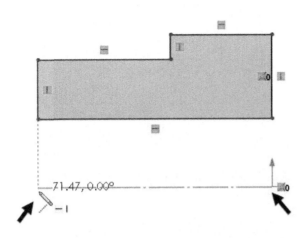

6. Activate the **Smart Dimension** tool and apply to two horizontal dimensions (refer to the **Adding Dimensions** section of Tutorial 1).

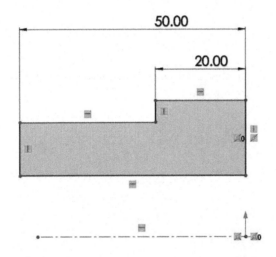

7. Click on the centerline and bottom horizontal line.

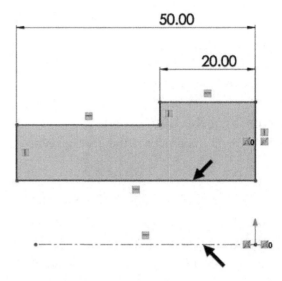

9. Move the pointer downwards, and then towards right. Click to position the dimension.

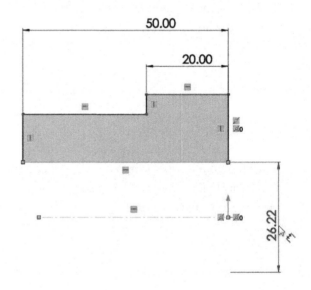

10. Type-in 30 in the **Modify** box and click **OK**.

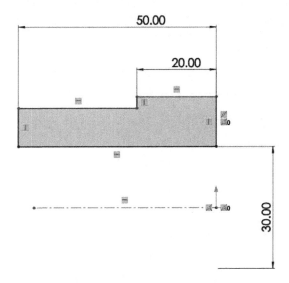

11. Create other symmetric dimensions, as shown.

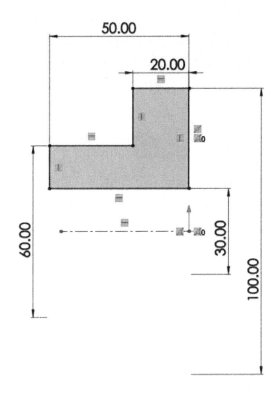

12. Click **Exit Sketch**.

Constructing the Revolved Boss

1. On the CommandManager, click **Features > Revolved Boss/Base**.

2. Select the sketch, if not already selected.

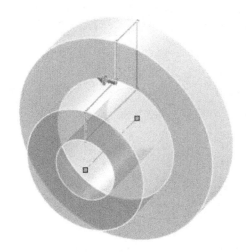

3. On the **Revolve** PropertyManager, set the **Direction1 Angle** value to **360**.

4. Click **OK**.

Constructing the Cut feature

1. Press and hold the Middle Mouse Button and drag the pointer to rotate the part.

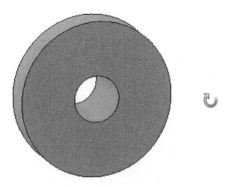

2. Click on the back face and click **Sketch**.

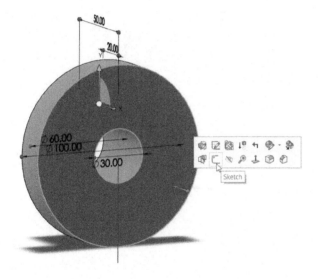

3. On the CommandManager, click **Sketch > Rectangle** drop-down **> Center Rectangle**.

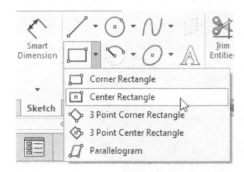

4. Select the origin to define the center point.

5. Move the pointer diagonally toward right and click to create the rectangle.

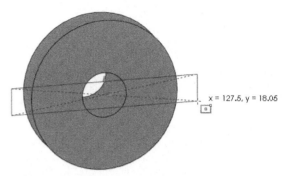

6. Add dimensions to the sketch.

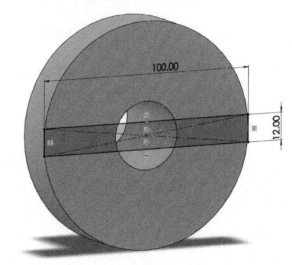

7. Click **Exit Sketch**.
8. On the CommandManager, click **Features > Extruded Cut**.

9. On the **Cut-Extrude** PropertyManager, set the **Depth** value to 10 and click **OK**.

SOLIDWORKS 2019 Learn by Doing

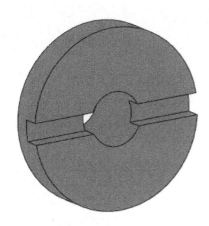

Constructing another Cut feature

1. On the Quick Access Toolbar, click **Options** drop-down > **Customize**.
2. On the **Customize** dialog, click the **Mouse Gestures** tab.
3. Select 8 gestures from the drop-down located at left side.

4. Click **OK** to close the **Customize** dialog.
5. Press the right mouse button and drag the mouse to display the Mouse gesture.
6. On the Mouse gesture, select Front.

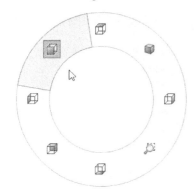

7. On the CommandManager, click **Sketch > Sketch** and click on the front face.
8. Press **S** on the keyboard.
9. On the Flyout Toolbar, click **Rectangle**.

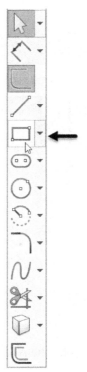

10. On the PropertyManager, select **Corner Rectangle** .
11. Specify the corners of the rectangle.

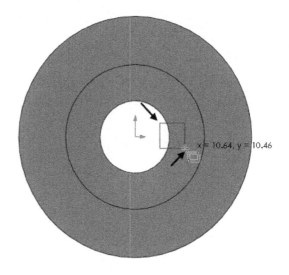

12. On the CommandManager, click **Sketch > Line > Centerline**.
13. Draw a horizontal centerline passing through the origin.
14. Press the Ctrl key and click on the horizontal lines of the sketch.

30

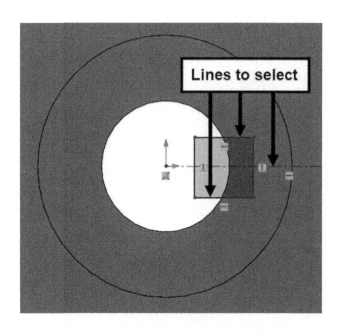

15. On the PropertyManager, under the **Add Relations** section, click **Symmetric**.

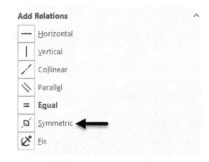

16. Click **OK** ✓.
17. Add dimensions to the sketch.

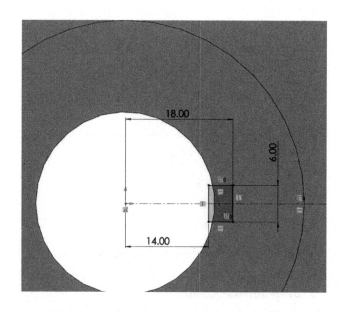

18. Click **Exit Sketch**.
19. On the CommandManager, click **Features > Extruded Cut**.
20. Click on the sketch.
21. On the **Cut-Extrude** PropertyManager, under the **Direction 1** section, select **End Condition > Through All**.

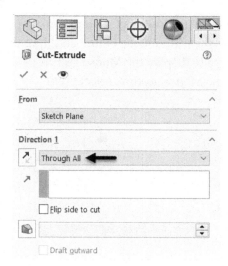

22. Click **OK** ✓ to construct the cutout.
23. Press Ctrl+7 on your keyboard to change the view to isometric.

SOLIDWORKS 2019 Learn by Doing

Adding a Fillet

1. Click on the circular edge of the model geometry and select **Fillet**.

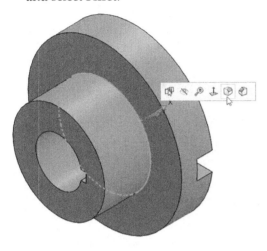

2. Enter **5** in the callout attached to the selected edge.

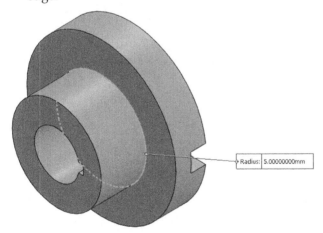

3. Click **OK** ✓ to add the fillet.

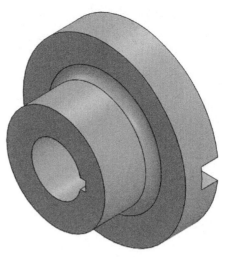

To display the part in different modes, use the options on the **Display Style** menu on the **View (Heads Up)** toolbar.

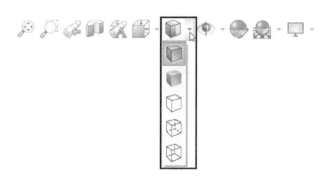

Shaded With Edges

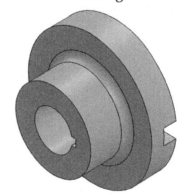

Shaded

Hidden Lines Removed

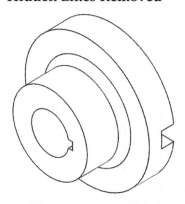

Hidden Lines Vissible

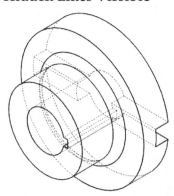

Wireframe

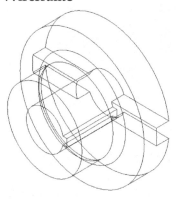

The default display mode for parts and assemblies is **Shaded With Edges**. You may change the display mode whenever you want.

Viewing Parent and Child relationships between features

In SOLIDWORKS 2019, you can view the parent and child relationships between part features using the **Dynamic Reference Visualization** options.

1. On the FeatureManager Design tree, click the right mouse button on the part name, and then select **Dynamic Reference Visualization (Parent).**

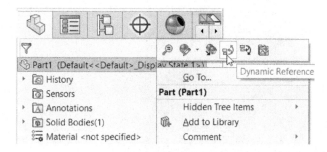

2. On the FeatureManager Design Tree, click the **Fillet** feature and notice an arrow pointing towards the **Revolve** feature. This indicates that the **Revolve** feature is the parent of the **Fillet** feature.

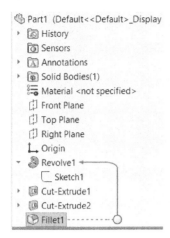

3. Click the right mouse button on the part and select the **Dynamic Reference Visualization (Child)** option.

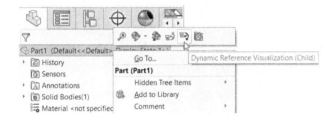

4. Click the **Revolve** feature in the FeatureManager Design Tree. Notice the arrows originating from the Revolve feature and pointing to the Right Plane and Origin. This indicates that they are the parents of the Revolve feature. In addition, notice the arrows pointing downwards to the Cut-Extrude and Fillet features. They are the child features of the Revolve feature.

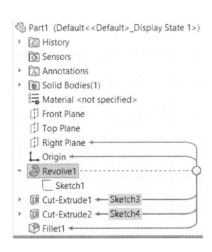

Saving the Part

1. Click the **Save** button on the **Quick Access Toolbar**.
2. Enter **Flange** in the **File name** field.
3. Browse to **C:\Users\Username\Documents\Oldham Coupling** folder.
4. Click **Save** to save the file.
5. Click **File > Close**.

TUTORIAL 3

In this tutorial, you will construct a Shaft by performing the following operations:

- Constructing a cylindrical feature
- Constructing a cut feature

Opening a New Part File

1. To open a new part, click **File > New** on the menu bar.
2. On the **New SOLIDWORKS Document** dialog, click the **Part** button.
3. Click **OK**.

Constructing the Cylindrical Feature

1. Activate the **Revolved Boss/Base** tool and click the right plane.
2. Construct the sketch, as shown in figure.

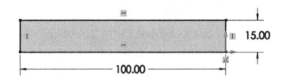

3. Click **Exit Sketch**.
4. Click on the bottom horizontal line of the sketch to define the axis of rotation.

34

SOLIDWORKS 2019 Learn by Doing

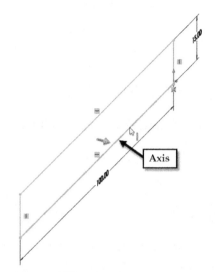

5. Click **OK** ✓ .

Constructing Cut feature

1. Activate the **Extruded Cut** tool and click on the front face of the model geometry.
2. On the CommandManager, click **Sketch > Center Rectangle** .
3. Click on the top quadrant point of the circular edge.

4. Move the pointer away and click to construct the rectangle.

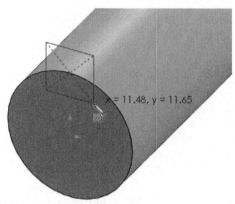

5. Create a vertical centerline from the origin point.
6. Press the Ctrl key, and then select the centerline and center point of the rectangle.
7. Select **Coincident** from PropertyManager.
8. Add dimensions and relations to fully constrain the sketch.

35

SOLIDWORKS 2019 Learn by Doing

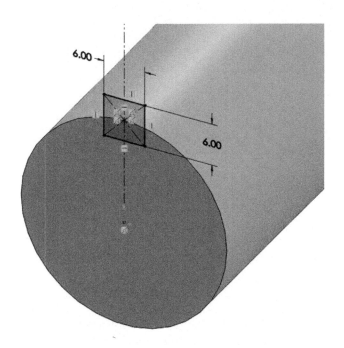

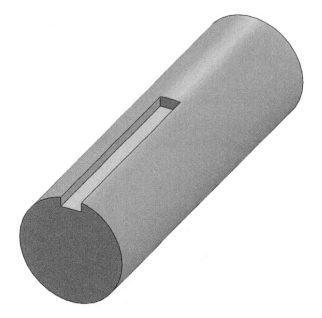

9. Click **Exit Sketch**.
10. Click on the extrude handle and drag. A scale appears on the model.
11. Release the pointed when the depth is set to 55.

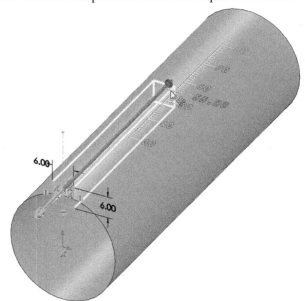

12. Click **OK** ✓.

Saving and Closing the Part

1. Click the **Save** 💾 button on the **Quick Access Toolbar**.
2. Enter **Shaft** in the **File name** field.
3. Browse to **C:\Users\Username\Documents\Oldham Coupling** folder.
4. Click **Save** to save the file.
5. Click **File > Close**.

TUTORIAL 4

In this tutorial, you construct a Key by performing the following operations:

- Constructing an Extruded Boss
- Applying draft

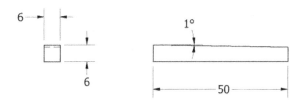

Constructing Extruded Boss

1. To open a new part, click **File > New** on the menu bar.

2. On the **New SOLIDWORKS Document** dialog, click the **Part** button.
3. Click **OK**.
4. On the CommandManager, click **Features > Extruded Boss/Base**.
5. Click on the front plane.
6. Construct the sketch, as shown in figure.

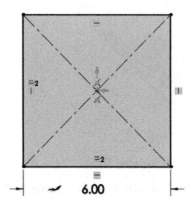

7. Click **Exit Sketch**.
8. On the **Boss-Extrude** PropertyManager, under the **Direction 1** section, set **End Condition** to **Mid Plane**.
9. Set the **Depth** value to 50.
10. Click **OK** to construct the extruded boss.

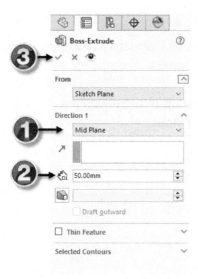

Applying Draft
1. On the CommandManager, click **Features > Draft**.
2. Click on the front face of the model geometry to define the neutral plane
3. Click on the top face to define the draft face.

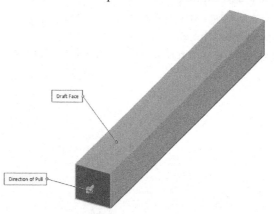

4. Type-in 1 in the **Draft Angle** box and click the **Reverse Direction** button.
5. Click **OK**.

Saving and Closing the Part
1. Click the **Save** button on the **Quick Access Toolbar**.
2. Enter **Key** in the **File name** field.

3. Browse to **C:\Users\Username\Documents\Oldham Coupling** folder.
4. Click **Save** to save the file.
5. Click **File > Close**.

Chapter 3: Assembly Basics

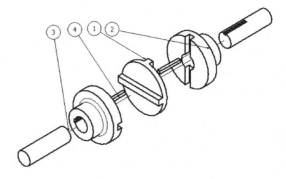

In this chapter, you will:

- Add Components to the assembly
- Apply constraints between components
- Create the exploded view of the assembly

TUTORIAL 1

This tutorial takes you through the creation of your first assembly. You create the Oldham coupling assembly:

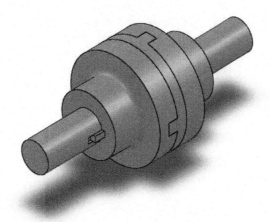

PARTS LIST		
ITEM	PART NUMBER	QTY
1	Disc	1
2	Flange	2
3	Shaft	2
4	Key	2

There are two ways to create an assembly model.

- Top-Down Approach
- Bottom-Up Approach

Top-Down Approach

In the Top-Down approach, you will start the assembly document, and then construct components in it.

Bottom-Up Approach

In this approach, you will create the components, and then add them to the assembly document. In this tutorial, you will create an assembly using this approach.

Opening a New Assembly File

1. To open a new assembly, click **New** on the **Quick Access Toolbar**.
2. On the **New SOLIDWORKS Document** dialog, click **Assembly**, and then click **OK**.

The Assembly window appears along with the **Begin Assembly** PropertyManager located on the left side.

Inserting the Base Component

1. On the **Begin Assembly** PropertyManager, under the **Part/Assembly to Insert** section, click the **Browse** button.

2. Browse to the location: **C:\Users\Username\Documents\Oldham Coupling**.
3. Double-click on **Flange.** This attaches the component to the pointer.
4. Click inside the graphics window to position the component.

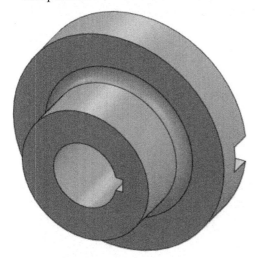

Adding the second component
1. To insert the second component, click **Assembly > Insert Component** on the CommandManager.
2. On the **Insert Component** PropertyManager, click the **Browse** button.
3. Browse to the location **C:\Users\Username\Documents\Oldham Coupling**, and then double-click on **Shaft**.
4. Click inside the graphics window to position the shaft.

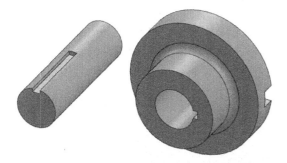

In SOLIDWORKS, you can view a component in separate preview window. This helps you to the rotate or move component independently, and apply mates. To view component in the preview window, click on it and select **Component Preview Window**.

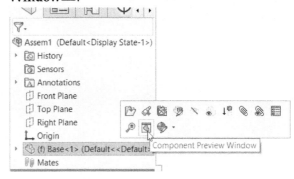

Applying Mates
After adding the components to the assembly window, you have to apply mates between them. By applying mates, you establish real contact and motion between components.

You can apply mates between parts using the **Mate** tool.

The following sections explain some of the assembly mates that you can apply using the **Mate** tool.

Coincident: Using this mate, you can align two faces such that they will point in the same direction.

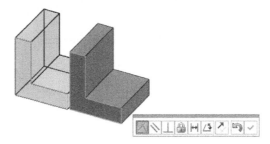

On the context toolbar that appears in the graphics window, click **Flip Mate Alignment** to flip the alignment direction.

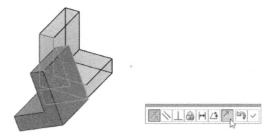

Parallel: Using this mate, you can make an axis, face, or edge of one part parallel to that of another part.

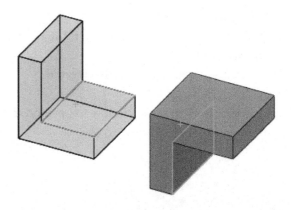

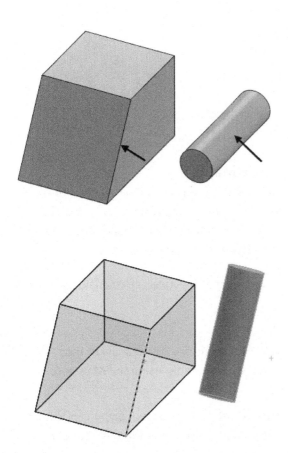

Concentric: Using this mate, you can align the centerlines of the cylindrical faces.

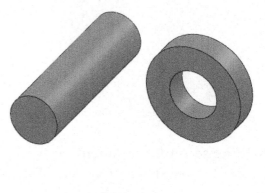

Perpendicular: Using this mate, you can make an axis, face or edge of one part perpendicular to that of another part.

Click **Flip Mate Alignment** to flip the alignment direction. Check the **Lock Rotation** option to lock the rotation between components.

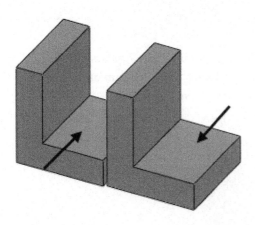

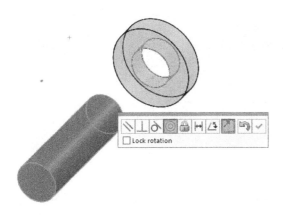

Lock: Makes parts to form a rigid set. As you move a single part in a rigid set, all the other parts will also be moved.

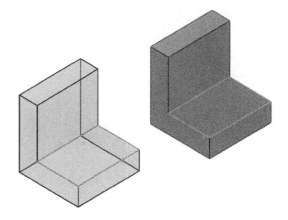

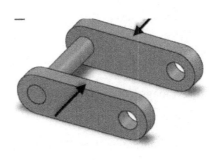 **Angle:** Applies the angle mate between two components.

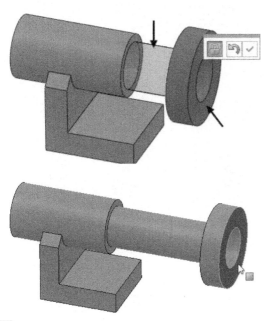

Click **Flip Dimension** to reverse the angle direction.

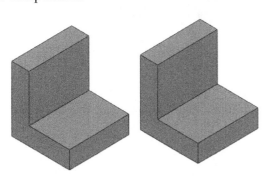

Distance: Applies the distance mate between two components.

Tangent: This mate makes two faces tangent to each other.

SOLIDWORKS 2019 Learn by Doing

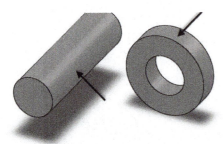

1. On the CommandManager, click **Assembly > Mate** .
2. On the **Mate** PropertyManager, click **Concentric** .
3. Click on the cylindrical face of the Shaft.
4. Click on the inner cylindrical face of the Flange

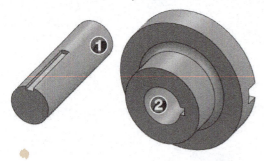

In SOLIDWORKS, the first selection is made transparent while applying mates. You can turn OFF the transparency by unchecking the **Make first selection transparent** option in the **Options** section of the **Mate** PropertyManager.

5. Click **Add/Finish Mate**.

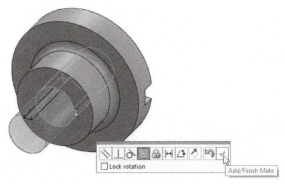

This aligns the Shaft and the Flange axially.

6. On the **Mate** PropertyManager, click **Coincident** .
7. Click on the front face of the shaft.

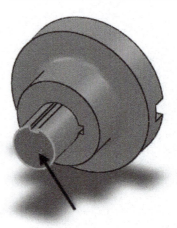

8. Rotate the model.
9. Click on the slot face of the flange, as shown in figure.

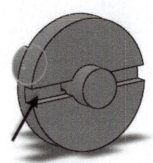

10. On the **Mate** PropertyManager, under the **Standard Mates** section, click the **Aligned** button.

43

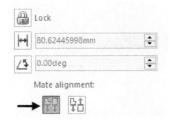

11. Click **OK** on the **SOLIDWORKS** message.

12. Click **Add/Finish Mate**.

This aligns front face of the Shaft and the slot face of the Flange.

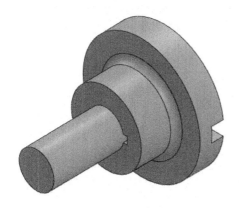

13. On the **Mate** PropertyManager, click **Coincident**.
14. In the **FeatureManager tree**, expand **Flange** and select **Top Plane**.
15. Expand Shaft and select **Right Plane**.

16. Click **Add/Finish Mate**.
17. Click **OK** on the **PropertyManager**.

This assembles the two components and fully constrains the Shaft.

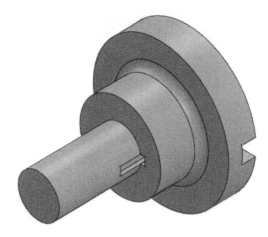

Adding the Third Component

In order to assemble the third component, you need to hide the Flange.

1. In the **FeatureManager Design Tree**, click the right mouse button on the Flange and select **Hide Components** to hide the Flange. Now, it is easy to assemble the third component.

SOLIDWORKS allows you to hide a body placing the cursor on it and pressing the Tab key. You can unhide the body by placing the cursor at its position and pressing Shift+Tab.

Tip: You can also hide a part face so that the obscured face is visible. To do this, activate the Mate tool, place the pointer on a face, and then Alt key; the face is temporarily hidden. Click in the graphics window to unhide the hidden face.

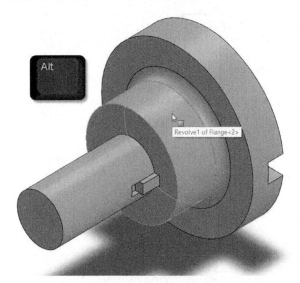

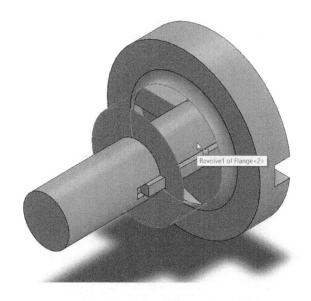

2. To insert the third component, click **Assembly > Insert Component**.
3. On the PropertyManager, click the **Browse** button.
4. Browse to the folder: **C:\Users\Username\Documents\Oldham Coupling**, and then double-click on the Key.
5. Click inside the graphics window to position the key.

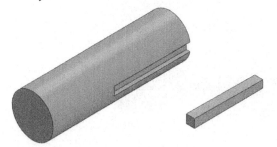

6. Activate the **Mate** tool.
7. On the **Mate** PropertyManager, click **Coincident**.
8. Right-click on the side face of the key and select **Select Other**.

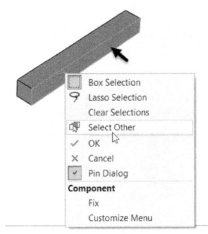

9. From the **Select Other** box, select the bottom face of the Key.

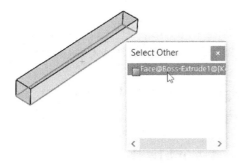

10. Select the bottom face of the slot.

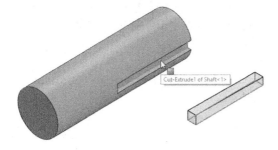

11. Click **Add/Finish Mate** .
12. This aligns the bottom face of the key with the bottom face of the slot.

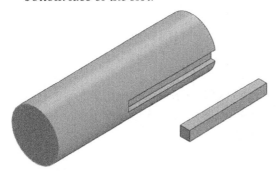

13. Select the front face of the Key and back face of the Shaft.

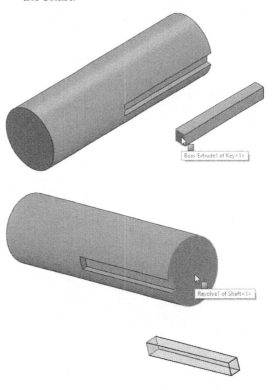

14. Click **Flip Alignment**.

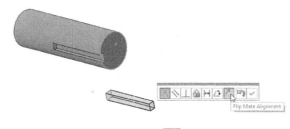

15. Click **Add/Finish Mate** .
16. This applies the mate between the selected faces.

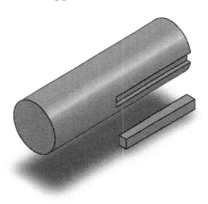

17. Click on the top face of the key.

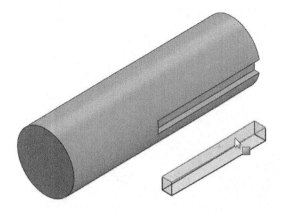

18. Rotate the shaft and select the side face of the slot.

19. Click **Add/Finish Mate**.

20. Click **OK** on the PropertyManager.
21. Now, you have to turn-on the display of the Flange.
22. Click the right mouse button on the Flange in the **FeatureManager** tree, and then select **Show Components** to display the Flange.

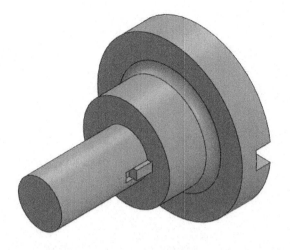

Checking the Interference

1. On the CommandManager, click **Evaluate > Interference Detection**.
2. On the PropertyManager, click **Calculate**.

The **Results** section shows **No Interferences.**

3. Click **OK**.

Saving the Assembly

1. Click **Save** on the **Quick Access Toolbar**.
2. Enter **Flange_subassembly** in the **File name** field.
3. Browse to **C:\Users\Username\Documents\Oldham Coupling** folder.
4. Click **Save** to save the file.
5. Click **File > Close**.

Starting the Main assembly

1. Click the **New** button on the **Quick Access Toolbar**.
2. On the **New SOLIDWORKS Document** dialog, click **Assembly**, and then click **OK**.

Adding Disc to the Assembly

1. On the **Begin Assembly** PropertyManager, click **Browse**.

2. Browse to the location **C:\Users\Username\Documents\Oldham Coupling** and double-click on **Disc.ipt**.
3. Click inside the graphics window to place the component at the origin.

Placing the Sub-assembly

1. To insert the sub-assembly, click **Assembly > Insert Components** on the CommandManager.
2. Click **Browse** on the PropertyManager.
3. Browse to the location **C:\Users\Username\Documents\Oldham Coupling** and double-click on **Flange_subassembly.asm**.
4. Click in the window to place the flange sub assembly.

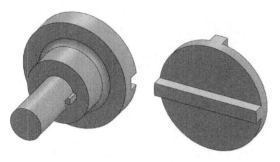

Adding Constraints

1. Activate the **Mate** tool.
2. Click on the front face of the disc and back face of the flange.

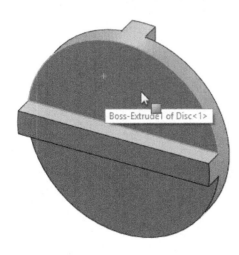

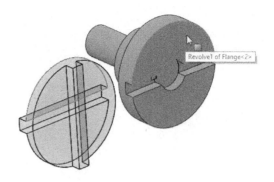

3. Click **Add/Finish Mate**.
4. Click on top flat face of the disc.

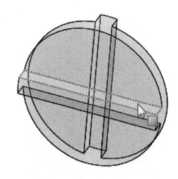

5. Rotate the model geometry and click on the slot face of the flange, as shown in figure.

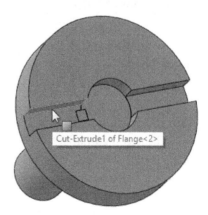

6. Click **Add/Finish Mate**.
7. Click on the cylindrical faces of the disc and flange.

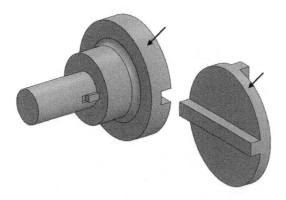

8. Click **Add/Finish Mate**.
9. Click **OK**.

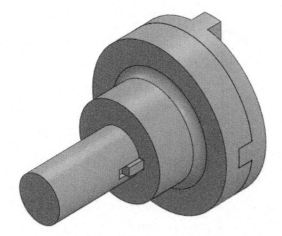

Placing the second instance of the Sub-assembly

1. In the FeatureManager Design Tree, click on the **Flange_subassembly**.
2. Press Ctrl+C on your keyboard to copy the assembly.
3. Press Ctrl+V on your keyboard to paste the assembly. Expand the copied flange assembly in the FeatureManager Design Tree and notice that it is copied along with mates between parts of the sub-assembly.
4. Change the orientation of the assembly, as shown.

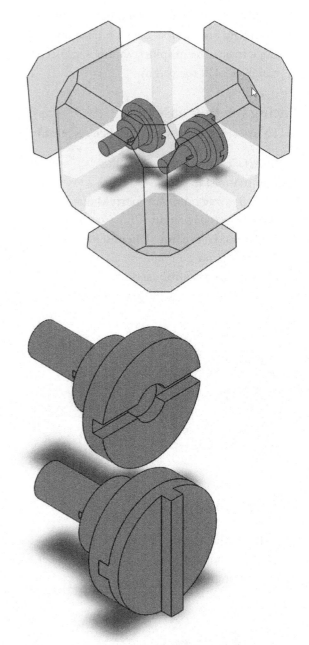

5. On the CommandManager, click **Assembly** tab > **Mate**.
6. Select the two faces of the assembly, as shown.

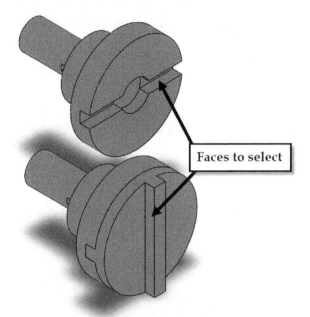

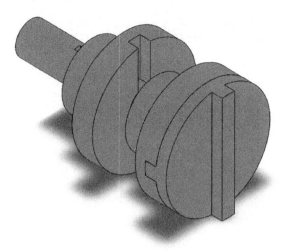

10. Select the flat faces of the assembly, as shown.

7. Click **OK** on the PropertyManager.
8. Click on the cylindrical faces of the assembly, as shown.

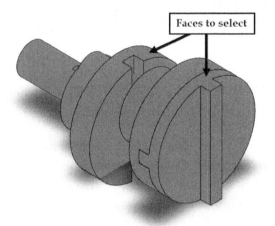

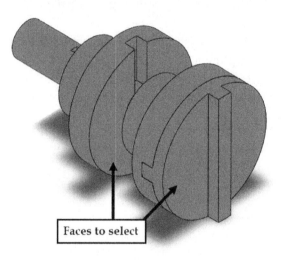

9. Click **OK** on the PropertyManager.

11. Click the **Anti Aligned** icon under the Mate Alignment section of the PropertyManager; the **SOLIDWORKS** dialog appears showing that the Concentric mate was reversed to prevent any errors.

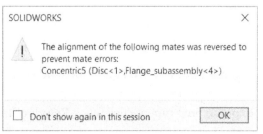

12. Click **OK** on the **SOLIDWORKS** dialog to close it.

13. Click **OK** on the PropertyManager to create the mate.
14. Change the assembly orientation to Isometric.

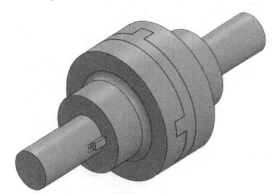

Saving the Assembly
1. Click **Save** on the **Quick Access Toolbar**.
2. Specify **Oldham_coupling** as **File name**.
3. Browse to **C:\Users\Username\Documents\Oldham Coupling** folder.
4. Click **Save** to save the file.

TUTORIAL 2
In this tutorial, you create the exploded view of the assembly:

Creating the Exploded View
1. To create the exploded view, click **Assembly > Exploded View** on the CommandManager.
2. On the **Explode** PropertyManager, under the **Explode Step type** section, click **Regular Step**.

3. On the **Explode** PropertyManager, under the **Options** section, check **Select the subassembly parts**.

4. Click on the shaft, and then click on the Z-axis.

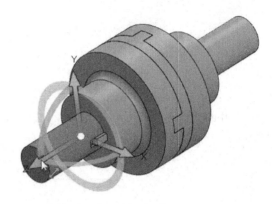

SOLIDWORKS has an improved triad, which helps you to rotate or translate parts easily.

5. On the PropertyManager, under the **Add a Step** section, set the **Explode Distance** value to **180**.
6. Click **Add Step**.

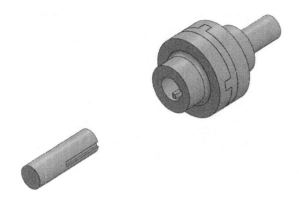

7. Click on the flange and set the **Explosion Distance** to 100.
8. Click **Add Step**, and then click **Done**.

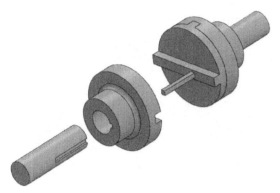

9. Click on the other shaft and set the **Explosion Distance** to -180.

10. Likewise, explode the other flange to -100 mm distance.

11. Click **OK** on the PropertyManager.

Creating Explode lines

1. To create explode lines; click **Assembly > Explode Line Sketch** .

2. Click on the circular edge of the flange.

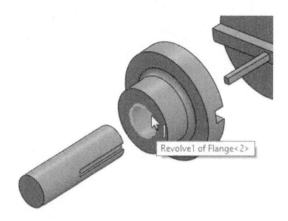

3. On the PropertyManager, under the **Options** section, check the **Reverse** option.

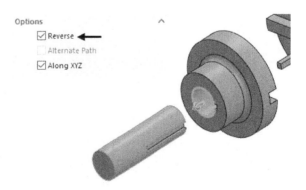

4. Click on the circular edge of the shaft.

SOLIDWORKS 2019 Learn by Doing

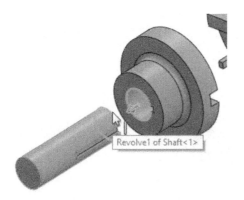

5. Click **OK**.

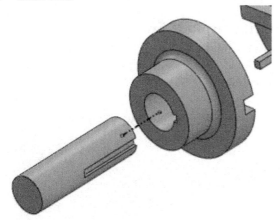

6. Click on the vertices of the flange and key, as shown in figure.
7. Click **OK**.

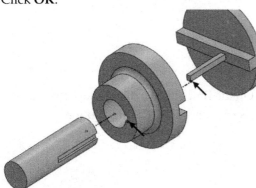

8. Click on the vertices of the flange and disc, as shown in figure.

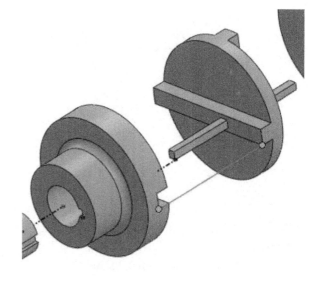

9. Click **OK**.
10. Click the **Jog Line** button located next to the PropertyManager.

11. Click on the explode line, as shown in figure.

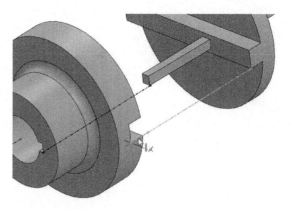

12. Drag the pointer to draw a rectangle.

53

SOLIDWORKS 2019 Learn by Doing

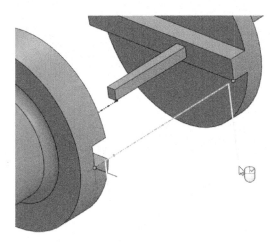

13. Press the Tab key to change the orientation of the sketch line.

14. Click to draw the jogged line.

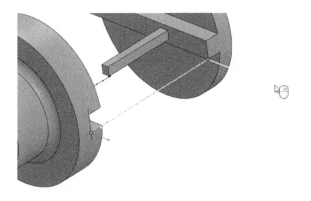

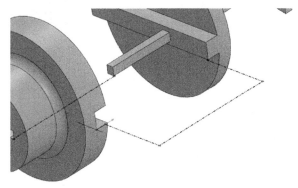

15. Click the **Route Line** icon located next to the PropertyManager.

16. Draw the other explode lines. Click **OK** on the PropertyManager.

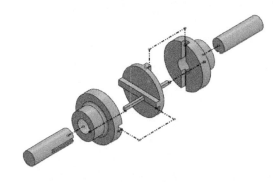

17. Click **Exit Sketch**.

The **ConfigurationManager** lists all the explode steps and exploded lines.

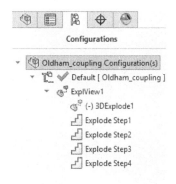

To edit an explode step, click the right mouse button on it and select **Edit Feature**.

To collapse the explosion, click the right mouse button on the exploded view and select **Collapse**.

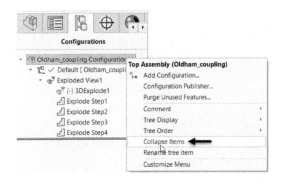

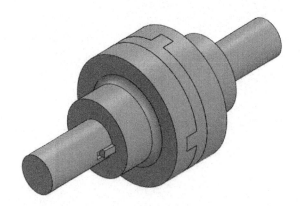

To animate the explosion, select it from the Configurations manager, click the right mouse button, and select **Animate Explode**.

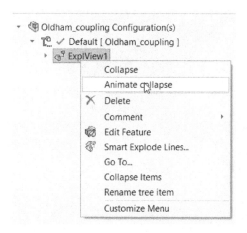

Use the options on the **Animation Controller** dialog to play, stop, or save the animation.

18. Save and close the assembly file.

Chapter 4: Creating Drawings

In this chapter, you create drawings of the parts and assembly from the previous chapters.

In this chapter, you will:

- Create model views
- Create section views
- Create detail views
- Add dimensions and annotations
- Create Custom templates
- Insert exploded view of the assembly
- Insert a bill of materials of the assembly
- Apply balloons to the assembly drawing

TUTORIAL 1

In this tutorial, you will create the drawing of the Flange.sldprt file created in the second chapter.

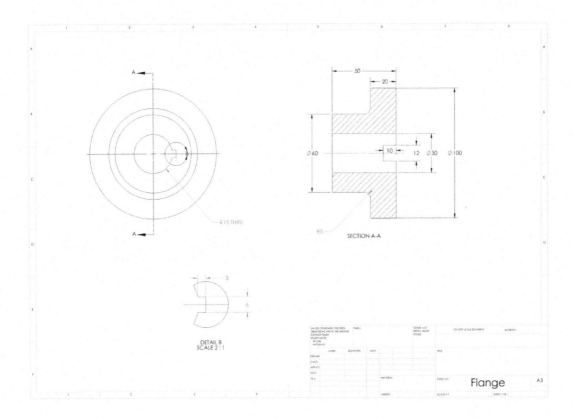

Opening a New Drawing File

1. To open a new drawing, click the **New** button on the **Quick Access Toolbar**.
2. On the **New SOLIDWORKS Document** dialog, select **Drawing** and click **OK**.

3. Select **A3 (ANSI) Landscape** from the list box in the **Sheet Format/Size** dialog.

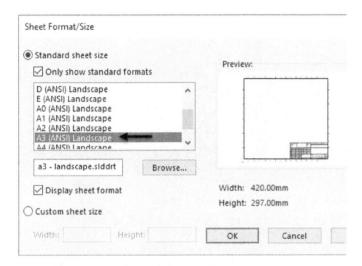

4. Click **OK**.
5. Click **Cancel** on the **Model View** PropertyManager.

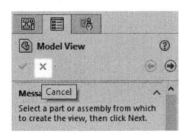

6. On the **FeatureManager Design Tree**, click the right mouse button on **Sheet1** and select **Properties**.
7. On the **Sheet Properties** dialog, set the **Type of projection** to **Third angle** (close the dialog if already selected).
8. Click **Apply Changes**.

Generating the Base View

1. On the CommandManager, click **View Layout > Model View**.
2. To generate the base view, click the **Browse** button on the **Model View** PropertyManager.

3. Browse to the location **C:/User/Document/Oldham_Coupling** and double-click on **Flange.sldprt**.
4. On the **Model View** PropertyManager, under the **Orientation** section, click **Front**.

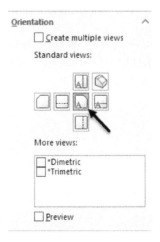

5. Click on the sheet to position the view. The **Projected View** tool gets active.

SOLIDWORKS 2019 Learn by Doing

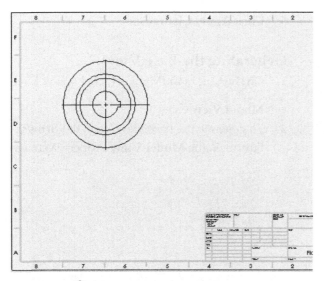

6. Click **OK** ✓ on the **PropertyManager**.
7. On the **View Heads-up** toolbar, click the **Hide** flyout and make sure that the **View Origin** icon is deactivated.

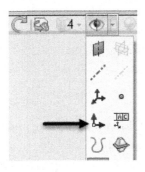

Creating the Section View

1. To create the section view, click **View Layout > Section View** ⇄ on the CommandManager.
2. Snap to the center point of the base view and click to position the section line.

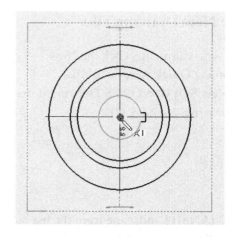

3. Click **OK**.

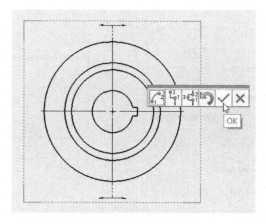

4. Move the pointer toward right and click to place the section view.
5. Click the green check on the PropertyManager.

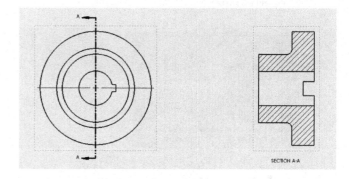

Creating the Detailed View

Now, you need to create the detailed view of the keyway that appears on the front view.

1. To create the detailed view, click **View Layout > Detail View** on the CommandManager.
2. Specify the center point and boundary point of the detail view, as shown in figure.

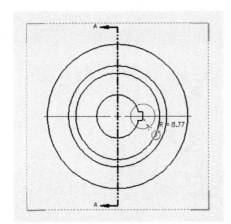

3. On the PropertyManager, under the **Detail Circle** section, set the options shown below.

4. Set the **Display Style** and **Scale** options, as shown below.

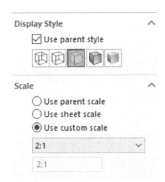

5. Place the detail view below the base view. Click **OK** on the PropertyManager.

In SOLIDWORKS, you can change the scale of the drawing views by using the drop-down available at the bottom right. Note that the scale of the detail view remains unchanged.

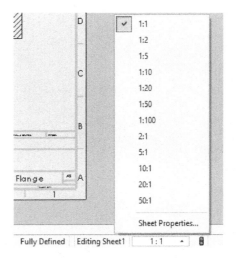

You can change the outline of the detail view by using the options in the **Detail View** section of the PropertyManager.

No outline

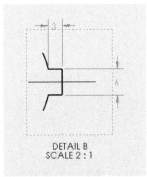

Full outline

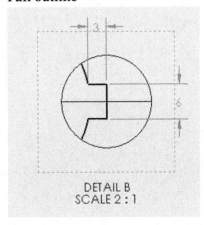

Jagged outline

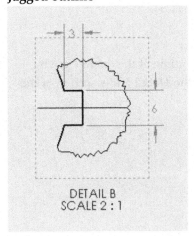

Use the **Shape Intensity** slider to change the size of the jagged shape.

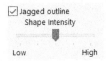

Creating the Centerline

1. On the CommandManager, click **Annotation > Centerline** .
2. Click on the inner horizontal edges of the section view, as shown in figure.

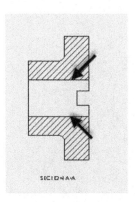

3. Click **OK** on the PropertyManager.

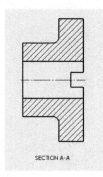

Specifying Dimension Settings

1. To specify the dimension settings, click **Options** on the **Quick Access Toolbar**.

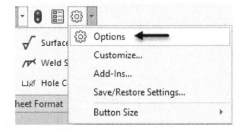

2. On the dialog, under the **Document Properties** tab, click **Drafting Standard**.
3. Select **Overall drafting standard > ANSI**.

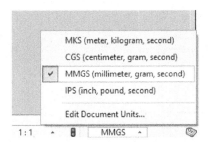

Retrieving Dimensions

Now, you will retrieve the dimensions that were applied to the model while creating it.

1. To retrieve dimensions, click **Annotation > Model Items** on the CommandManager.
2. On the PropertyManager, select **Source > Entire model**.
3. Uncheck the **Import Items into all views** option.
4. Under the **Dimensions** section, select **Marked for drawing**.

4. Under **Drafting Standard**, click **Dimensions**.
5. Under **Primary Precision**, select **Unit Precision > None**.

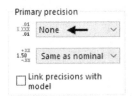

6. At the bottom of the dialog, check the **Center between extension lines**.

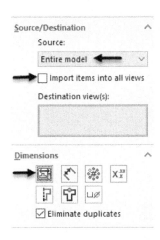

5. Click on the view boundary of the section view and click **OK** on the PropertyManager.

7. Click **OK**.
8. At the bottom of the window, set the **Unit System** to **MMGS**.

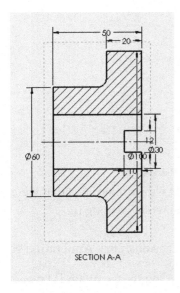

Adding additional dimensions

1. To add dimensions, click **Annotation > Smart Dimension** on the CommandManager.
2. On the section view, click on the fillet edge and position the radial dimension.

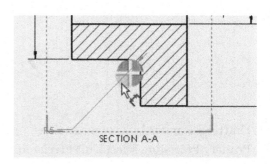

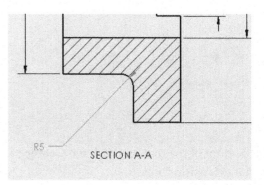

3. Select the radial dimension and click on the arrow to change its direction.

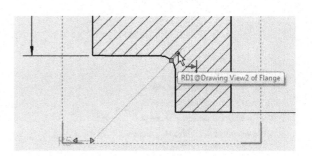

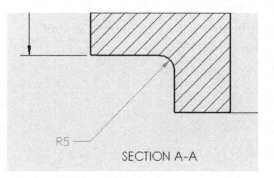

6. Drag and arrange the dimensions.

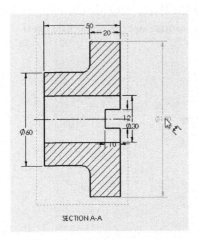

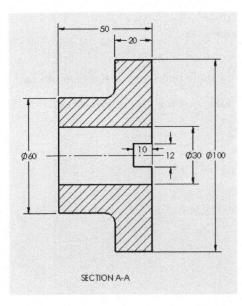

4. On the detail view, click on the vertical edge of the slot and position the dimension.

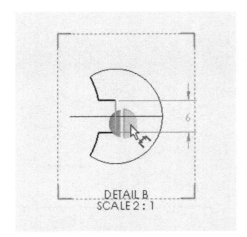

5. Likewise, add dimension to the horizontal edge of the slot.

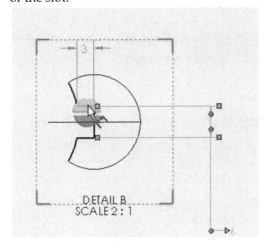

6. On the CommandManager, click **Annotation > Hole Callout**.
7. Click on the innermost circular edge of the front view and position the hole callout.
8. Click **Close Dialog** on the PropertyManager

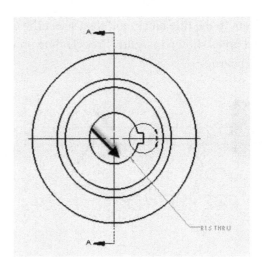

Saving the Drawing
1. Click **Save** on the **Quick Access Toolbar**.
2. Specify **Flange** as **Name**.
3. Browse to **C:\Users\Username\Documents\Oldham Coupling** folder.
4. Click **Save** to save the file.
5. Click **File > Close**.

TUTORIAL 2
In this tutorial, you will create the drawing of Disc.sldprt file created in the second chapter.

Creating a Custom Sheet Format
1. On Quick Access Toolbar, click the **New** button.
2. On the **New SOLIDWORKS Document** dialog, select **Drawing** and click **OK**.
6. Select **A3 (ANSI) Landscape** from the list box in the **Sheet Format/Size** dialog.
7. Click **OK**.
8. Close the **Model View** PropertyManager.
9. On the **FeatureManager Design Tree**, click the right mouse button on **Sheet1** and select **Properties**.
10. On the **Sheet Properties** dialog, set the **Type of projection** to **Third angle**. Click **Apply Changes**.
11. On the CommandManager, click **Sheet Format > Edit Sheet Format**.

12. Zoom to the title block, and then select the lines and notes shown in figure. Press **Delete** on your keyboard.

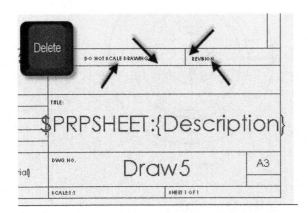

3. On the CommandManager, click **Sketch > Line** and draw a line on the title block.

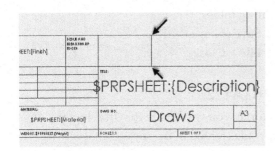

4. On the CommandManager, click **Annotation > Note**.
5. On the PropertyManager, under the **Text Format** section, select **Link to Property**.

6. On the **Link to Property** dialog, select **Current document**.
7. Select **SW-Author (Author)** from the **Property name** drop-down, and then click **OK**.

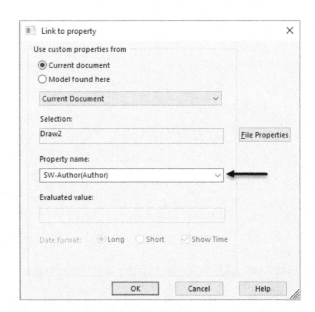

8. On the PropertyManager, under the **Leader** section, select **No Leader**.

9. Click inside the box, as shown in figure.

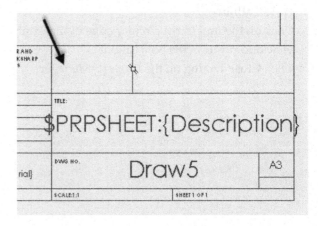

10. On the **Formatting** toolbar, set the font size to 8 and type **Author**.
11. Click **OK** on the PropertyManager.

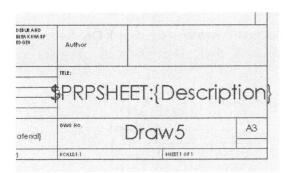

12. On the Menu bar, click **Insert > Picture**.
13. Select your company logo and click **Open**.
14. Resize (click and drag the top right corner of the image) and position the image on the title block.

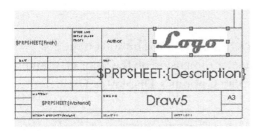

15. Click **OK** on the PropertyManager.
16. Click **Exit Sheet Format**.

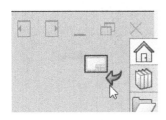

17. On the **Quick Access Toolbar**, click **Options**.

18. On the dialog, under the **Document Properties** tab, click **Drafting Standard**.
19. Select **Overall drafting standard >ANSI**.
20. Click **Units** and set the **Unit System** to **MMGS**.
21. Click **OK**.
22. Click **File > Save**.
23. On the **Save As** dialog, select **Save as type > Drawing Templates**.
24. Browse to **C:\Users\Username\Documents\Oldham Coupling** folder.
25. Type-in **Sample** in the **File name** box and click **Save**.
26. On the Menu bar, click **File > Close**.

Starting a New drawing

1. On the Quick Access Toolbar, click the **Options** button.
2. On the **System Options** dialog, click **File Locations**.
3. Select **Show folders for > Document Templates** and click the **Add** button.

4. Browse to **C:\Users\Username\Documents\Oldham Coupling** folder. Click **Select Folder**.
5. Click **OK** on the **System Options** dialog, and then click **Yes**.
6. On the Quick Access Toolbar, click the **New** button.
7. On the **New SOLIDWORKS Document** dialog, click the **Advanced** button.
8. Under the **Oldham Coupling** tab, select **Sample** and click **OK**.

SOLIDWORKS 2019 Learn by Doing

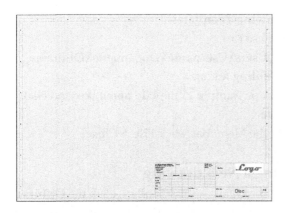

Generating the Drawing Views

1. On the **Model View** PropertyManager, click the **Browse** button and browse to the location: C: /User/Document/Oldham_Coupling
2. Double-click on **Disc.sldprt**.
3. On the PropertyManager, under the **Orientation** section, check the **Create multiple views** option.
4. Select the **Front** and **Bottom** views.

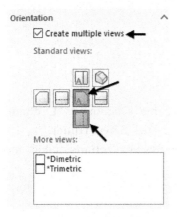

5. Click **OK** on the PropertyManager.

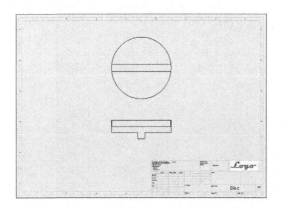

6. On the CommandManager, click **Annotation > Model Items**.
7. On the PropertyManager, select **Source > Entire model**.
8. Click on the two views and click **OK**.

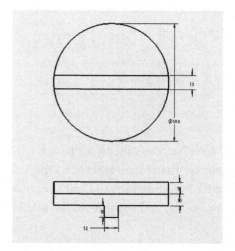

9. Click the right mouse button on the 100-diameter dimension on the front view and select **Display Options > Display as Diameter**.

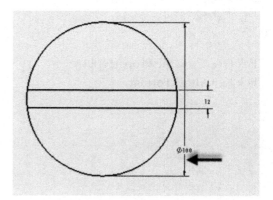

10. Arrange the dimensions by dragging them.

67

SOLIDWORKS 2019 Learn by Doing

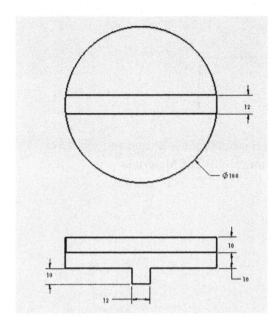

11. Save and close the drawing file.

TUTORIAL 3

In this tutorial, you will create the drawing of Oldham coupling assembly created in the previous chapter.

Creating the Isometric View

1. Start a new drawing file using the **Sample** template.
2. On the **Model View** PropertyManager, click the **Browse** button.
3. Browse to the location C: /User/Document/Oldham_Coupling folder and double-click on **Oldham_Coupling.sldasm**.
4. On the **Model View** PropertyManager, under the **Reference Configuration** section, uncheck the **Show in exploded or model break state** option.
5. Under the **Orientation** section, select **Isometric**.

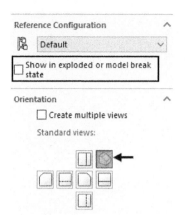

6. Under the **Scale** section, select **Use custom scale** and set the scale factor to **1:2**.

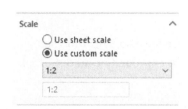

7. Click on the sheet to position the view.

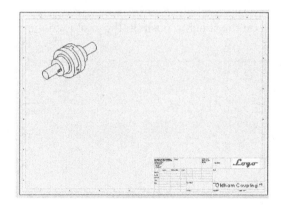

8. Click the green check on the PropertyManager.

Generating the Exploded View

1. On the CommandManager, click **View Layout > Model View**.
2. On the PropertyManager, under the **Part/Assembly to Insert** section, double-click on **Oldham Coupling**.

SOLIDWORKS 2019 Learn by Doing

3. Under the **Reference Configuration** section, enable **Shown in exploded or model break state**.
4. Under the **Orientation** section, select **Isometric**.
5. Under the **Scale** section, select **Use custom scale** and set the scale factor to **1:2**.
6. Click on the sheet to position the exploded view.

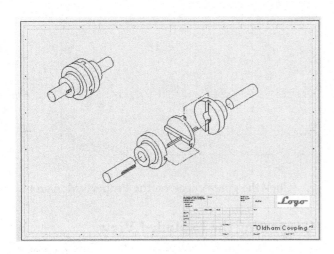

7. Click **Close Dialog** on the Property Manager.

Creating the Bill of Materials

1. Click the right mouse button on the sheet and select **Edit Sheet Format**.
2. Click on the top right corner of the sheet border.

3. Click the right mouse button and select **Set Anchor as > Bill of Materials**.

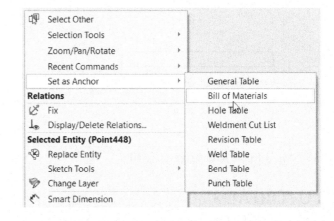

4. Click **Close Dialog** on the **Point** PropertyManager.
5. Click the right mouse button on the sheet and select **Edit Sheet**.
6. To create a parts list, click **Annotation > Tables > Bill of Materials** on the CommandManager.

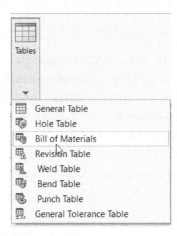

7. Click on the exploded view.
8. On the PropertyManager, under the **Table Position** section, check the **Attach to anchor point** option.

69

9. Set the **BOM Type** to **Parts only**.

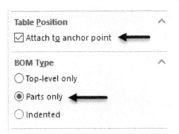

10. Click **OK**. You will notice that the BOM appears outside the sheet.

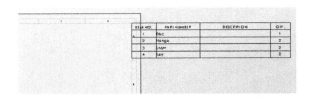

11. Click on the anchor point of the BOM.

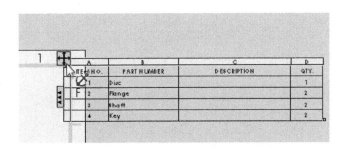

12. On the PropertyManager, under the **Table Position** section, select **Top Right**.

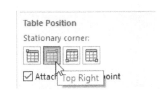

Creating Balloons

1. To create balloons, click **Annotation > Auto Balloon** on the CommandManager.
2. On the PropertyManager, under **Balloon Layout** section, select **Layout Balloons to Right**.
3. Click on the exploded view and click **OK**.

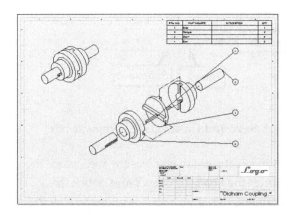

Adding Comments to the Drawing

SOLIDWORKS allows you to add comments to the drawing. This helps you in the inspection process.

1. Place the pointer on the exploded view.
2. Right click when the boundary of the view appears.
3. Select **Comment > Add Comment** from the shortcut menu.
4. Type a comment in the comment box.

In addition, you can add a timeline, image, or snapshot in the comment.

13. Click the green check on the PropertyManager.

SOLIDWORKS 2019 Learn by Doing

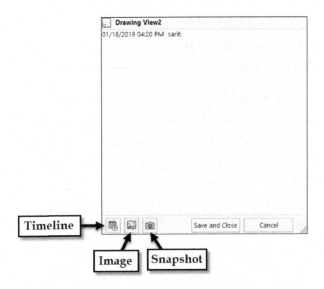

5. Click **Save and Close** on the comment box.

6. On the FeatureManager Design Tree, place the pointer the Drawing View2 and notice the comment.

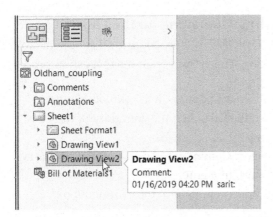

7. Save and close the drawing file.

Chapter 5: Sketching

In this chapter, you will learn the sketching tools. You will learn to create:

- Rectangles
- Polygons
- Resolve Sketch
- Relations
- Splines
- Ellipses
- Move, rotate, scale, copy, and stretch entities
- Circles
- Arcs
- Circular pattern
- Trim Entities
- Fillets and Chamfers

Creating Rectangles

A rectangle is a four-sided object. You can create a rectangle by just specifying its two diagonal corners. However, there are various tools to create a rectangle. You can access these tools from the **Rectangle** drop-down available on the **Sketch** CommandManager. These tools are explained next.

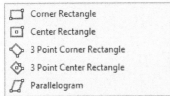

1. On the CommandManager, click **Sketch > Sketch** and select the Front plane.
2. On the CommandManager, click **Sketch > Rectangle Drop-down > Corner Rectangle** .
3. Select the origin point to define the first corner.
4. Move the pointer diagonally and click to define the second corner.

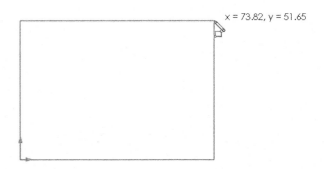

5. On the PropertyManager, click the **Center Rectangle** icon under the **Rectangle Type** section.
6. Click in the graphics window to define the center point.
7. Move the pointer and click to define the corner.

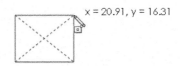

8. On the PropertyManager, select **From Midpoints** under the **Rectangle Type** section.
9. Select the center point and corner point of the rectangle. Two construction lines are created from the midpoints of the rectangles.

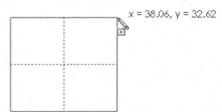

10. On the PropertyManager, click the **3 Point Corner Rectangle** icon under the **Rectangle type** section. This option creates a slanted rectangle. You can also check the **Add construction lines** option to add construction lines between the corners or midpoints.
11. Select two points to define the width and inclination angle of the rectangle.

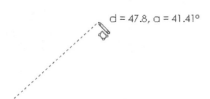

12. Select the third point to define its height.

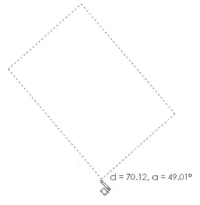

13. On the PropertyManager, click the **3 Point Center Rectangle** icon under the **Rectangle Type** section.
14. Click to define the center point of the rectangle.
15. Move the pointer and click to define the midpoint of one side.

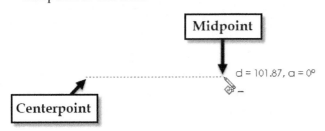

16. Move the pointer and click to define the corner point.

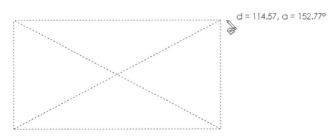

17. On the PropertyManager, click the **Parallelogram**  icon under the **Rectangle Type** section. This option creates a parallelogram by using three points that you specify.
18. Select two points to define the width of the parallelogram.

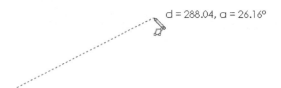

19. Drag the pointer and click to define the height of parallelogram.

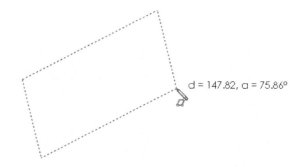

20. Click **Close Dialog** on the PropertyManager.

Lasso Selection

The **Lasso Selection** tool helps you to select multiple elements by dragging the pointer over them.

1. Click the right mouse button in the graphics window and select **Selection Tools > Lasso Selection**.

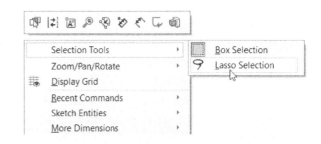

2. Click the left mouse button and drag the pointer covering the three elements of the rectangle, as shown.

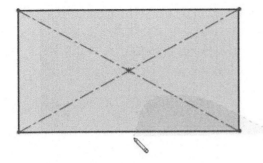

The three elements will be selected.

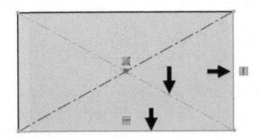

3. Press **Delete** to erase the elements of the rectangle.
4. Press Ctrl+A to select all the sketch elements.
5. Press **Delete** to erase the elements.

Creating Polygons

A Polygon is a shape having many sides ranging from 3 to 1024. In SOLIDWORKS, you can create regular polygons having sides with equal length. Follow the steps given next to create a polygon.

1. Activate the **Sketch** mode.
2. On the CommandManager, click **Sketch > Polygon**.
3. On the PropertyManager, type **8** in the **Number of Sides** box under the **Parameters** section.
4. Select **Inscribed circle**. This option creates a polygon with its sides touching a dotted circle. You can also select the **Circumscribed circle** option to create a polygon with its vertices touching a dotted circle.
5. Click to define the center of the polygon.
6. Move the pointer and click to define the size and angle of the polygon.
7. Press Esc to deactivate the tool.

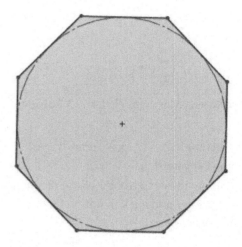

Resolve Sketch

When creating sketches for a part, SOLIDWORKS will not allow you to over-constrain the geometry. The term 'over-constrain' means adding more dimensions than required. The following figure shows a fully constrained sketch. If you add another dimension to this sketch (e.g. diagonal dimension), the **Make Dimension Driven** dialog appears.

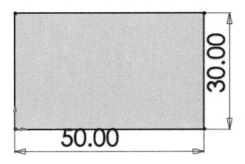

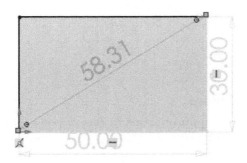

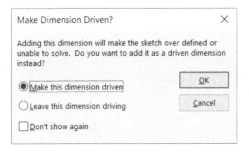

Now, you have to convert the new dimension into driven. Select **Make this dimension driven** and click **OK**.

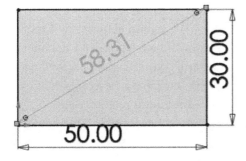

Now, if you change the value of the width, the reference dimension along the diagonal updates, automatically.

Relations

Relations are used to control the shape of a sketch by establishing relationships between the sketch elements. You can add relations using the **Add Relation** tool or pop-up toolbar or by selecting sketch elements.

Merge

This relation connects a point to another point.

1. On the **Sketch** tab of the CommandManager, click **Delete/Display Relations > Add Relation**.
2. Select two points.
3. Click **Merge** on the PropertyManager. The selected points will be merged together.

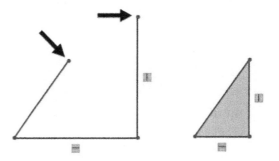

▬ Horizontal

To apply the **Horizontal** relation, click on a line and click the **Horizontal** icon on the context toolbar.

You can also align two points or vertices horizontally. Press the Ctrl key and select the two points. Click the **Horizontal** icon on the PropertyManager.

76

SOLIDWORKS 2019 Learn by Doing

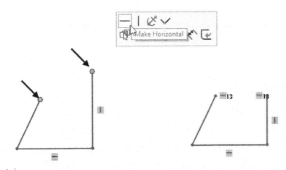

Vertical
Use the **Vertical** relation to make a line vertical. You can also use this relation to align two points or vertices vertically.

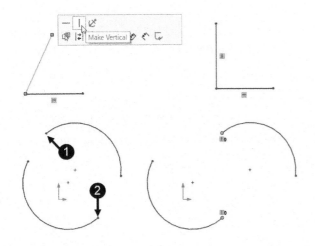

Tangent
This relation makes an arc, circle, or line tangent to another arc or circle. Select a circle, arc, or line. Press the Ctrl key and select another circle, or arc. Click the **Tangent** icon on the PropertyManager. The two elements will be tangent to each other.

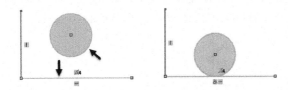

Parallel
Use the **Parallel** relation to make two lines parallel to each other. To do this, press and hold the Ctrl key and select the two lines to be parallel. Next, click the **Parallel** icon on the PropertyManager.

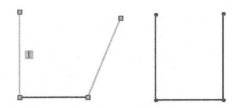

Perpendicular
Use the **Perpendicular** relation to make two entities perpendicular to each other.

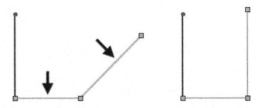

Midpoint
Use the **Midpoint** relation to make a point coincide with the midpoint of a line or arc.

1. Press the Ctrl key and select and line/arc and a point.
2. Click the **Midpoint** icon on the PropertyManager.

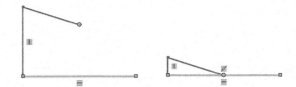

Automatic Relations
SOLIDWORKS automatically adds relations when you create sketch elements.

1. Start a new sketch and activate the **Line** tool from the **Sketch** CommandManager.
2. Click to specify the start point of the line.
3. Move the pointer in the horizontal direction and notice the **Horizontal** relation flag.
4. Click to create a line with the **Horizontal** relation.

5. Likewise, create a line with the **Vertical** relation.

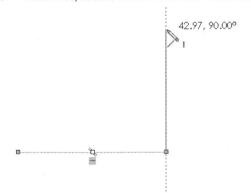

6. Create an inclined line as shown.

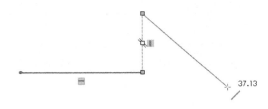

7. Move the pointer along the inclined line and notice the **Collinear** relation flag.

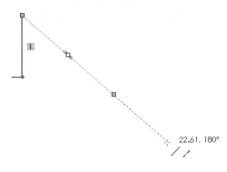

8. Move the pointer in the direction perpendicular to inclined line and notice the Perpendicular relation flag.
9. Click to create the line with the Perpendicular relation.

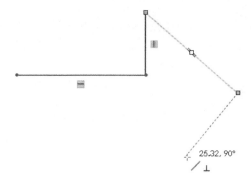

10. Press Esc to deactivate the **Line** tool.
11. Select the perpendicular line.

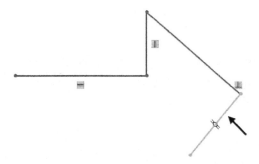

12. Right click and select **Sketch Entities > Line**.
13. Click in the graphics window to specify the start point of the line. Notice the yellow inferred lines with reference to the selected line.
14. Move along the yellow inferred line notice the **Parallel** relation flag.

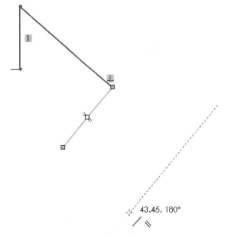

15. Click to create a line parallel to the selected line.
16. Press Esc to deactivate the **Line** tool.

17. On the CommandManager, click **Sketch > Circle**, and then create circle.
18. Activate the **Line** tool and click on the circle.
19. Move the pointer around the circle and notice that the line maintains the **Tangent** relation with the circle.

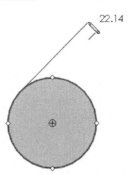

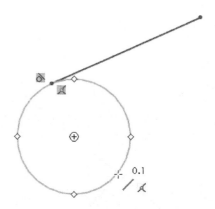

20. Click to create a line which is tangent and coincident to the circle. Right click and select **End chain**.

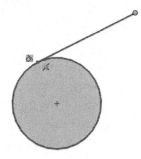

Deleting Relations

You can delete relations by using the following methods.

- Select the relation and press **Delete**.
- Select the sketch entity to view all its relations in the PropertyManager. Select the relations from the **Existing Relations** section of the PropertyManager and press **Delete**.
- On the CommandManager, click **Sketch > Display/Delete Relations**. On the PropertyManager, select the relations from the Relations section and click **Delete**. You can also use the **Delete All** button to delete all the relations.

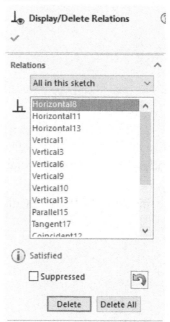

21. Activate the **Line** command.
22. Select a point on the circle and move the pointer.
23. Move the pointer back to the start point of the line.
    Notice the **Coincident** relation flag and the yellow inferred lines. You can create a line which is tangent or normal to the circle using the inferred lines.

Hiding Relations

To hide sketch relations by clicking the **Hide/Show Items** drop-down on the **View Heads-Up** Toolbar, and then deactivating the **View Sketch Relations** icon.

Sketch Numeric Input

The **Sketch Numeric Input** tool automatically adds dimensions to the sketch elements when you create them.

1. Click the Right Mouse button and select **Sketch Numeric Input** from the shortcut menu.

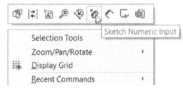

2. Activate a sketching tool and check the **Add Dimensions** option on the PropertyManager. In case of a circle, you can select the **Diameter dimensions** option to add the diameter dimension to the circle.
3. Start creating the sketch elements. Notice that you can enter the dimension values of the sketch elements. Use the Tab key to walk through the dimension values.

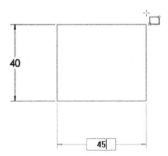

You can change the dimension units from flyout located at the bottom right corner of the window. The dimension units are reflected in the sketch.

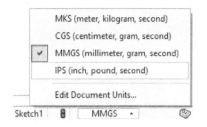

Replace Entity

The **Replace Entity** tool replaces a sketch entity with another one. You can use this tool instead of deleting a sketch entity and creating another one. This tool transfers all the associated features of the replaced entity to the replacement entity. This will avoid any parent-child errors when you modify the sketch. The following example shows the significance of this tool.

1. Start a new sketch on the Front plane and create the sketch, as shown.

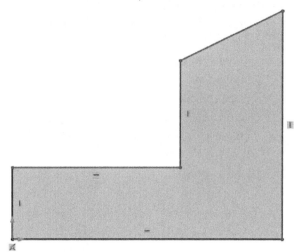

2. On the **Sketch** CommandManager, click the **Smart Dimension** tool.
3. Select the inclined line and the vertical line connected to it.

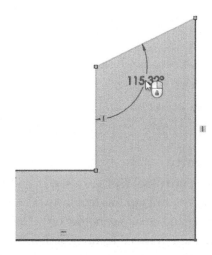

4. Place the dimension, type 115 in the **Modify** box, and then click **OK**.
5. Select the inclined line and move the pointer. Notice that the orientation of the dimension changes as per the movement of the pointer.
6. Move the pointer vertically upward and right click to lock the orientation of the dimension. Now, the orientation of the dimension does not change with the cursor movement.
7. Place the dimension and the specify its value as 35.
8. Likewise, add other dimensions to the sketch.

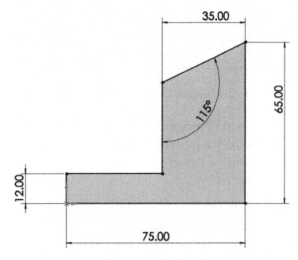

9. Exit the sketch, and then extrude it up to 50 mm distance.

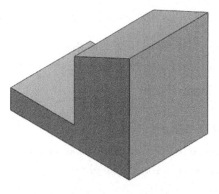

10. Activate the **Extrude Boss/Base** tool and click on the horizontal face of the model.

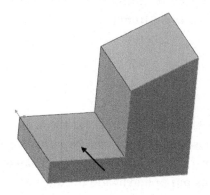

11. Create the sketch as shown. Exit the sketch.

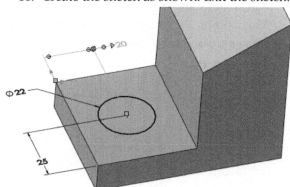

12. On the PropertyManager, select **Up To Surface** from the **Direction 1** drop-down.

13. Select the inclined face of the model, and then click **OK**.

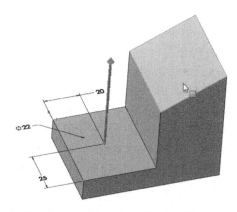

14. In the FeatureManager Design Tree, expand the Boss-Extrude1, click on the Sketch1, and then select the **Edit Sketch**.

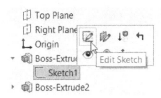

15. Select the inclined line and press **Delete** on your keyboard.

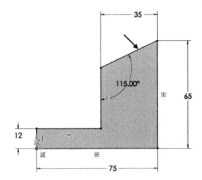

16. Click **Yes**.

17. Create a 3-point arc closing the sketch loop, as shown.

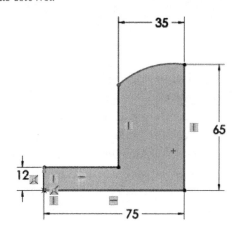

18. Click **Exit Sketch**. The **What's Wrong** dialog pops up on the screen. Its shows that the end face cannot terminate the extruded feature.

19. Close the dialog box, and press Ctrl+Z thrice to undo the changes.

20. Create an arc, as shown. Press Esc to deactivate the **3 Point Arc** command.

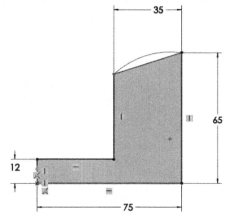

21. Right click in the graphics window and select **Replace Entity** from the shortcut menu.

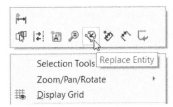

22. Select the inclined line as the entity to be replaced.
23. Select the arc as the replacing entity.
24. Check the **Make construction** option on the PropertyManager, and the click **OK**.
25. Apply 50 mm radius dimension to the arc.

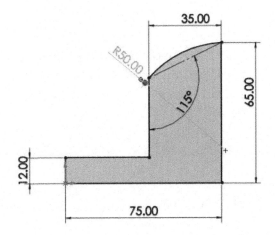

26. Exit the sketch and notice that end face of the extruded feature is replaced.

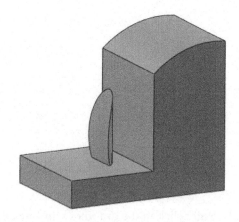

Make Path

The Make Path tool creates path combining all the sketch entities. When you apply a relation between anyone of the entity of the path and other individual entity, the relation will be persistent through all the entities of the path.

1. Create a closed sketch and a circle, as shown.

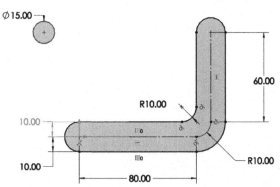

2. On the Menu bar, click **Tools > Sketch Tools > Make Path** ⌒.
3. Select all the entities of the closed loop, and then click **OK** on the PropertyManager.
4. Apply the **Tangent** relation between the circle and anyone of the entity of the closed loop.
5. Click and drag the circle notice that it maintains the **Tangent** relation with all the entities of the path.

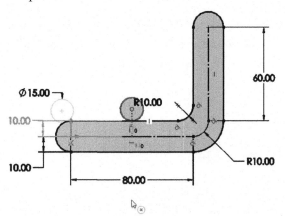

Path Length Dimension

The **Path Length Dimension** tool defines a fixed length for all the sketch entities combined together.

1. Create the sketch as shown.

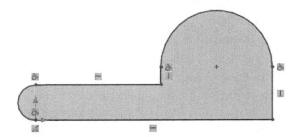

2. On the **Sketch** CommandManager, click **Smart Dimension > Path Length Dimension** ∑.
3. Drag a selection box across all the sketch entities to select them.
4. Click **OK** on the PropertyManager.
5. Double click on the Path Length dimension, type 200, and press Enter.
6. Click and drag the bottom horizontal line of the sketch. Notice that the path length is fixed and the sketch shape changes.

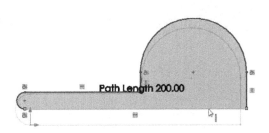

Convert Entities

The **Convert Entities** tool helps you to use the edges of the part geometry to create sketch elements.

1. Download the Chapter 5: Sketching folder from the Companion website.
2. Open the Convert_entities part file from the folder.
3. Start a sketch on the plane offset to the model face, as shown.
4. On the **Sketch** CommandManager, click the **Convert Entities** button.
5. Select the face of the model, as shown.

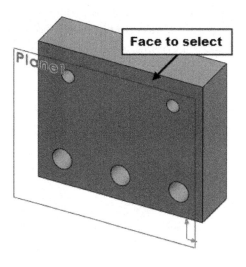

6. On the PropertyManager, click the **Select all inner loops** button to select the inner loops of the face.
7. Click on **Face<1>** in the **Entities to convert** selection box, and then select **Delete**.

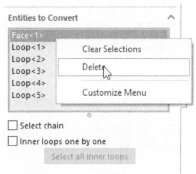

8. Click **OK** on the PropertyManager. All the internal loops of the selected face are projected onto the sketch plane.

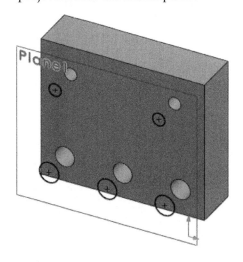

9. Select the previously selected face, and then click the **Convert Entities** button on the **Sketch** CommandManager. The outer loop of the face is converted into sketch elements.

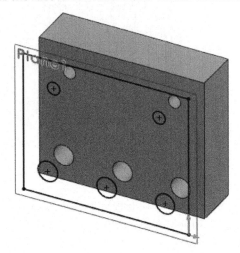

Midpoint line, Perimeter Circle, and SketchXpert

In this tutorial, you will create a sketch using the **Midpoint line** and **Perimeter Circle** tools.

1. Activate the **Sketch** mode.
2. On the CommandManager, click **Sketch > Line drop-down > Midpoint Line**.
3. Click on the origin point to define the midpoint of the line.
4. Move the pointer horizontally toward right and click.

5. Move the pointer upward and click when a dotted line appears.

6. Move the pointer away from the endpoint of the vertical line.
7. Move the pointer and place it on the end point of the vertical line.
8. Move the pointer horizontally toward left.
9. Move the pointer diagonally toward top left corner and click. Next, right click and select **Select**.

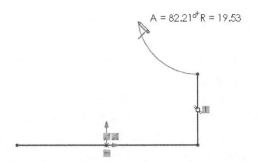

10. On the CommandManager, click **Sketch > Line drop-down > Centerline**.
11. Select the origin point of the sketch, move the pointer vertically upwards, and click. Press Esc.

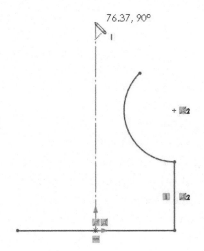

12. On the CommandManager, click **Sketch > Mirror Entities**.
13. Select the arc and right vertical line.
14. On the PropertyManager, click in the **Mirror about** selection box and select the vertical centreline. Click **OK**.

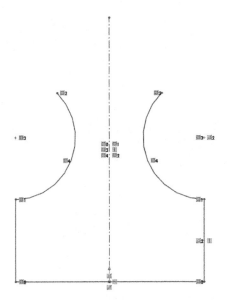

15. Right click and select **Sketch Entities > 3 Point Arc**.

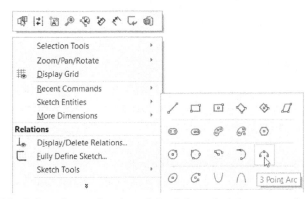

16. Select the end point of the left and right arc, and then move the pointer upward.
17. Click to create a three-point arc.

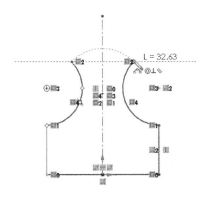

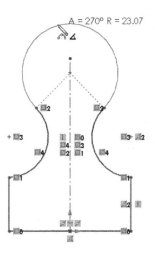

18. On the CommandManager, click **Sketch > Circle**.
19. Place the pointer on the three-point arc to display its centerpoint.
20. Select the centerpoint of the three-point arc, move the pointer outward, and click to create the circle.

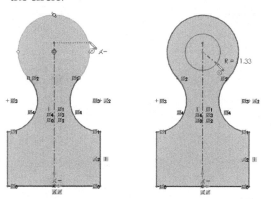

21. Add dimensions to the sketch, as shown. Press ESC to deactivate the **Smart Dimension** command.

SOLIDWORKS 2019 Learn by Doing

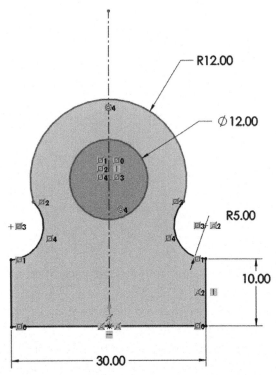

22. Press the Ctrl key and select the two arcs, as shown.

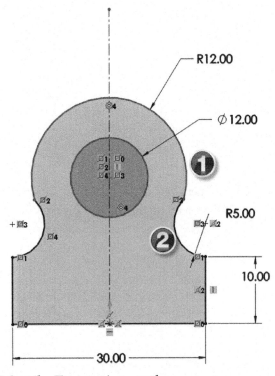

23. Select the **Tangent** icon on the PropertyManager, and click **OK**; the tangent relation is applied between the selected arcs. Also, the sketch is fully constrained.

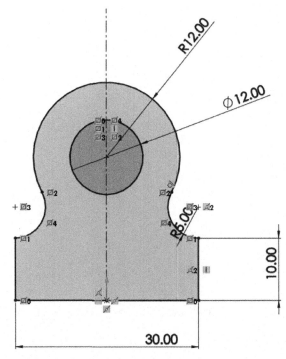

24. Exit the sketch.

Ellipses

Ellipses are also non-uniform curves, but they have a regular shape. They are actually splines created in regular closed shapes.

1. Activate the **Sketch** mode.
2. On the CommandManager, click **Sketch > Ellipse** drop-down **> Ellipse**.
3. Pick a point in the graphics window to define the center of the ellipse.
4. Move the pointer and click to define the radius and orientation of the first axis.

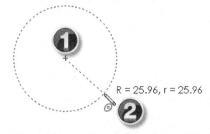

5. Move the pointer and click to define the radius of the second axis.

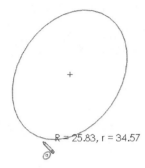

Click and drag the ellipse the notice that it is under-defined. You need to add dimensions and relations to fully define the ellipse.

6. Activate the **Line** tool and select the top quadrant point of the ellipse.
7. Move the pointer downward and select the centerpoint.
8. Move the pointer toward right and select the quadrant point.

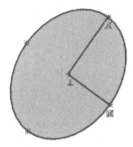

9. Press the Ctrl key and select the two lines.
10. Select **Perpendicular** from the PropertyManager.
11. Right click and select **Construction Geometry**.

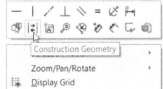

12. On the **Sketch** CommandManager, click the **Smart Dimension** tool.
13. Select the major axis line of the ellipse.
14. Select the origin point of the sketch. Notice the horizontal and vertical vectors of the sketch.
15. Select the horizontal vector of the sketch. The angled dimension is attached to the pointer.

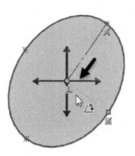

16. Move the pointer and place the angled dimension.

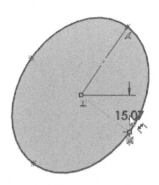

17. Type 15 and click **OK**.
18. Add the major and minor axes dimensions to the sketch. This fully-defines the sketch.

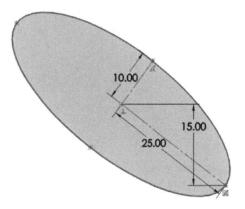

Partial Ellipse

1. On the CommandManager, click **Sketch > Ellipse drop-down > Partial Ellipse**.
2. Click to define the center of the partial ellipse.
3. Move the pointer and click to define the radius and orientation of the first axis.

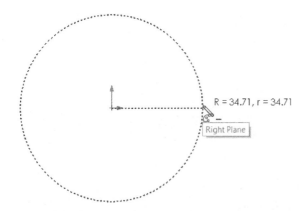

4. Move the pointer and click to define the radius of the second axis and start point.

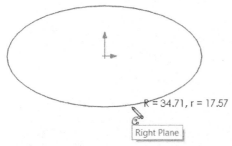

5. Rotate the pointer and click to define end point.

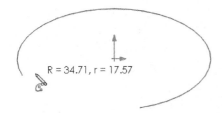

6. Click **Close Dialog** on the PropertyManager.

Conic

The **Conic** tool is used to create conic curve. You can use a conic curve to connect two open sketch entities.

1. Create a line and arc, as shown.

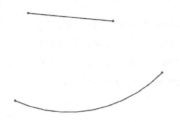

2. On the **Sketch** CommandManager, click **Ellipse** drop-down > **Conic**.
3. Select the endpoints of the line and arc.
4. Move the pointer and notice the dotted lines. These lines are tangent to the line and arc.
5. Select the intersection point of the dotted tangent lines. Move the pointer and notice the rho value displayed. The rho value defines the type of conic created.

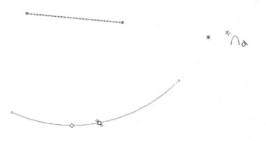

6. Click to the create the conic curve. Now, you have to specify the Rho value of the conic curve.
7. Expand the Parameters section of the PropertyManager, and then type 0.5 in the ρ box.
8. Click **Close Dialog** on the PropertyManager.

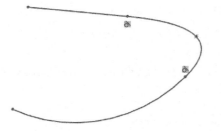

Move and Rotate Entities

The **Move Entities** tool moves a selected object(s) from one location to a new location without changing its orientation. To move objects, you must activate this tool and select the objects from the graphics window. After selecting objects, you must define the 'base point' and 'destination point'.

1. Create the sketch, as shown below.
2. Turn ON the **Shaded Sketch Contours** icon on the **Sketch** tab of the CommandManager.

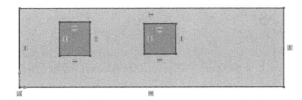

3. Click **Sketch > Move Entities** on the CommandManager.
4. Select the square located at the right-side by clicking inside it.
5. On the PropertyManager, under the **Parameter** section, select **From/To**.
6. Click in the **Start point** selection box, and then select the lower corner point as the base point.
7. Move the pointer toward right and pick a point as shown below. This moves the square to the new location.

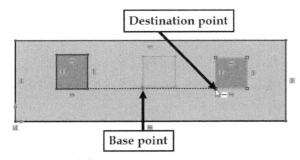

Rotate Entities

The **Rotate Entities** tool rotates an object or a group of objects about a base point.

1. On the CommandManager, click **Sketch > Move Entities > Rotate Entities**.
2. Drag a selection box covering the sketch elements, and click the right mouse button.
3. Click to define the base point of the rotation.
4. Click again to specify the second point.

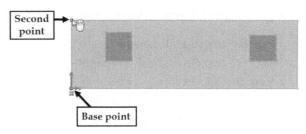

5. Press and hold the left mouse button, and drag the cursor; the select sketch elements to rotate. You can also type-in the rotation angle on the PropertyManager.

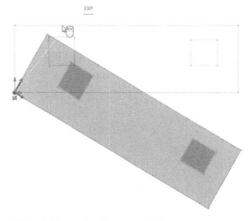

6. Click **OK** on the PropertyManager.

Copy Entities

The **Copy Entities** tool is used to copy objects and place them at a required location. This tool is similar to the **Move Entities** tool, except that object will remain at its original position and a copy of it will be placed at the new location.

1. Start a new sketch on anyone of the planes.
2. Turn OFF the **Shaded Sketch Contours** icon on the **Sketch** tab of the CommandManager.
3. Draw two circles of 80 mm and 140 mm diameter, respectively.

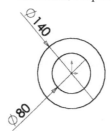

4. Click **Sketch > Move Entities > Copy Entities** on the CommandManager.
5. Select the two circles, and then right-click to accept the selection.
6. Select the center of the circle as the base point.
7. Move the pointer toward right and click.

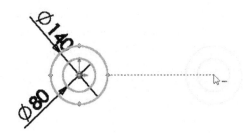

This creates a copy of the circles at the new location.

Scale Entities

The **Scale Entities** tool changes the size of objects. It reduces or enlarges the size without changing the shape of an object.

1. Click **Sketch > Move Entities > Scale Entities** on the CommandManager.
2. Select the circles shown below and right-click to accept the selection.

3. Select the center point of the selected circles as the base point.
4. Type 0.6 in the **Scale Factor** box under the **Parameters** section of the PropertyManager.
5. Uncheck the **Copy** option on the PropertyManager and click **OK**.

6. Click **Sketch > Circle drop-down > Perimeter Circle** on the CommandManager.
7. Select the two circles shown below to define the tangent points.

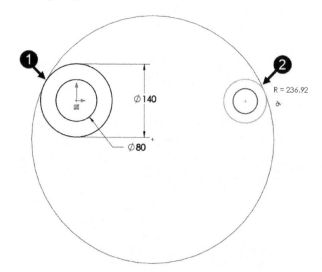

8. Move the pointer down and click to create the circle.

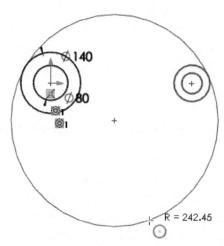

9. Likewise, create another circle by selecting the points as shown.

91

SOLIDWORKS 2019 Learn by Doing

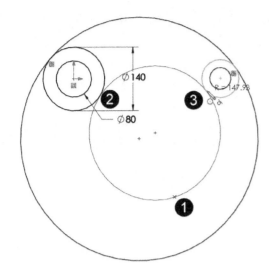

10. Click **Close Dialog** on the PropertyManager.

Trim Entities

When an object intersects with another object, you can remove its unwanted portion by using the **Trim Entities** tool.

1. Click **Sketch > Trim Entities** on the CommandManager.
2. On the PropertyManager, click the **Power trim** icon.
3. Press and hold the left mouse button and drag the pointer across the unwanted portions of the circles as shown.

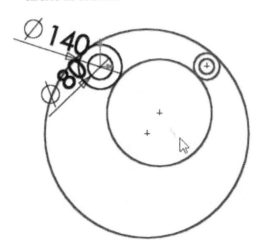

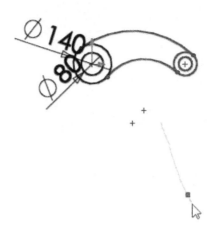

Check the **Keep trimmed entities as construction geometry** option, if you want to convert trimmed entities as construction geometry.

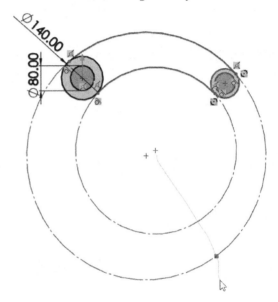

Check the **Ignore trimming of construction geometry** option, if you want to leave the construction geometry untrimmed.

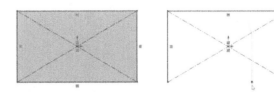

4. On the PropertyManager, click the **Trim Closest** icon.
5. Click on the inner portions of the circles, as shown.

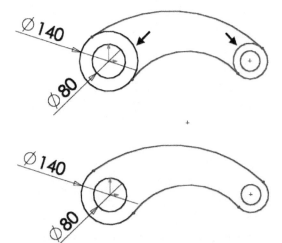

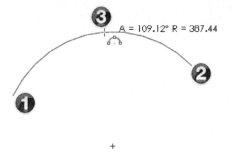

6. Click **Close Dialog** on the PropertyManager.
7. On the CommandManager, click **Sketch > Arc drop-down > 3 Point Arc**.
8. Select three points in the graphics window, as shown.

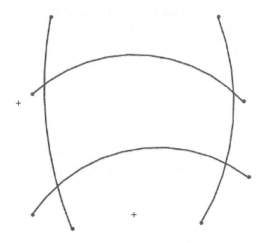

9. Create other arcs using the **3 Point Arc** tool, as shown.

10. On the CommandManager, click **Sketch > Trim Entities**.
11. On the PropertyManager, click the **Trim away inside** icon.
12. Click on the boundary entities, as shown.
13. Click on the entities to trim, as shown.

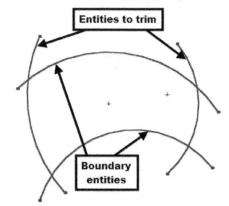

The inner portions of the entities are trimmed.

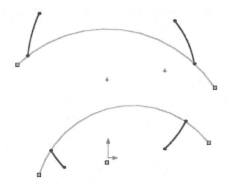

14. Press Ctrl+Z twice to undo the trim operations (or) click **Undo** twice on the Quick Access Toolbar.
15. Activate the **Trim Entities** tool and click the **Trim away outside** icon on the PropertyManager.
16. Click on the boundary and trim entities. The outer portions are trimmed, as shown.

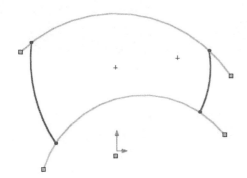

17. Undo the trim operations.
18. Activate the **Trim Entities** tool and click the **Corner** icon on the PropertyManager.
19. Click on the intersecting entities, a shown.

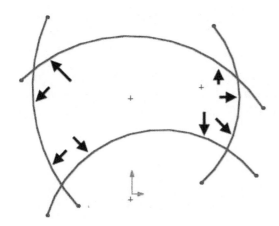

The entities are trimmed to form a corner.

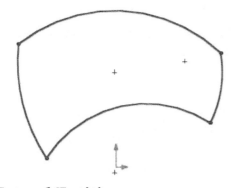

Extend Entities

The **Extend Entities** tool is similar to the **Trim Entities** tool but its use is opposite of it. This tool is used to extend lines, arcs and other open entities to connect to other objects.

1. Create a sketch as shown below.

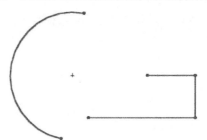

2. Click **Sketch > Trim Entities > Extend Entities** on the CommandManager.
3. Select the horizontal open line. This will extend the line up to arc.

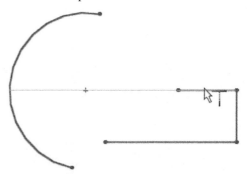

Likewise, extend the other elements, as shown.

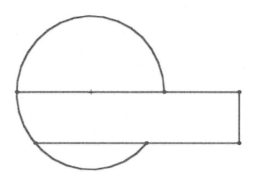

4. Trim the unwanted portions.

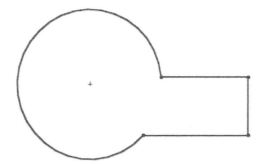

Offset Entities

The **Offset Entities** tool creates parallel copies of lines, circles, arcs and so on.

1. On the CommandManager, click **Sketch** tab > **Offset Entities**.
2. Check the **Select Chain** option on the PropertyManager to select connected elements.
3. Select an entity and notice that all the connected entities are selected.
4. Type-in the offset distance on the PropertyManager.
5. Click inside or outside the sketch to define the offset side.

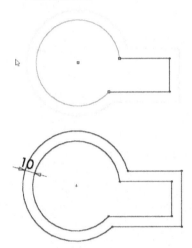

You can also reverse the offset direction by double-clicking on the offset dimension and selecting the **Reverse the sense of direction** button.

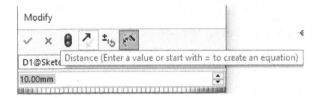

6. Create a line chain as shown.

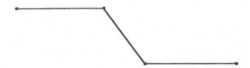

7. Activate the **Offset Entities** tool.
8. Select a line segment and notice that entire chain is selected.
9. Check the **Bi-directional** option. Notice that the offset preview appears on both sides.

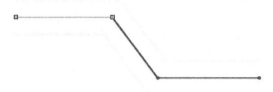

10. Check the **Cap ends** option and select **Arcs**. Notice that the ends are capped with arcs.

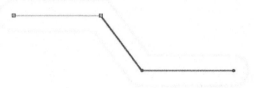

11. Check the **Base geometry** option under the **Construction geometry** section and click **OK**. The line chain is offset on both sides, and then converted into construction entity.

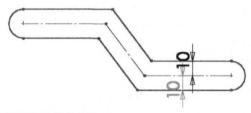

TUTORIAL 1

This tutorial teaches you to use **Sketch Fillet**, **Sketch Chamfer**, **Mirror Entities**, and **Tangent Arc** tools.

Sketch Fillet

The **Sketch Fillet** tool converts the sharp corners into round corners.

1. Draw the lines as shown below.

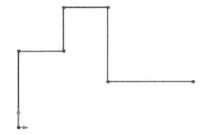

2. Click **Sketch > Sketch Fillet** on the CommandManager.
3. On the PropertyManager, type-in a value in the **Radius** box.
4. Click on the corner, as shown.

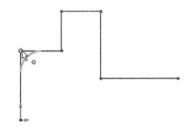

5. Select the vertical and horizontal lines, as shown.

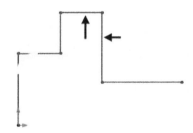

The **Keep constrained corners** option retains all the existing constraints.

The **Dimension each fillet** option dimensions all the fillets created in single instance. If you uncheck this option, only a single fillet is dimensioned and the **Equal** relation is applied between all other fillets.

6. Click **OK** on the PropertyManager. The fillets are created. The **Keep visible** icon on the PropertyManager will keep it open. You can select other corners or click the **Close** icon.

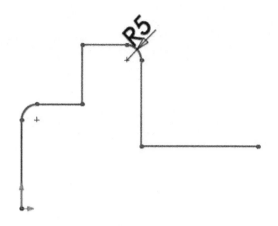

Sketch Chamfer

The **Sketch Chamfer** tool replaces the sharp corners with an angled line. This tool is similar to the **Sketch Fillet** tool, except that an angled line is placed at the corners instead of rounds.

1. Click **Sketch > Sketch Fillet > Sketch Chamfer** on the CommandManager.
2. On the PropertyManager, select the **Distance-distance** option and check the **Equal distance** option.
3. Type-in a value in the **Distance** box.
4. Click on the corner as shown.

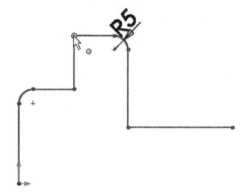

5. Click **OK** on the PropertyManager.

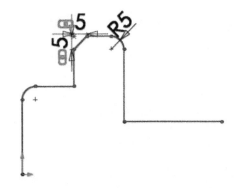

Mirror Entities

The **Mirror Entities** tool creates a mirror image of objects. You can create symmetrical sketches using this tool.

1. Create a horizontal centerline passing through the origin.

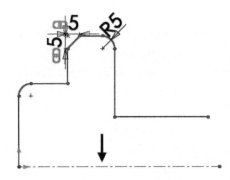

2. On the Command Manager, click **Sketch > Mirror Entities**.
3. Drag a selection box covering all the sketch entities.

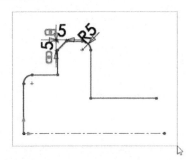

4. On the PropertyManager, click in the **Mirror about** box and select the centerline passing through the origin.
5. Click **OK** to mirror the selected entities.

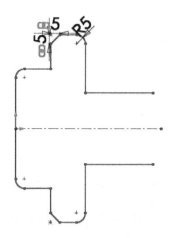

6. On the CommandManager, click **Sketch > Arc drop-down > Tangent Arc**.
7. Select the start point of the arc as shown below.

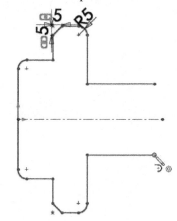

8. Move the pointer and select the end point of the arc, as shown below.

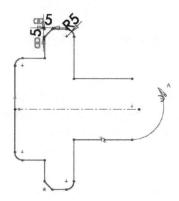

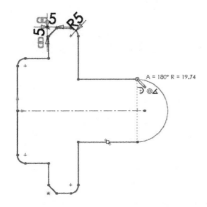

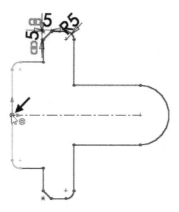

9. Click **OK** on the PropertyManager.

Stretch Entities

The **Stretch Entities** tool lengthens or shortens drawings or parts of sketches. Note that you cannot stretch circles using this tool. In addition, you must select the portion of the drawing to be stretched by dragging a selection box.

1. On the CommandManager, click **Sketch > Move Entities > Stretch Entities** .
2. Drag a crossing window to select the objects of the sketch, as shown. Click the right mouse button.

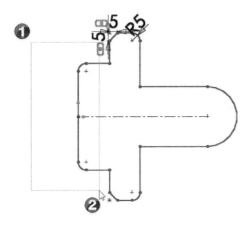

- Select the base point as shown below.

- Move the pointer toward left and click to stretch the sketch.

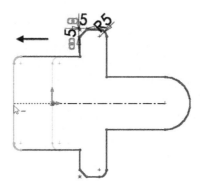

Circular Sketch Pattern

The **Circular Sketch Pattern** tool creates an arrangement of objects around a point in circular form.

1. Create two concentric circles of 140 and 50 diameters.

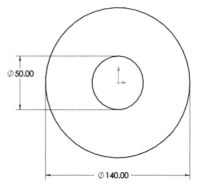

2. On the CommandManager, click **Sketch > Arc drop-down > Centerpoint Arc** .

3. Select the quadrant point of the circle as shown below.

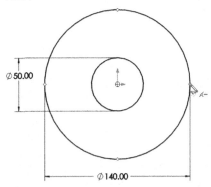

4. Move the pointer down and click on the circle when the **Coincident** symbol appears.

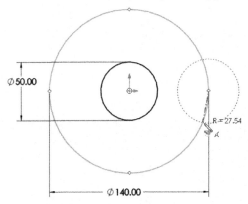

5. Move the pointer leftwards and up.
6. Click on the circle when the Coincident symbol appears.

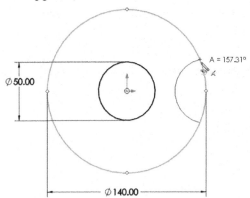

7. Click **Close Dialog** on the PropertyManager.
8. Dimension the arc with radius 30.

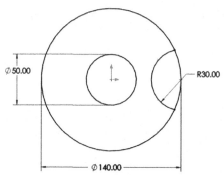

9. On the CommandManager, click **Sketch > Linear Sketch Pattern > Circular Sketch Pattern**.
10. Select the arc. The preview of the circular pattern appears as the center of the pattern is selected, automatically.

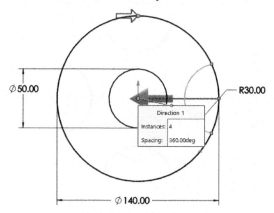

11. Leave the default options on the PropertyManager and click **OK**.
12. Trim the unwanted portions as shown below.

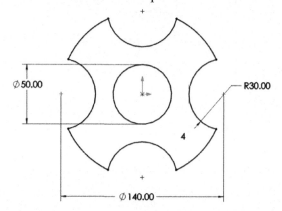

Text

Texts are used to provide information on the models such as company name, model specifications, and so on.

1. Start a new sketch.
2. Create the circle and two lines perpendicular to each other, as shown. Note that you need to check the **For Construction** option in the **Options** section of the PropertyManager while creating sketch elements.

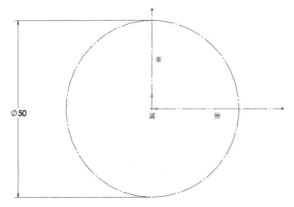

3. On the **Sketch** CommandManager, click the **Text** tool.
4. Select the horizontal line as the supporting curve.
5. Click in the **Text** box in the PropertyManager and type SOLIDWORKS. On the PropertyManager, use the **Alignment** options (**Left Align**, **Center Align**, **Right Align**, and **Full Justify**) to change the alignment of the text. Use the **Flip** options (**Flip Vertical** and **Flip Horizontal**) to the flip the text.

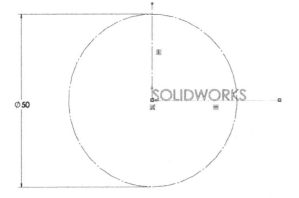

6. Uncheck the **Use document font** option; the font option is available.
7. Click the **Font** button to open the **Choose Font** dialog.
8. On the **Choose Font** dialog, change the font type, font style, height, and spacing between the text. Also, you can apply effects such as strikeout and underline.
9. Click **OK** on the **Choose Font** dialog.
10. Click right mouse button in the **Curve** box and select the **Clear Selections** option. Next, click on the vertical construction line.

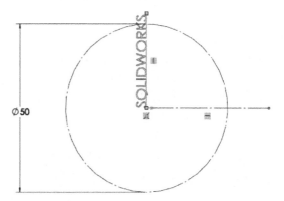

11. Select the text from **Text** box and click **Rotate**.
12. Change the rotation angle value in the **Text** box, as shown.

13. Right click in the **Curve** box and select **Clear Selections**.
14. Select the circle as the alignment curve.
15. Select the rotation angle value of the text 0.

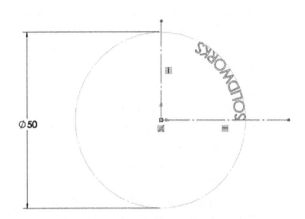

16. Click the **OK** on the PropertyManager.

3D Sketch

3D sketches are created without selecting any plane and sketch elements spread over the 3D space instead of a single plane. However, you can also use planes to create 3D sketch.

1. On the CommandManager, click **Sketch > Sketch drop-down > 3D Sketch** .
2. On the CommandManager, click **Sketch > Line** .
3. Select the origin point to define the start point.

4. Move the pointer along the X-axis and click to create a line.

5. Move the pointer along the Y-axis and click.

6. Press the Tab key to change the plane.
7. Move the pointer in the Z-direction and click.

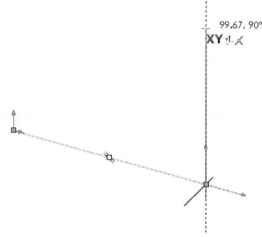

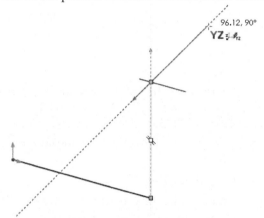

8. Press the Tab key to change the plane.
9. Move the pointer in the X-direction and click.

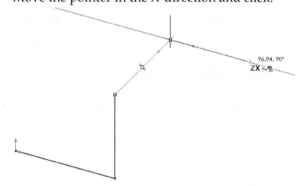

10. Click the right mouse button and select **Select**.
11. On the CommandManager, click **Sketch > Plane** .
12. Press the Ctrl key and select the end points as shown.
13. Click **OK** on the PropertyManager.

SOLIDWORKS 2019 Learn by Doing

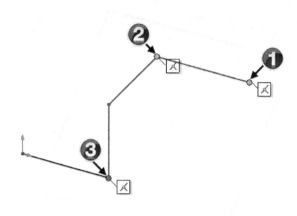

14. Activate the **Line** tool and click the end of the previous line.
15. Move the pointer and click when the **Vertical** symbol appears next to the pointer.

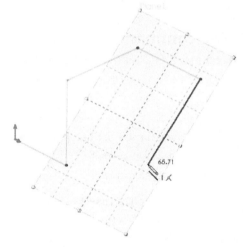

16. Move the pointer and click when the **Horizontal** symbol appears.

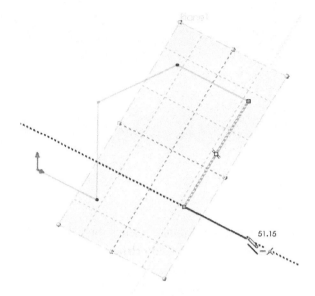

17. Click the right mouse button and select **Select**.
18. Add dimensions and relations, and then click **Exit Sketch**.

Mirroring Entities in a 3D Sketch

In a 3D sketch, you can mirror entities located on a same plane.

1. On the CommandManager, click the **Sketch** tab > **Sketch** drop-down > **3D Sketch**.
2. On the CommandManager, click the **Sketch** tab > **Plane** .
3. Select the Front Plane from the FeatureManager Design Tree.
4. Click the **Coincident** icon on the PropertyManager.
5. Click **OK**.

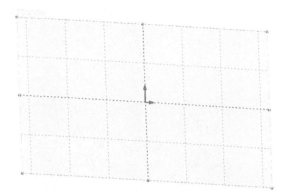

6. On the CommandManager, click the **Sketch** tab > **Line** drop-down > **Centerline**.
7. Select the sketch origin, move the pointer upward, and then click.

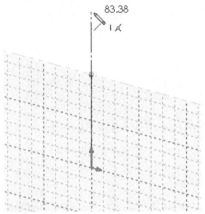

8. Right click and select **Select** from the shortcut menu.
9. Activate the **Line** command, and then create the sketch entities, as shown.

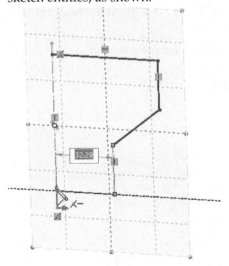

10. Press **Esc** to deactivate the **Line** command.
11. Click in the **Mirror about** selection box, and then select the centreline.
12. Click **OK** to mirror the entities.

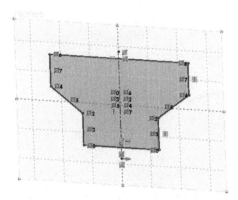

13. Click the **Exit Sketch** icon located at the top right corner in the graphics window.
14. Save and close the part file.

The Slicing command

The **Slicing** command is used to create sketch using the cross-section at the intersection of a plane and model geometry.

1. Download the Chapter 5: Sketching files from the companion website.
2. Open the Slicing.sldprt file.
3. On the Menu bar, click **Insert > Slicing**.
4. Selec the plane intersecting with the model, as shown.
5. Type 4 in the **Number planes to create** box.
6. Type 20 in the **Offset** box.
7. In the **Options** section, check the **Preview slices (slower)** option to preview the slices.

SOLIDWORKS 2019 Learn by Doing

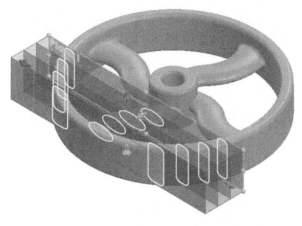

8. Click on the right arrow of the bounding box, and then drag it inside the model.

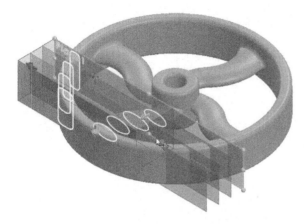

9. Likewise, click and drag the left arrow of the bounding box.

10. Click **OK**.

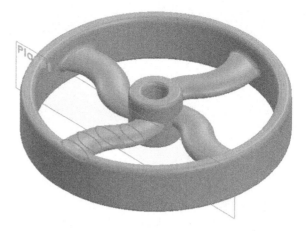

11. Expand the **Slice** folder in the FeatureManager Design Tree, and then notice the sketches and planes created.

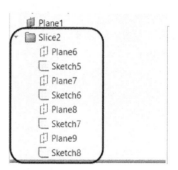

Generic Splines

The generic splines are created when you try to offset or project a spline, or create an intersection curve. This makes it easy to edit an entity created by projected or offsetting a spline.

1. Create a spline on the Front plane, as shown.

2. Create a plane offset to the Front plane.

104

SOLIDWORKS 2019 Learn by Doing

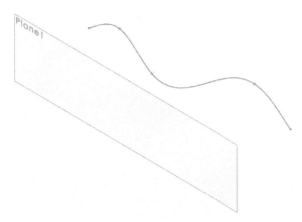

3. On the CommandManager, click **Sketch > Sketch**.
4. Select the newly created plane.
5. On the CommandManger, click **Sketch > Convert Entities**.
6. Select the spline and click **OK** on the PropertyManager.

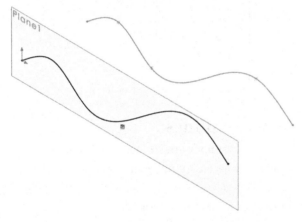

7. Select the projected spline and notice that the **Genetric Spline** PropertyManager appears.

On the **Generic Spline** PropertyManager, notice the **On Edge** relation in the **Existing Relations** box.

8. Select the **On Edge** relation in the **Existing Relation** box, and then press **Delete**; the relation is removed and the generic spline can be edited using the spline editing tools.

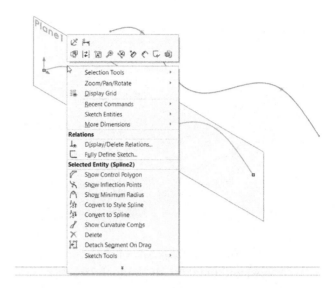

9. Click **Exit Sketch** on the CommandManager.

105

Chapter 6: Additional Modeling Tools

In this chapter, you construct models using additional modeling tools. You will learn to:

- Construct Helixes
- Add Reference Planes
- Construct Swept features
- Construct Revolved Cuts
- Mirror Features
- Construct Loft features
- Create multibody parts
- Add Indent Features
- Shell Models
- Create Helical threads
- Construct rib features
- Insert Holes
- Create Patterns

TUTORIAL 1

In this tutorial, you will construct a helical spring using the **Helix** and **Swept Boss/Base** tools.

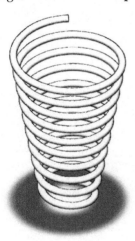

Constructing the Helix

1. Open a new SOLIDWORKS file using the **Part** template.
2. To construct a helix, click **Features > Curves > Helix and Spiral** on the CommandManager.

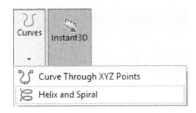

3. Click on the top plane.
4. Draw a circle of diameter 30.

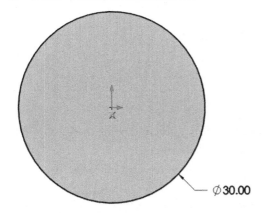

5. Click **Exit Sketch** and change the view to Isometric.

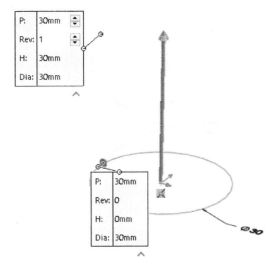

6. On the PropertyManager, set **Pitch** to 10 mm.
7. Set **Revolutions** to 10.
8. Select **Clockwise**.
9. Check the **Taper Helix** option and set **Taper Angle** to 10.
10. Click **OK**.

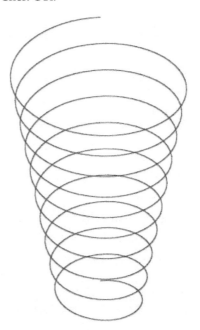

Adding the Reference Plane

1. To add a reference plane, click **Features > Reference Geometry > Plane** on the CommandManager.

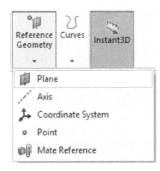

2. Select the helix from the graphics window.
3. Select the end of the helix.

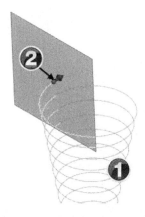

4. Leave the default values and click **OK** ✓.

Constructing the Swept feature

1. On the CommandManager, click **Sketch > Sketch**.
2. Select the plane created normal to helix.
3. On the **View (Heads Up)** Toolbar, click **View Orientation > Normal To**.

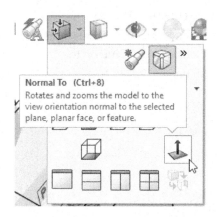

4. Draw circle of 4 mm diameter.

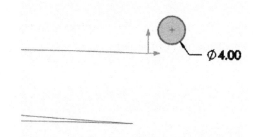

5. On the CommandManager, click **Sketch > Display/Delete Relations > Add Relations**.
6. Click on the center point of the circle and helix.
7. On the PropertyManager, under the **Add Relations** section, select **Pierce**.

8. Click **OK** ✓.

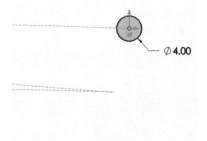

9. Click **Exit Sketch** and change the view orientation to Isometric.
10. To construct a Swept feature, click **Features > Swept Boss/Base** on the CommandManager.
11. Select the circle to define the profile.
12. On the PropertyManager, click in the **Path** selection box and select the helix to define the path.
13. Leave the default settings and click **OK** to construct the Swept feature.
14. On the **View Heads-Up** toolbar, click the **Visibility** drop-down and turn off the **Plane** and **Curves** icons.

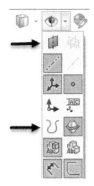

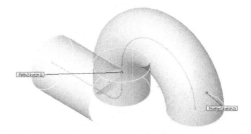

Note: In the above figure, the cross-section plane is normal to the path.

In SOLIDWORKS, you can create a profile anywhere along the path. For example, create a profile at the middle of the path, as shown. Activate the Swept tool and select the profile and path. On the PropertyManager, use the **Direction 1**, **Bidirectional**, and **Direction 2** icons to Swept the profile.

Direction 1

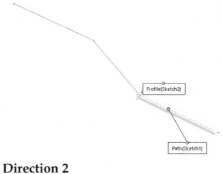

Direction 2

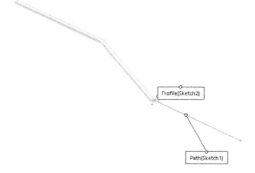

15. Save and close the file.

You need to make sure that the size of the cross section is not larger than the curves on the path, the resulting geometry will intersect and the Swept will fail.

Bidirectional

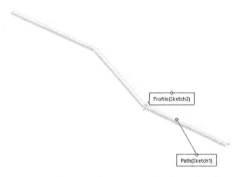

In SOLIDWORKS, you can select the face of a model to define the swept profile.

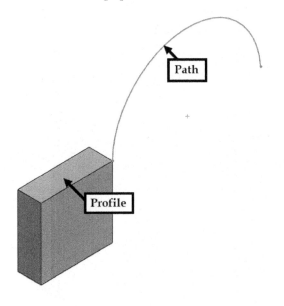

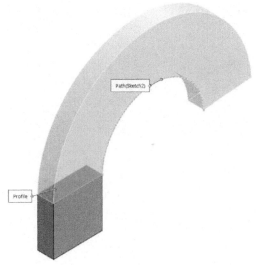

TUTORIAL 2

In this tutorial, you construct a pulley wheel using the **Revolve Boss/Base** and **Revolved Cut** tools.

1. Open a new file in the **Part** Environment.
2. On the CommandManager, click **Sketch > Sketch**.
3. Click on the right plane.
4. On the CommandManager, click **Sketch > Line > Centerline**.
5. Construct a horizontal centerline passing through origin.
6. Construct the sketch, as shown in figure.

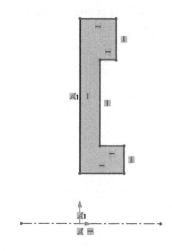

7. Add dimensions to the sketch.
8. Add the **Coincident** relation between the origin

and the vertical line at the center. Next, exit the sketch.

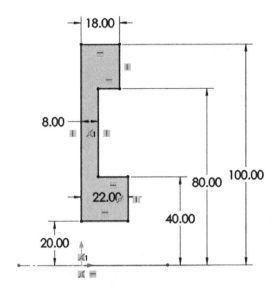

9. Construct the revolved boss.

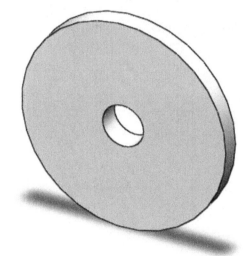

Constructing a Revolved Cut

1. To construct a revolved cut, click **Features > Revolved cut** on the CommandManager.
2. Expand the **FeatureManager Design Tree** and select the right plane.
3. Under the **FeatureManager Design Tree**, click the right mouse button on the sketch and select **Normal To**.

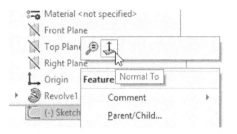

4. On the CommandManager, click **Sketch > Convert Entities**.
5. Click on the horizontal edge of the model. Click **OK**.

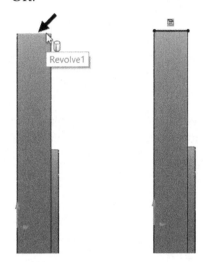

6. Activate the **Line** command.
7. Select the left endpoint of the converted edge.
8. Move the pointer vertically downward and click.
9. Move the pointer horizontally toward right and click.
10. Move the pointer upward and select a point on the converted edge.

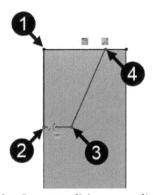

11. On the CommandManager, click **Sketch > Trim**

Entities.

12. On the PropertyManager, click the **Power Trim** icon.
13. Click and drag the left mouse button across the unwanted portion of the converted edge, as shown. Next, press Esc.

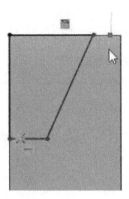

14. Select the inclined and horizontal lines, move the pointer toward left and click to place the dimension.

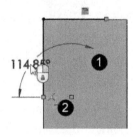

15. Type 110 and press Enter.
16. Select the upper horizontal line, move the pointer upward and click to place the dimension. Type 13 and press Enter.
17. Select the lower horizontal line, move the pointer downward and click to place the dimension. Type 5 and press Enter.
18. Create a horizontal centreline passing through the origin.

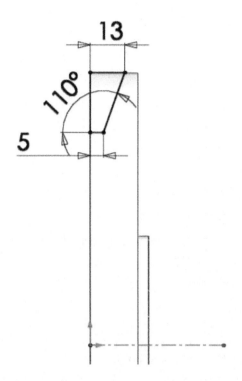

19. Click **Exit Sketch** and click **OK**.

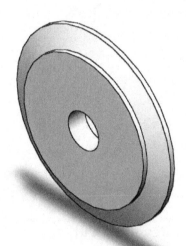

Constructing a Mirror Feature

1. To construct the mirror feature, click **Features > Mirror** on the CommandManager.
2. Click on the front flat face to define the mirror face.

SOLIDWORKS 2019 Learn by Doing

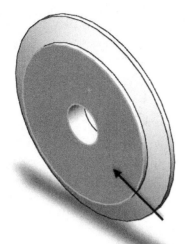

3. On the PropertyManager, expand the **Bodies to Mirror** section and click on the model geometry.
4. Click **OK**.

5. Save and close the model.

TUTORIAL 3

In this tutorial, you construct a shampoo bottle using the **Loft**, **Extrude**, **Shell**, **Indent**, and **Swept** tools.

Creating Sections and Guide curves

To construct a lofted boss, you need to create sections and guide curves.

1. Open a new file in the **Part** Environment.
2. On the CommandManager, click **Sketch > Sketch**.
3. Select the top plane.
4. On the CommandManager, click **Sketch > Ellipse**.
5. Select the origin point of the sketch.
6. Move the pointer horizontally and left click.
7. Move the pointer vertically and left click.

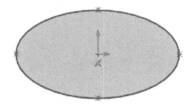

8. Create two centerlines passing to the origin and perpendicular to each other, as shown.

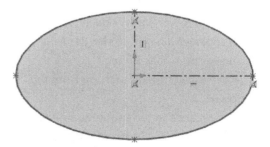

114

9. Activate **Smart Dimension** tool and add dimensions to the centerlines, as shown.

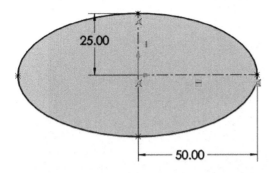

10. Click **Exit Sketch**.
11. Change the orientation to Isometric.
12. On the CommandManager, click **Sketch > Sketch**.
13. Select the front plane.
14. On the CommandManager, click **Sketch > Spline**.
15. Draw a spline similar to the one shown in figure.

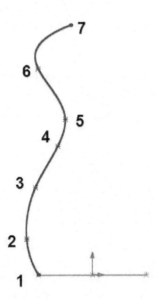

16. Press the Ctrl key and click on the first point of the spline and the previous sketch.
17. On the PropertyManager, under the **Add Relations** section, click **Pierce**.
18. Draw a vertical centreline starting from the origin point.
19. Apply dimensions to the spline, as shown in figure. First, create the horizontal dimensions, and then create the vertical dimensions in the descending order.

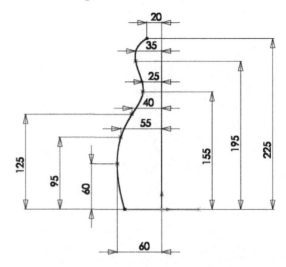

20. On the CommandManager, click **Sketch > Mirror Entities**.
21. Select the spline.
22. On the PropertyManager, click **Mirror about**, and then select the vertical centerline.
23. Click **OK**.

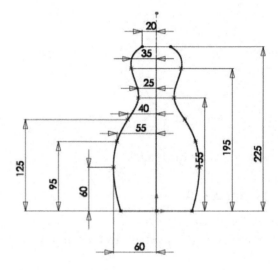

24. Click **Exit Sketch**.
25. Change the view orientation to Isometric.

Creating another section

1. On the CommandManager, click **Features > Reference Geometry > Plane**.
2. Select the top plane from FeatureManager Design Tree.

3. On the PropertyManager, type-in **225** in the **Offset Distance** box.

4. Click **OK**.
5. Start a sketch on the new reference plane.
6. Draw a circle of 40 mm diameter.

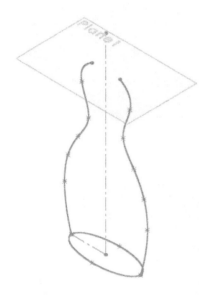

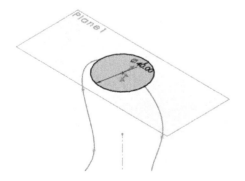

7. Click **Exit Sketch**.
8. Change the view to Isometric.

Constructing the swept feature

1. On the CommandManager, click **Features > Lofted Boss/Base**.
2. Select the circle and ellipse.
3. On the PropertyManager, click in the **Guide Curves** selection box, select the first guide curve, as shown. Next, click **OK** on the box.

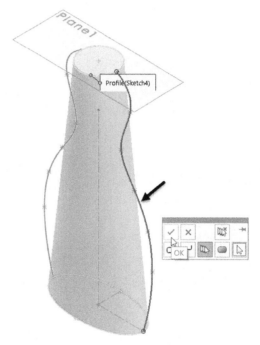

4. Select the second guide curve and click **OK** on the box.

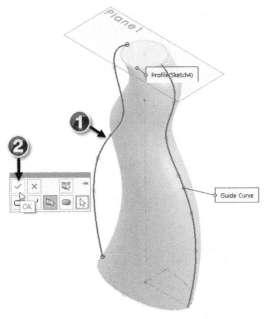

2. Press the Ctrl key and select the reference plane located at the top of the lofted feature.
3. On the Menu bar, click **Insert > Derived Sketch**.

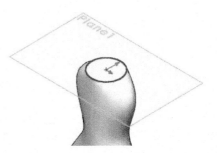

4. Click **Exit Sketch**.
5. Activate the **Extrude Boss/Base** tool and extrude the sketch up to 25 mm depth.

5. Click **OK**.

Constructing the Extruded feature

1. In the **FeatureManager Design Tree**, expand the Loft feature and select the Sketch 3.

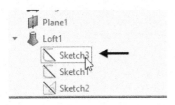

Adding Fillets

1. On the CommandManager, click **Features > Fillet**.
2. On the PropertyManager, click the **FilletXpert** tab.
3. Click on the bottom and top edges of the loft feature.

4. Set **Radius** to 5 mm.

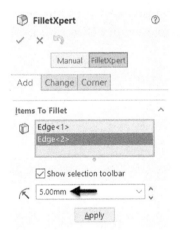

5. Click **OK** to add the fillet.

Shelling the Model

1. On the CommandManager, click **Features > Shell** .
2. On the PropertyManager, set **Thickness** to 2 mm.
3. Select the top face of the cylindrical feature.

4. Click **OK** to shell the geometry.

Adding the Indent feature

1. On the CommandManager, click **Features > Reference Geometry > Plane** .
2. In the **FeatureManager Design Tree**, select the Front plane.

SOLIDWORKS 2019 Learn by Doing

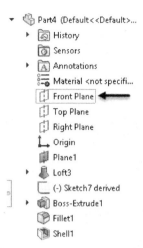

3. On the PropertyManager, type-in **50** in the **Offset distance** box.

4. Click **OK**.

5. Create a sketch on the plane, as shown in figure.

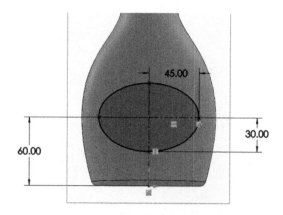

6. Click **Exit Sketch**.
7. On the CommandManager, click **Features > Extruded Boss/Base**.
8. Select the sketch.
9. On the PropertyManager, under the **Direction1** section, select **End Condition > Up To Surface**.
10. On the **PropertyManager**, under **Direction 1**, uncheck **Merge result**.

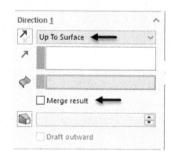

11. Rotate the model and select the inner face of the model geometry.

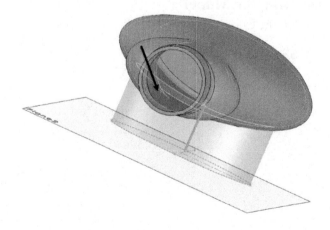

119

12. Click **OK** to create separate extruded body.

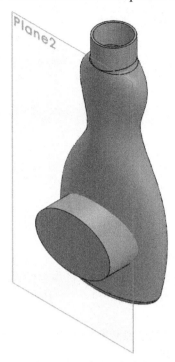

13. On the Menu bar, click **Insert > Features > Indent**.

14. Click on the loft feature to define the target body.
15. Click on the extruded body to define the tool body.
16. On the PropertyManager, select **Remove Selections**.
17. Under the **Parameters** section, set the **Thickness** value to 2 and **Clearance** value to 1.

18. Click **OK** to indent the extruded body onto the lofted body.
19. Hide the extruded body, sketch, and plane.

20. Add 1 mm fillet to the inner and outer edges of the indent.

120

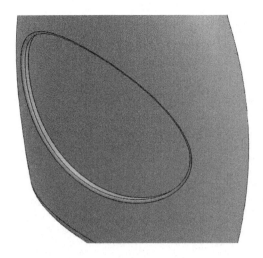

Adding Threads

1. On the CommandManager, click **Features > Reference Geometry > Plane**.
2. Click on the top face of the model geometry.
3. Set the **Distance** value to 5 and check the **Flip offset** option.
4. Click **OK**; a new reference plane is created.

5. Start sketch on the new reference plane.
6. On the CommandManager, click **Sketch > Convert Entities**.
7. Click on the outer edge of the cylindrical feature and click **OK**.

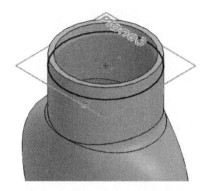

8. Click **Exit Sketch**.
9. On the CommandManager, click **Features > Curves > Helix and Spiral**.
10. Select the circular sketch.
11. On the PropertyManager, select **Constant pitch**.
12. Type-in 7 in the **Pitch** box and check the **Reverse Direction** option.
13. Type-in 2 in the **Revolutions** box.
14. Set the **Start Angle** value to **0**.
15. Uncheck the **Taper Helix** option.
16. Click **OK**.

17. On the CommandManager, click **Features > Reference Geometry > Plane**.
18. Click on the helix and its start point.

19. Click **OK**.
20. Start a sketch on the new reference plane.
21. On the Heads-Up toolbar, click **View Orientation drop-down > Normal To**.
22. Activate the **Line** command and specify the points of the line-chain, as shown.

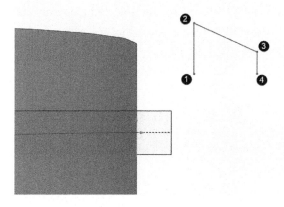

23. Activate the **Centerline** command and create a horizontal line.

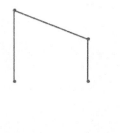

24. Press the Ctrl key and select the left endpoint of the centerline. Next, select the helix.

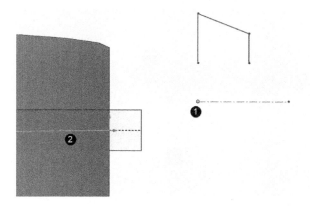

25. On the PropertyManager, click the **Pierce** icon; the endpoint of the centreline is pierced with the endpoint of the helix.

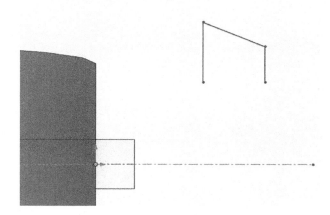

26. Press the Ctrl key and select the lower endpoint of the vertical line of the sketch. Next, select the centreline.

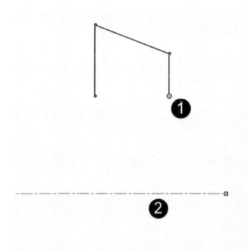

27. Click the **Coincident** icon on the PropertyManager.
28. Click and drag the left vertical line of the sketch such that it is inside the model geometry.

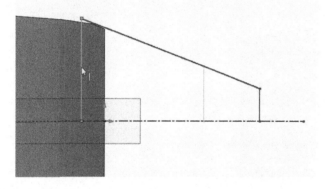

29. Activate the **Sketch Fillet** command and type **0.5** in the **Fillet Radius** box on the PropertyManager.
30. Select the corner point of the right vertical and inclined line, as shown.

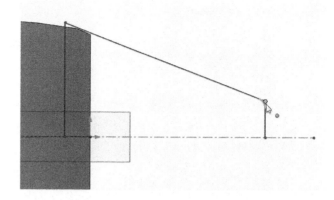

31. Click **OK** on the PropertyManager.
32. On the CommandManager, click the **Mirror Entities** button, and then select all the sketch elements except the centreline.
33. On the PropertyManager, click in the **Mirror about** selection box, and then select the centreline.
34. Click **OK** to mirror the selected elements about the centreline.

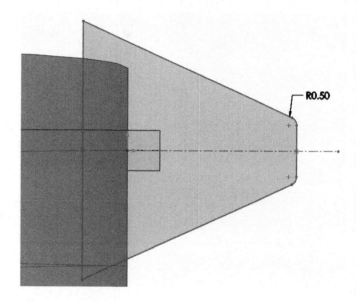

35. Add dimensions to sketch using the **Smart Dimension** command.

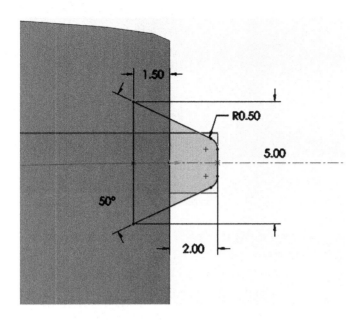

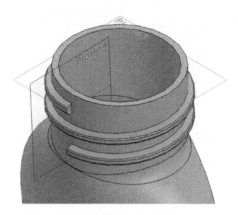

41. Start a sketch on the end face of the thread.

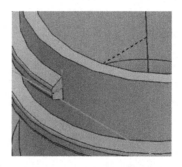

36. Click **Exit Sketch**.
37. On the CommandManager, click **Features > Swept Boss/Base** .
38. Click on the thread profile and the helix.

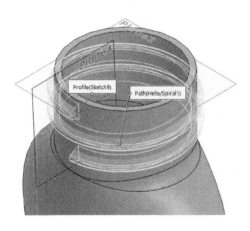

42. On the CommandManager, click **Sketch > Covert Entities** and select the thread profile of the Swept feature from the FeatureManager Design Tree.

43. Click **OK**.

39. On the PropertyManager, expand the **Options** section and check **Merge result**.
40. Click **OK**.

124

SOLIDWORKS 2019 Learn by Doing

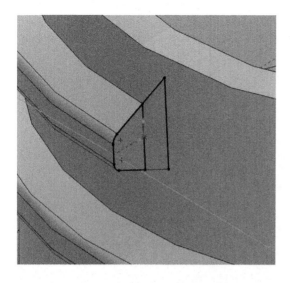

44. Click **Exit Sketch**.

45. Activate the **Revolved Boss/Base** tool and click on the vertical line of the sketch.

46. On the PropertyManager, set **Direction 1 Angle** to **100**.

47. Use the **Reverse Direction** button, if the preview of the revolved feature is displayed inside the model.

48. Check the **Merge result** option.

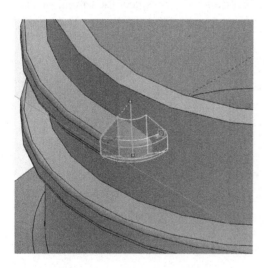

49. Click **OK**.
50. Rotate the model and click on the other end of the thread.

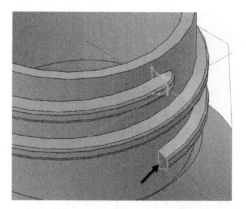

51. Press the Ctrl key and select the sketch used for the previous revolved feature.
52. On the Menu bar, click **Insert > Derived Sketch**; the sketch is projected onto the sketch plane.

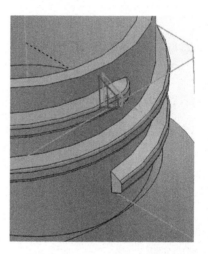

53. Press Esc to deselect the sketch.
54. On the CommandManager, click **Display/Delete Relations > Add Relations**.
55. Click on the inclined line of the sketch and the inclined edge of the end face.

125

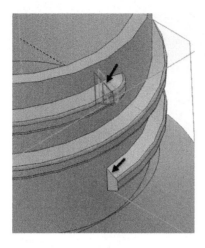

56. On the PropertyManager, click **Collinear**.
57. Press the Ctrl key and click on the end-points, as shown in figure.

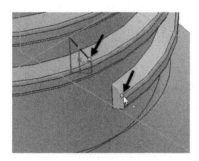

58. On the PropertyManager, click **Coincident**.

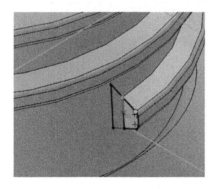

59. Click **Exit Sketch** on the Command Manager.
60. Create a revolved boss using the sketch.

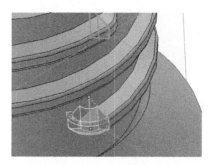

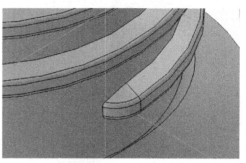

61. Save the model and close it.

TUTORIAL 4

In this tutorial, you construct a patterned cylindrical shell.

SOLIDWORKS 2019 Learn by Doing

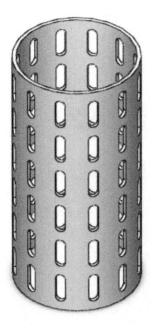

Constructing a cylindrical shell

1. Start a new file using the **Part** template.
2. Create a sketch on the top plane.

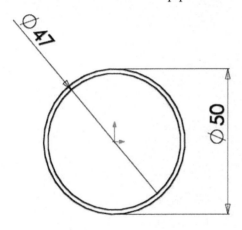

3. Extrude the sketch up to 100 mm depth.

Adding a Slot

1. Activate the **Extruded Cut** tool.
2. Click on the front plane.
3. On the CommandManager, click **Sketch > Straight Slot**.
4. Click to define the first point of the slot.

5. Move the pointer up and click to define the second point.

127

6. Move the pointer and click to create a slot.
7. Add dimensions to the slot.

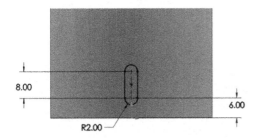

8. Click **Exit Sketch**.
9. On the PropertyManager, select **End Condition > Through All**.
10. Click the **Reverse Direction** button next to the **End Condition** drop-down.

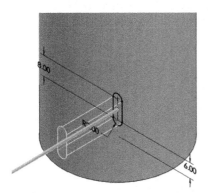

11. Click **OK**.

Constructing the Axis

1. On the CommandManager, click **Features > Reference Geometry > Axis**.
2. Click on the inner cylindrical face of the model geometry.

3. Click **OK** to construct the axis.

Constructing the Linear pattern

1. On the CommandManager, click **Features > Linear Pattern**.
2. On the PropertyManager, under the **Features and Faces** section, click in the **Features to Pattern** box, and then select the slot.
3. In the FeatureManager Design Tree, select the newly created axis. You can also select the Top Plane from the FeatureManager Design Tree.

4. On the PropertyManager, under the **Direction1** section, set the **Spacing** value to 16.

SOLIDWORKS 2019 Learn by Doing

5. Set **Number of Instances** to 6.

6. Click **OK**.

Constructing the Circular pattern

1. On the CommandManager, click **Features > Linear Pattern > Circular Pattern**.
2. In the FeatureManager Design Tree, select the linear pattern and the cut-extrude feature.

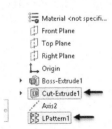

3. On the PropertyManager, click in the **Pattern Axis** selection box and select the cylindrical face of the model.

4. Type-in **12** in the **Number of Instances** box.
5. Check the **Equal Spacing** option.
6. Click **OK** to make the circular pattern.

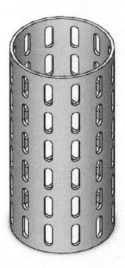

11. Save and close the model.

129

TUTORIAL 5

In this tutorial, you construct the model shown in figure.

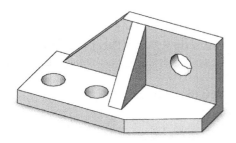

Constructing the first feature
1. Open a new part file.
2. Construct the first feature on the top plane (extrude the sketch up to a distance of 10 mm).

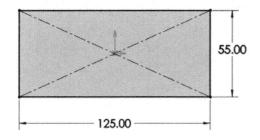

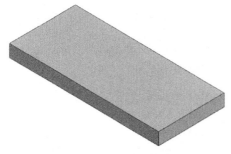

Constructing the Second Feature
1. Draw the sketch on the top face of the first feature.

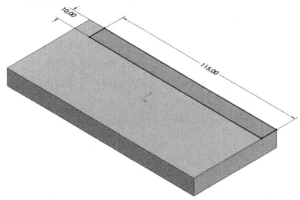

2. Click **Exit Sketch**.
3. On the CommandManager, click **Features > Extruded Boss/Base** .
4. Type-in **45** in the **Depth** box.

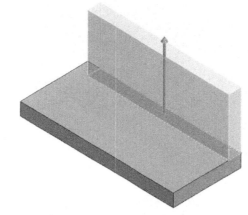

5. Click **OK**.

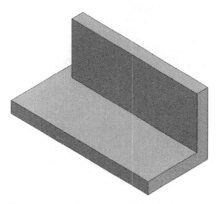

Constructing the third feature
1. On the CommandManager, click **Features > Reference Geometry > Plane**.
2. Click on the right-side face of the model geometry.

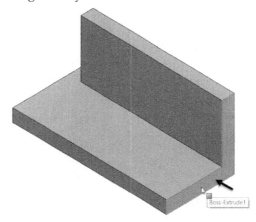

3. Click on the left-side face of the second feature.

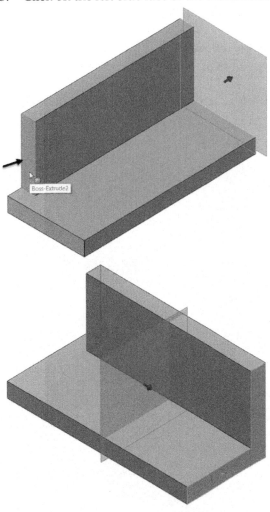

4. Click **OK**.
5. Draw the sketch on the new reference plane.

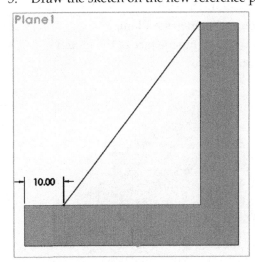

6. Click **Exit Sketch**.
7. On the CommandManager, click **Features > Rib** .

8. On the PropertyManager, click **Thickness > Both Sides**.
9. Set **Rib Thickness** to 10.
10. Select **Extrusion direction > Parallel to Sketch**.
11. Check the **Flip material side** option.
12. Click **OK**.

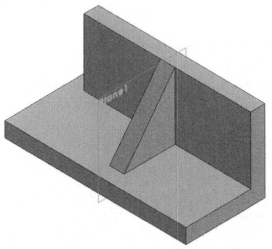

Inserting Holes

1. To insert holes, click **Features > Hole Wizard** on the CommandManager.
2. On the **Hole Specification** PropertyManager, select the **Hole** icon.
3. Select **Standard > ANSI Metric**.
4. Select **Type > Drill Sizes**.
5. Under the **Hole Specifications** section, select **Size > 16**.
6. Select **End Condition > Through All**.
7. Expand the **Tolerance/Precision** section.
8. Select the **Tolerance Type > Bilateral**.
9. Type **0.05** in the **Maximum Variation** box.
10. Type **-0.02** in the **Minimum Variation** box.
11. Click the **Positions** tab and click on the top face of the base feature.
12. Place two holes on the top face.

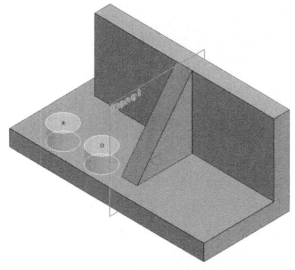

13. Add dimensions to define the hole location.

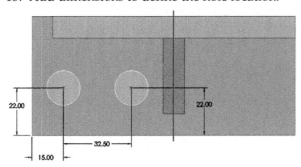

14. Click **OK**.

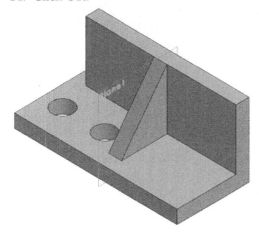

15. Insert another hole on the front face of the second feature.

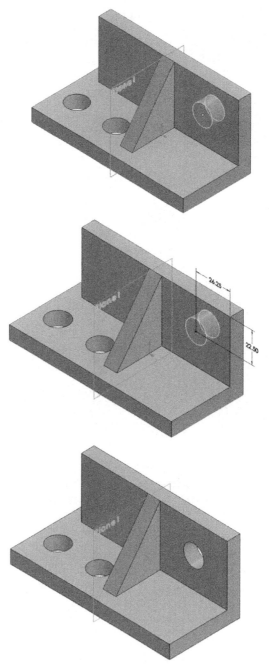

Adding Chamfers

1. To add a chamfer, click **Features > Fillet Chamfer** on the CommandManager.
2. On the PropertyManager, select **Distance Distance**.
3. Select **Asymmetric** from the **Chamfer Method** drop-down available in the **Chamfer Parameters** section.
4. Type-in **45** and **25** in the **Distance 1** and **Distance 2** boxes.

SOLIDWORKS 2019 Learn by Doing

5. Click on the corner edge of the first feature.

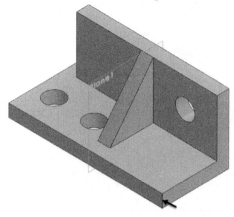

6. Click **OK** to add the chamfer.

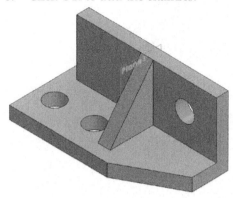

7. Activate the **Chamfer** tool.
8. On the PropertyManager, select **Angle distance**.
9. Type-in **45** in the **Distance** and **Angle** boxes.
10. Click on the corner edge of the second feature.

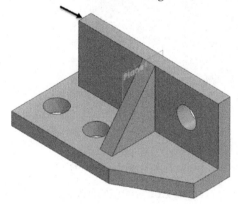

11. Click **OK**.

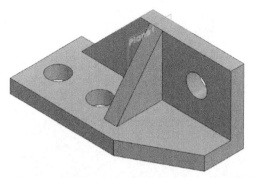

Creating Bounding Box

1. To create a bounding, click **Features > Reference Geometry > Bounding Box** on the CommandManager.
2. On the PropertyManager, select **Best Fit** under the **Reference Face/Plane** section.
3. Click **OK** to create the bounding box.

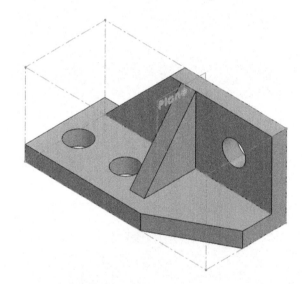

TUTORIAL 6

In this tutorial, you create the model shown in figure.

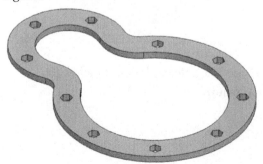

133

SOLIDWORKS 2019 Learn by Doing

Constructing the first feature
1. Open a new part file.
2. On the CommandManager, click **Features > Extruded Boss/Base** .
3. Click on the top plane.
4. Construct two circles and add dimensions to them.

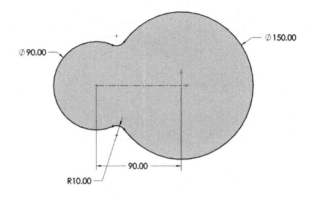

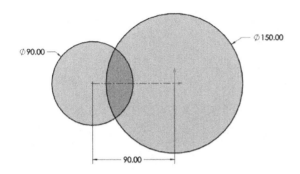

5. On the CommandManager, click **Sketch > Trim Entities** and trim the intersecting entities.

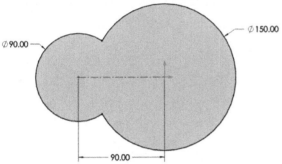

6. On the CommandManager, click **Sketch > Sketch Fillet** and set the **Fillet Radius** value to 10.
7. Select the intersecting corners of the circles, and then click **OK**.

8. Click **Exit Sketch**.
9. On the PropertyManager, type 5 in the **Depth** box.
10. Check the **Thin Feature** option and select **Type > One Direction**.
11. Type 20 in the Thickness box.
12. Use the **Reverse Direction** button next to the **Type** drop-down to make sure that the extruded feature is thickened from inside.
13. Click **OK**.

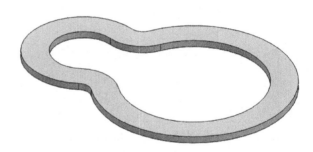

Constructing the Extruded cut
1. On the CommandManager, click **Features > Extruded Cut**.
2. Click on the top face of the model geometry.
3. On the CommandManager, click **Sketch > Polygon**.
4. On the PropertyManager, type-in 6 in the **Number of Sides** box.
5. Select the **Inscribed circle** option.
6. Click to define the center point of the polygon.

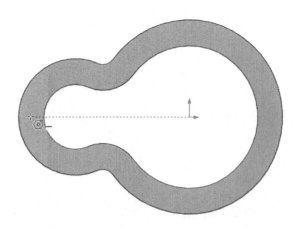

7. Move the pointer and click to construct the polygon.
8. Draw a horizontal centerline connecting the center point of the polygon and sketch origin.

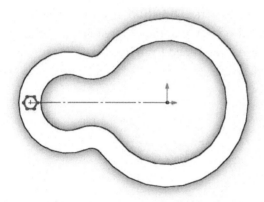

9. On the CommandManager, click **Sketch > Display/Delete Relations > Add Relation**.
10. Click on the horizontal line of the polygon.

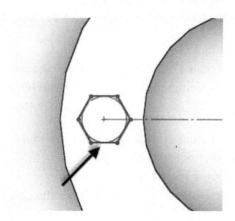

11. On the PropertyManager, click **Horizontal**, and then click **OK**.
12. Activate the **Smart Dimensions** command, zoom into the polygon, and select the construction circle.
13. Place the dimension, type 8, and press Enter.
14. Select the horizontal construction line, place the dimension, and type 125. Next, press Enter.

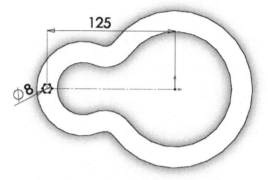

15. Click **Exit Sketch**.
16. Create the cut throughout the body.

Making the Curve Driven Pattern

1. On the CommandManager, click **Features > Linear Pattern > Curve Driven Pattern**.
2. In the FeatureManager Design Tree, select the sketch used to create Extrude-Thin1.

TUTORIAL 7

In this tutorial, you create a bolt.

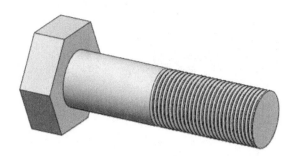

3. Select the polygonal cut to define the feature to pattern.
4. Type-in **10** in the **Number of Instances** box.
5. Check the **Equal Spacing** option.

Start a new part file

1. Start a new part file using the **Part** template.
2. Construct a cylindrical feature of 20 mm diameter and 75 mm length.

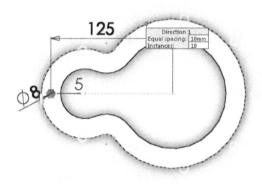

Creating the second feature

1. Start a sketch on the left face of the cylinder.
2. On the CommandManager, click **Sketch > Polygon**.
3. Create a hexagon and dimension it as shown.

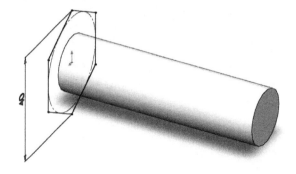

6. Set **Curve method** to **Offset Curve**.
7. Set **Alignment method** to **Tangent to curve**.
8. Click **OK**.

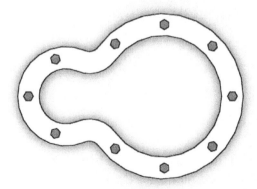

4. Exit the sketch.
5. Extrude the sketch up to 12 mm depth.

9. Save and close the file.

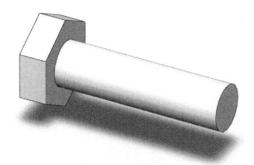

Adding Cosmetic Threads

1. On the CommandManager, click **Features > Hole > Thread** .
2. Click on the right circular edge of the model geometry.
3. Select **End Condition > Blind** and type-in 40 in the **Depth** box.
4. On the PropertyManager, select **Type > Metric Die**.
5. Select **Size > M20x1.5**.
6. Click the **Override Diameter** icon below the **Size** drop-down. This will enable you to override the thread diameter.
7. Click **OK** to add the thread.

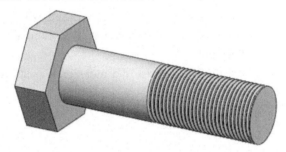

Notice that the starting of thread is created inside the model.

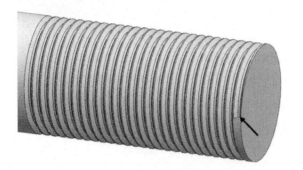

SOLIDWORKS 2019 has some new options to avoid this undesirable result.

8. On the FeatureManager Design Tree, click on the **Thread** feature and select **Edit Feature**.

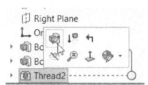

9. On the PropertyManager, under the **Thread Location** section, check the **Offset** option, and then type 1.5 the **Offset Distance** box.
10. Click the **Reverse Direction** button next to the **Offset Distance** box; the thread is offset outside the model.
11. Go to the **Thread Options** section, and then check **Trim with start face** option; the thread feature is aligned with the start face of the model.
12. Click **OK** on the PropertyManager.

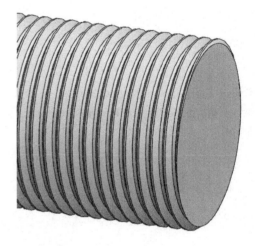

13. Save the file as Tutorial7.sldprt.

Creating Configurations Table

Configurations Table allows you to design a part with different variations, sizes, materials and other attributes. Now, you will create different variations of the bolt created in the previous section.

1. Click the **Configurations** tab on the left-side of the window. Notice that there is only one configuration available in the tree.

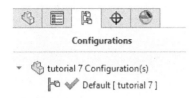

2. Click the **FeatureManager Design Tree** tab.
3. In the FeatureManager Design Tree, expand **Boss-Extrude1** and click the right mouse button on **Sketch1**.
4. Select **Configure Feature** from the shortcut menu.

5. On the **Modify Configurations** dialog, click the down-arrow next to **Sketch1** and check **D1**. Click on the dialog to display the Diameter dimension.

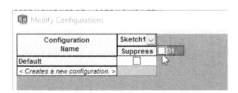

6. On the **Modify Configurations** dialog, click the right mouse button on **Sketch1** and select **Rename**.

7. Type-in **Bolt Diameter** and right-click on the **Modify Configurations** dialog.
8. On the **Modify Configurations** dialog, click in the < *Creates a new configuration.* > cell and type-in Small Diameter. Click on the table to create a new configuration.

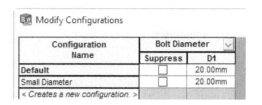

9. Type **12** in the **D1** cell of Small Diameter configuration.

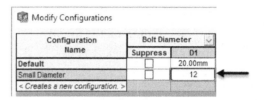

10. In the FeatureManager Design Tree, double-click on **Thread1**, **Boss-Extrude2**, and **Sketch2** to add them to the table.
11. On the **Modify Configurations** dialog, click the right mouse button on **Boss-Extrude2** column and select Delete. The column is removed from the table.
12. Add the dimensions of **Thread1** and **Sketch2** by clicking the down-arrows next to columns and checking the dimensions.
13. Modify the D6 value of Thread1 for Small Diameter configuration to 12.
14. Modify the D1 value of the Sketch2 for Small Diameter configuration to 20.

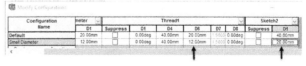

15. On the **Modify Configurations** dialog, type-in **Custom Table** in the box located at the bottom, and then click the **Save table view** button next to it.

16. Click **OK** to close the dialog.
17. Click the **Configurations** tab on the left-side pane and notice two configurations along with a configurations table.

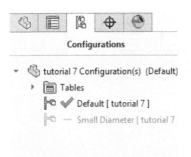

18. Click the right mouse button on the **Small Diameter** configuration and select **Show Configuration**.

19. To edit the configuration table, click the right mouse button on **Custom Table** and select **Show Table**. The **Modify Configurations** dialog appears. Change the values or create new configurations, and then click the **Save the table view** icon.

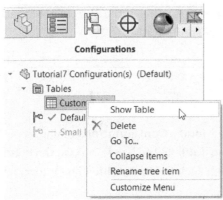

20. Save as **Configurations Table.sldprt** and close the file.

TUTORIAL 8

In this tutorial, you create a plastic casing.

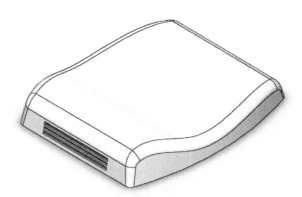

Creating the First Feature

1. Open a new Part file.
2. Create a sketch on the Top Plane, as shown in figure.

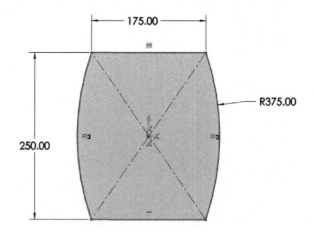

3. Click **Exit Sketch**.
4. Click the **Features > Extruded Boss/Base** 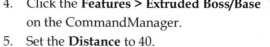 on the CommandManager.
5. Set the **Distance** to 40.
6. Click the **Draft on/off** icon and set the **Draft Angle** to 10.
7. Click **OK**.

139

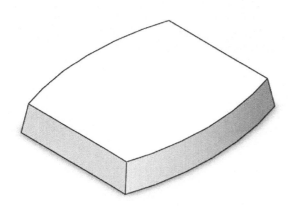

Creating the Extruded surface

1. On the CommandManager, click the right mouse on anyone of the tabs and select **Surfaces**.

2. Click **Surfaces > Extruded Surface** on the CommandManager and select the Right Plane.

3. On the View Heads up toolbar, click **View Orientation > Normal To**.

4. Click **Sketch > Spline** on the CommandManager.

5. Create a spline, as shown in figure.

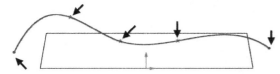

6. Apply dimensions to the spline, as shown below.

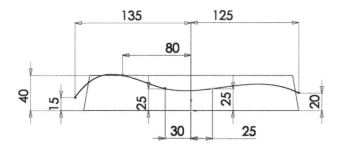

7. Click **Exit Sketch**.

8. Set the **End Condition** type to **Mid Plane**.
9. Type 215 in the **Depth** box and click **OK**.

Replacing the top face of the model with the surface

1. On the CommandManager, click **Surfaces > Replace Face** .

Now, you need to select the face to be replaced.

2. Select the top face of the model.

Next, you need to select the replacement face or surface.

3. Click in the **Replacement Face(s)** box on the PropertyManager and select the extruded surface.
4. Click **OK** to replace the top face with a surface.

5. Hide the extruded surface by clicking on it and selecting **Hide**.

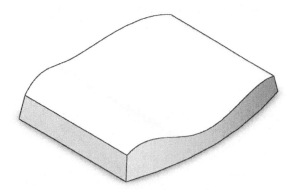

Creating a Face fillet

1. On the CommandManager, click the **Fillet** icon on the **Features** tab.
2. On the PropertyManager, click the **Manual** tab.
3. Click the **Face Fillet** button on the **Fillet** PropertyManager.
4. Select the top surface as the first face.
5. On the PropertyManager, click in the **Face Set 2** box and select the inclined front face as the second face.

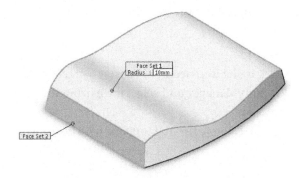

6. On the PropertyManager, under the **Fillet Parameters** section, select **Symmetric** from the drop-down and type 20 in the **Radius** box. Click **OK** to create the face fillet.

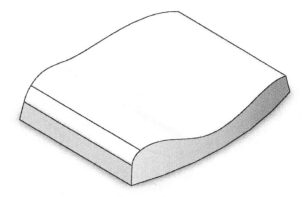

7. Likewise, apply a face fillet of 20 mm radius between top surface and the back inclined face of the model.

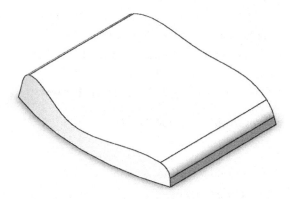

Creating a Variable Radius fillet

1. Click the **Fillet** icon on the **Features** tab.
2. Click the **Variable Size Fillet** icon on the **Fillet** PropertyManager.
3. Click the right mouse button on the curved edge and select **Select Tangency**.

SOLIDWORKS 2019 Learn by Doing

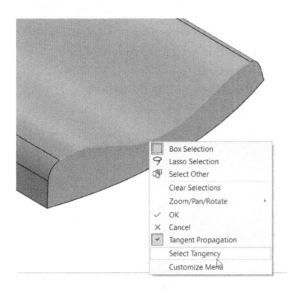

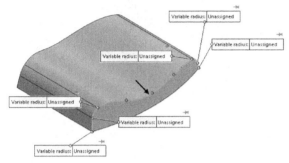

4. Modify the radii values in callouts as shown.

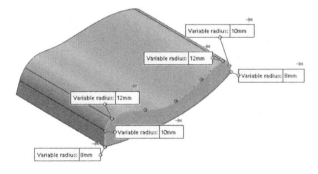

6. Make sure the **Smooth transition** option is checked under the **Profile** drop-down.
7. Click **OK** to create the variable fillet.

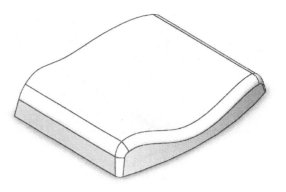

8. Create a variable fillet on other curved edge as shown.

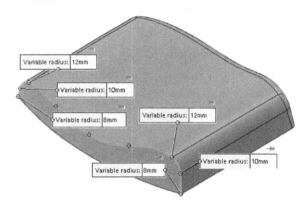

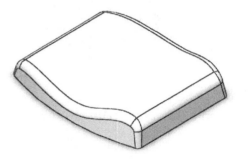

Shelling the Model

1. Click the **Shell** icon on the **Features** tab.

2. On the PropertyManager, type 2.5 mm in the **Thickness** box.

3. Change the orientation of the model and select the bottom face.

SOLIDWORKS 2019 Learn by Doing

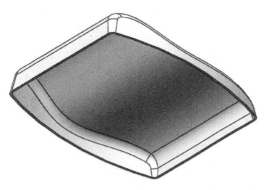

4. Click **OK**.

Creating the Mounting Bosses

1. On the CommandManager, click **Features > Reference Geometry > Axis** .
2. Press the Ctrl key and select the Right and Front planes from the FeatureManager Design Tree.

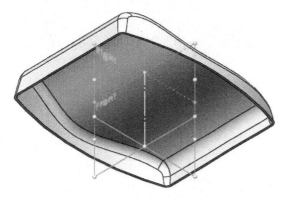

3. Click **OK** on the PropertyManager.
4. Click **Insert > Fastening Feature > Mounting Boss** on the Menu bar and select the inner side of top surface.

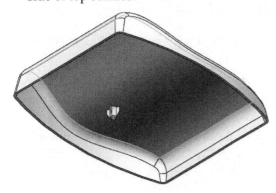

5. Click in the **Select Direction** box on the PropertyManager and select the **Axis** from the FeatureManager Design Tree.

6. Click the **Reverse Direction** icon next to the **Select Direction** box, if the mounted boss appears upwards.
7. Set the **Boss Type** to **Hardware Boss**.
8. Select the **Thread** icon.
9. In the **Boss** section, select **Select mating face**.
10. Select the bottom face of the model geometry.

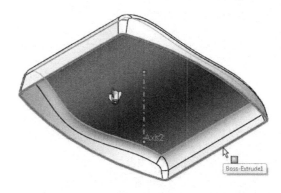

11. Specify the parameters in the **Boss** section as shown.

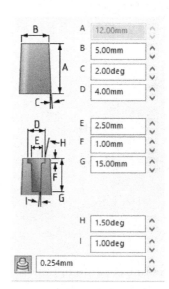

12. Specify the parameters in the **Fins** section, as shown.

143

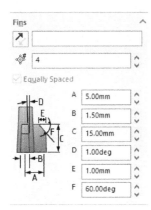

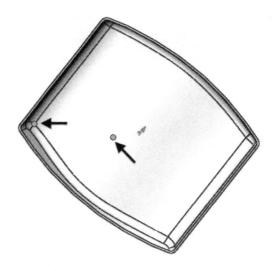

13. Click **OK** on the PropertyManager to create the boss.

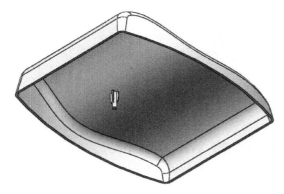

14. In the FeatureManager Design Tree, expand **Mounting Boss1** and notice that a 3D sketch is created.
15. Select **3DSketch1** and click **Edit Sketch**.

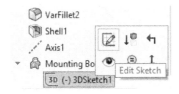

16. Press the Ctrl key and select the points as shown.

17. Click the **Coincident** icon on the PropertyManager, and click **OK**.
18. Click **Exit Sketch**. The position of the mounting boss is changed.

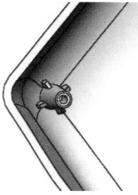

19. Likewise, create other mounting bosses as shown.

SOLIDWORKS 2019 Learn by Doing

Creating the Vent Feature

1. Create a sketch on the front inclined face.

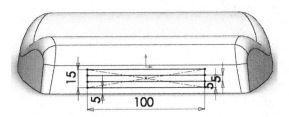

2. Click **Exit Sketch**.
3. On the Menu bar, click **Insert > Fastening Feature > Vent**.
4. Select the four lines of the rectangle to define the boundary.

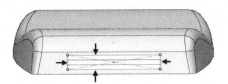

5. Click in the **Ribs** selection box and select the two horizontal lines.
6. Set the rib parameters, as shown below.

7. Click **OK** to create the vent.

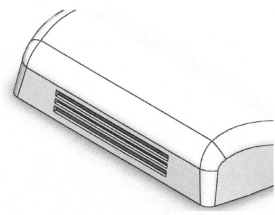

Creating the Wrap Feature

1. On the CommandManager, click **Sketch > Sketch**, and then select the Top plane from the FeatureManager Design Tree.
2. Right click in the graphics window and select **Sketch Entities > Centerline**.
3. Create a horizontal centreline passing through the origin.

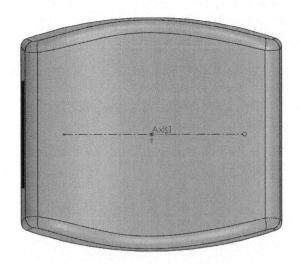

4. On the CommandManager, click **Sketch > Text**.

145

5. Select the horizontal centreline from the graphics window.
6. Click in the **Text** box on the PropertyManager.
7. Type SOLIDWORKS in the **Text** box.
8. On the PropertyManager, uncheck the **Use document font** option, and then click the **Font** button.
9. Select **SOLIDWORKS GDT** from the **Font** list.
10. Set the **Font Style** to **Regular**.
11. Type 20 in the **Units** box of the **Height** section.
12. Click **OK**.
13. Click **OK** on the PropertyManager.

14. On the CommandManager, click **Sketch > Exit Sketch**.
15. On the CommandManager, click **Features > Wrap**.
16. Click on the centreline of the sketch.

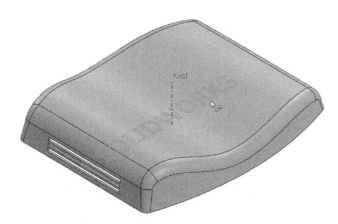

17. On the PropertyManager, click the **Spline Surface** icon under the **Wrap Method** section.
18. Select the **Emboss** icon from the **Wrap Type** section.
19. Click on the top surface of the model.
20. Type 1 in the Thickness box.
21. Click in the **Pull Direction** selection box, and then select the Top plane; the direction perpendicular to the selected plane is defined as the pull direction.
22. Leave the other default options, and then click **OK**.

23. Save the model as Plastic cover.sldprt and close it.

TUTORIAL 9

In this tutorial, you create Advanced Holes.

1. Open a new Part file.
2. Create a 50 X 50 X 35 box, as shown.

3. On the FeatureManager Design Tree, click the right mouse button on the **Boss-Extrude1** feature, and then select **Change Transparency**.

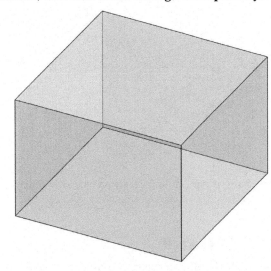

4. On the CommandManager, click **Features > Hole Wizard > Advanced Hole**.
5. Click on the top face of the model.
6. On the **Near Side** toolbar, click the down-arrow next to **Counterbored hole** button, and then select **Near Side Counterbore**.

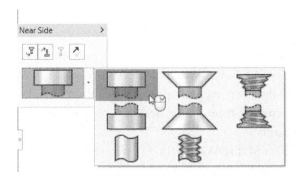

7. On the PropertyManager, select **ISO** from the **Standard** drop-down.
8. Select **Type > Hex Bolt Grade C ISO 4016**.
9. Select **M5** from the **Size** drop-down.
10. Click the **End Condition Override** icon.
11. Type **5** in the **Depth** box.

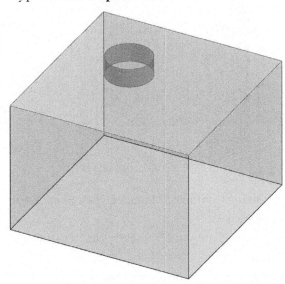

12. On the **Near Side** toolbar, click **Insert Element Below Active Element**; an element is added below the first one.

13. Click on the down-arrow next to the second element, and then select **Near Side Countersink**.

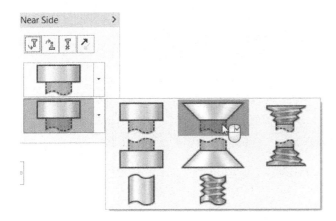

14. Again, click **Insert Element Below Active Element** .
15. Click on the down-arrow next to the third element, and then select **Hole**.

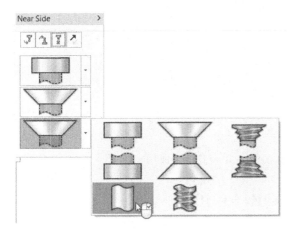

16. Select **Type > Screw Clearances**.
17. Select **M5** from the **Size** drop-down.
18. Select **Up To Next** from the **End Condition** drop-down.
19. Set the **End Shape** to **Flat bottom**.

20. Check the **Far Side** option from the **Near And Far Side Faces** section.
21. Rotate the model and select the bottom face of the model geometry.

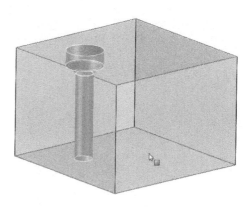

22. Click the down arrow next to the first element of the far side, and then select **Far Side Counterbore**.

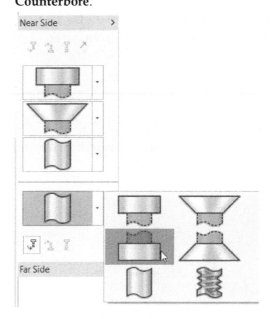

Notice that the model is highlighted in red, which means that there is an error. The third element (hole) extends up to the bottom face of the model. This intersects the far side element. To solve this problem, you need to change the **End Condition** of the third element.

SOLIDWORKS 2019 Learn by Doing

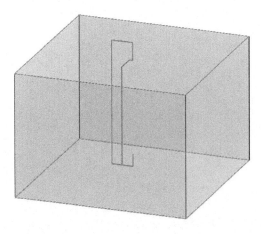

23. Select the third element (Hole) from the **Near Side** toolbar.
24. On the PropertyManager, select **Up To Next Element** from the **End Condition** drop-down.

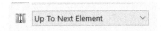

25. Select the far side element.
26. Specify the option in the **Element Specification** section of the PropertyManager.

27. Click the **Positions** tab on the PropertyManager.
28. Select the origin point to specify the location of the hole.

29. Click **OK** on the PropertyManager.

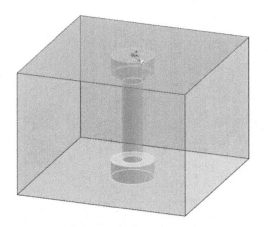

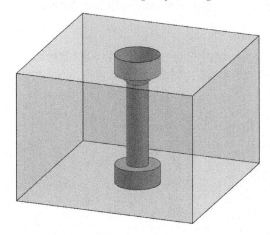

30. Save and close the part file.

TUTORIAL 10

In this tutorial, you create a partial chamfer.

1. Download the Chapter 6: Additional Modeling Tools files from the companion website.
2. Open the Tutorial 10.sldprt file.
3. On the CommandManager, click **Features** tab > **Fillet** drop-down > **Chamfer**.
4. Click the **Offset Face** icon in the **Chamfer Type** section on the PropertyManager.
5. Select the front edge of the model, as shown.

149

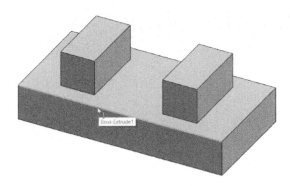
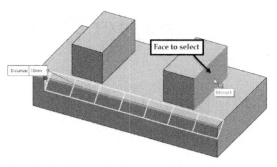

6. Check the **Partial Edge Parameters** option in the PropertyManager.
7. Select the **Distance Offset** option from the **Start condition** drop-down. You can also select the Percentage Offset or Reference Offset options. The Percentage Offset option allows you to specify the offset distance from the start port. The Reference Offset option allows you to create partial chamfer up to the selected reference face.
8. Type-in 10 in the **Offset distance** box.
9. Select **Reference Offset** from the **End condition** drop-down.
10. Select the flat face of the model, as shown.

11. Click **OK** on the PropertyManager.

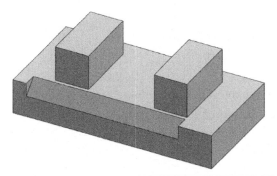

12. Close the file without saving.

Chapter 7: Sheet metal Modeling

This chapter will show you to:

- Construct Base Flange
- Construct Edge Flange
- Construct Miter Flange
- Close Corners
- Apply Corner Treatments
- Add Tab features
- Add Jogs
- Unfold and refold the bends
- Cut across bends
- Perform Forming Operations
- Add Hems
- Add Vents
- Add Gussets
- Make Fill Patterns
- View Flat Pattern

TUTORIAL 1

In this tutorial, you construct the sheet metal model shown in figure.

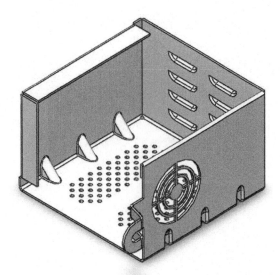

Opening a New File

1. Open a new part file.
2. On the CommandManager, click the right mouse button on anyone of the tabs and select **Sheet Metal**, if the **Sheet Metal** tab is displayed.

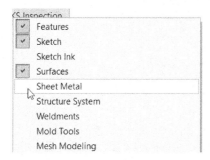

The **Sheet Metal** tab appears.

Constructing the Base Flange

1. To construct a base flange, click **Sheet Metal > Base Flange/Tab** on the CommandManager.
2. Select the front plane.
3. Construct the sketch, as shown. Note that the vertical lines should be symmetric about the centreline.

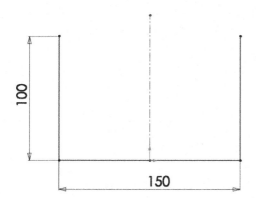

4. Click **Exit Sketch**.
5. On the PropertyManager, under **Direction 1** section, type-in 150 in the **Depth** box.
6. Check the **Use gauge table** option.
7. Select **SAMPLE TABLE –ALUMINIUM-METRIC UNITS**.
8. On the PropertyManager, under the **Sheet Metal Parameters** section, select **Gauge 14**.
9. Set the **Bend Radius** value to **2**.
10. Leave the **Auto Relief** section to default settings.
11. Click **OK** to construct the base flange.

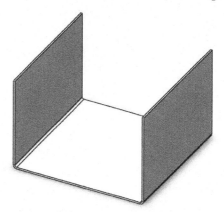

Adding an Edge flange

1. To add the flange, click **Sheet Metal > Edge Flange** on the CommandManager.
2. Select the edge on the top face.

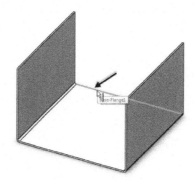

3. Move the pointer upward and click.
4. On the PropertyManager, under the **Flange Length** section, set **Length** to 100.
5. Click on the **Inner Virtual Sharp** icon in the **Flange Length** section. This measures the flange length from the outer face.
6. Under the **Flange Position** section, click the **Material Outside** icon.
7. Click **OK** to add the flange.

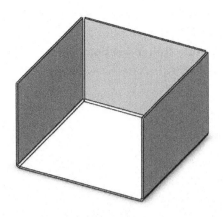

In SOLIDWORKS, you can use the **Edit Flange Profile** button available on the PropertyManager to change the shape of the flange. The sketch mode is activated when you click this button. Use the sketch tools to change the flange shape.

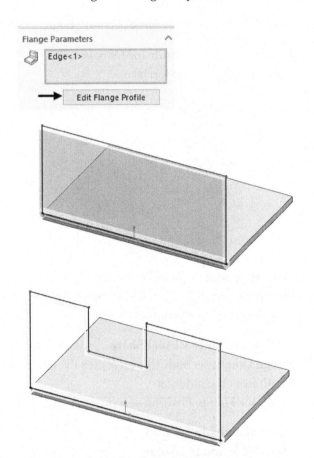

Constructing the Miter Flange

1. To construct the miter flange, click **Sheet Metal > Miter Flange** on the CommandManager.
2. Click the top edge left flange.

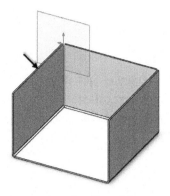

3. Draw the sketch, as shown.

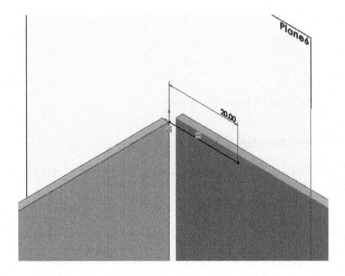

4. Click **Exit Sketch**.
5. Click on the vertical edge of the left flange.

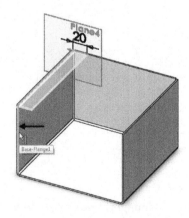

6. On the **Miter Flange** PropertyManager, set the **Flange Position** to **Material Inside** and **Gap distance** to 1.25.
7. Under the **Start/End Offset** section, set the **Start**

153

Offset Distance and End Offset Distance to 10.
8. On the PropertyManager, check the **Custom Relief Type** option.

Notice the three options in the **Relief Type** drop-down: **Rectangular**, **Obround**, and **Tear**. The **Tear** option has two more options under it: **Rip** and **Extended**.

Rectangular

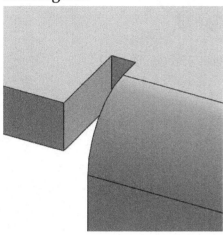

Obround

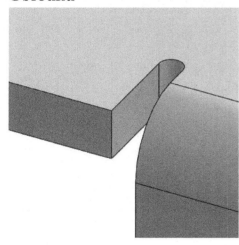

Tear

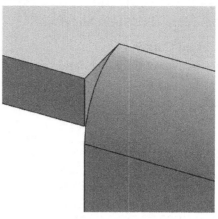

Tear (Extended)

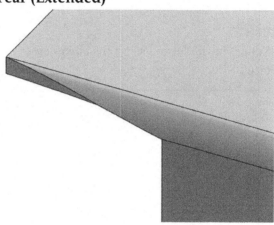

9. Select the **Rectangular** option from the **Relief Type** drop-down.
10. Check the **Use relief ratio** option.
11. Leave the **Ratio** value to 0.5.
12. Click **OK** to construct the miter flange.

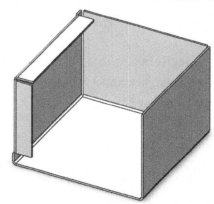

SOLIDWORKS 2019 Learn by Doing

Closing the Corners

1. To close the corners, click **Sheet Metal > Corners > Closed Corner**.
2. Select the corner face of the miter flange.

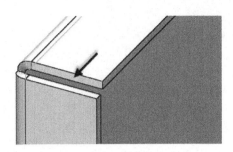

3. On the PropertyManager, set the **Corner type** to **Butt**.
4. Rotate the model and select the other corner faces.

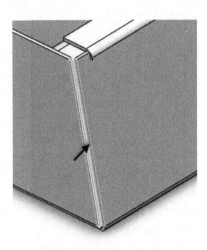

5. Click **OK** to close the corners.

Adding Corner Reliefs

1. To add corner reliefs, click **Sheet Metal > Corners > Corner Relief**. This selects the entire part.
2. Select **2 Bend Corner** from the PropertyManager.
3. On the PropertyManager, under the **Corners** section, click **Collect all corners**.
4. Under the **Relief Options** section, set the **Relief** type **Circular**.
5. Type **2** in the **Slot Width** box.
6. Click **OK** to add the corner relief.

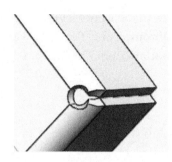

The different types of the reliefs are:

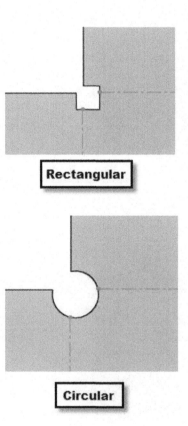

155

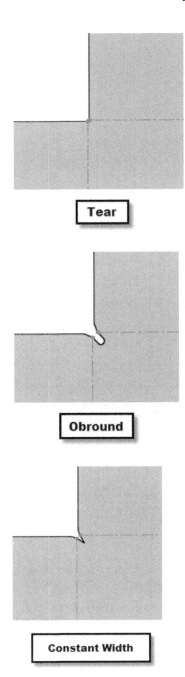

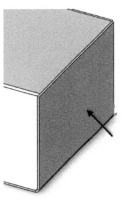

3. On the CommandManager, click **Sketch > Line**.
4. Click on the vertical edge of the face and move the pointer toward left.
5. Again, click to draw a horizontal line.

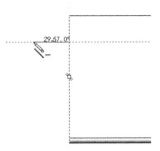

6. Move the pointer toward endpoint of the line. The arc mode gets active.

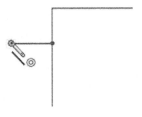

7. Move the pointer toward left, and then downwards.
8. Click to create an arc.

Adding a Tab feature

1. To add a tab, click **Sheet Metal > Base Flange/Tab** on the CommandManager.
2. Click on the right side of the base flange.

SOLIDWORKS 2019 Learn by Doing

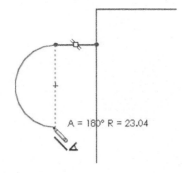

9. Close the sketch and add dimensions.

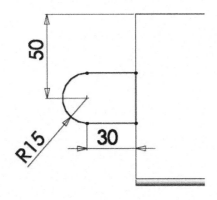

10. Exit the sketch.
11. Select the **Merge result** option and click **OK** on the PropertyManager.

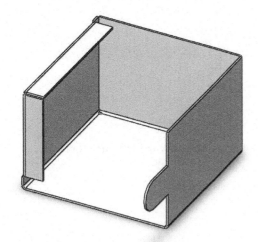

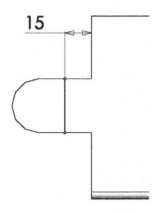

3. Click **Exit Sketch**.
4. Click on the base flange to define the fixed face.

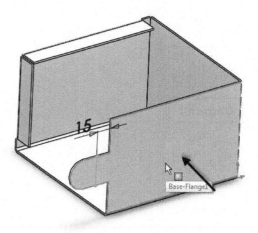

5. On the PropertyManager, under the **Jog Offset** section, set the **Offset Distance** to 20.
6. Set the **Dimension position** to **Outside Offset**.
7. Set the **Jog Position** to **Bend Centerline**.
8. Set the **Jog Angle** to **75**.
9. Click **OK**.

Adding a Jog

1. To add a jog, click **Sheet Metal > Jog** on the CommandManager.
2. Click on the tab face and draw a line.

157

Unfolding the bends
1. To unfold a bend, click **Sheet Metal > Unfold**

2. Click on the tab face to define the fixed face.
3. Click on the bends of the jog feature.

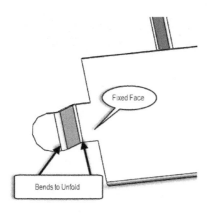

4. Click **OK**.

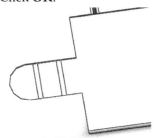

Make sure that the arc is concentric to the circular edge.

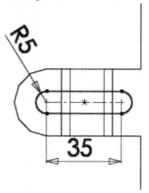

3. Click **Exit Sketch**.
4. Set the **End Condition** to **Up To Next**.
5. Click **OK** on the PropertyManager.

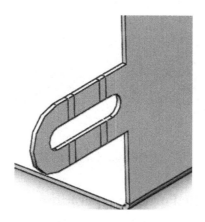

Folding the Unfolded bends
1. To fold the unfolded bends, click **Sheet Metal > Fold** on the CommandManager.
2. Click on the jog bends.

Creating Cuts across bends
1. To create cuts across bends, click **Sheet Metal > Extruded Cut** on the CommandManager.
2. Click on the tab and draw the sketch, as shown.

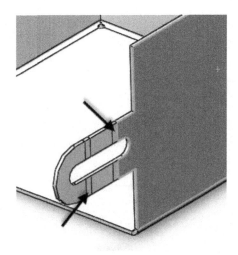

3. Click **OK**.

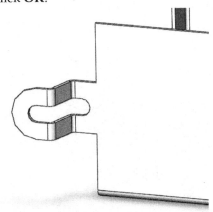

Performing the Forming Operations

1. To perform forming operations, click **Design Library** on the Task pane.

2. If the Design Library is not displayed, click **Add File Location** .
3. Browse to the location:

C:\ProgramData\SOLIDWORKS\SOLIDWORKS 2019\design library

4. Click **OK**.
5. In the **Design Library**, click the right mouse button on the **forming tools** folder and select **Forming Tools Folder**.
6. Click **Yes** on the **SOLIDWORKS** message box.

7. Double-click on the **Louvers** folder.

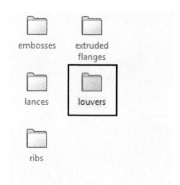

8. Click and drag the Louver onto the flange face.

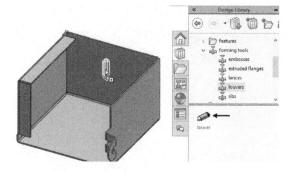

9. On the PropertyManager, type-in 90 in the **Rotation Angle** box.
10. Under the **Link** section, uncheck the **Link to form tool** option.
11. Under the **Flat Pattern Visibility** section, check the **Override document settings** option.

12. On the PropertyManager, click the **Position** tab and add dimensions to position the louver.

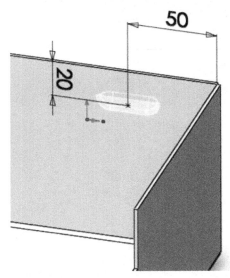

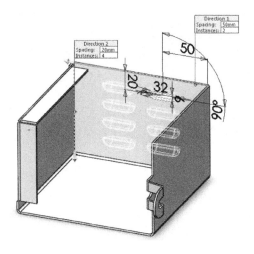

8. Click **OK** to construct the pattern.

13. Click **OK**.

Making the Linear Pattern

1. On the CommandManager, click **Features > Linear Pattern**.
2. Click on the horizontal edge of the flange to define the first direction.
3. On the PropertyManager, under the **Direction 1** section, type-in 50 in the **Spacing** box and 2 in the **Number of Instances** box.
4. Click the **Reverse Direction** button.
5. Click on the vertical edge of the flange feature to define the second direction.
6. Under the **Direction 2** section, type-in **20** in the **Spacing** box and 4 in the **Number of Instances** box.
7. Select the louver feature.

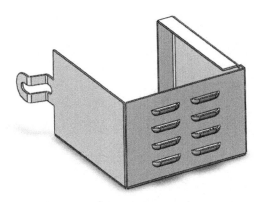

Adding a Hem

1. To add a hem, click **Sheet Metal > Hem** on the CommandManager.
2. Click on the inner edge of the right-side flange.

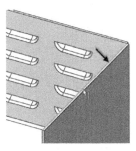

3. On the PropertyManager, under the **Type and Size** section, click the **Closed** icon.
4. Type-in **15** in the **Length** box.
5. Click **OK** to add the hem.

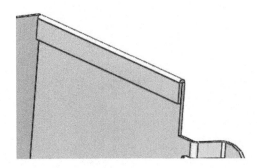

Adding a vent

1. Construct a sketch on the right side face of the base flange.

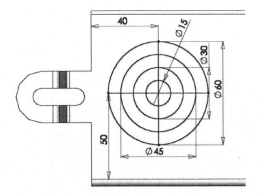

2. Click **Exit Sketch**.
3. On the CommandManager, click **Sheet Metal > Vent**.
4. Click on the outer most circle of the sketch to define the boundary of the vent.

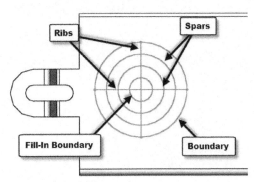

5. On the PropertyManager, click in **Ribs** selection box and select the line segments from the sketch.
6. Type-in 2 in the **Width** box.
7. Click in the **Spars** selection box and select the two middle circles.

8. Type-in 2 in the **Width** box.
9. Click in the **Fill-In Boundary** selection box and select the inner most circle.
10. Click **OK**.

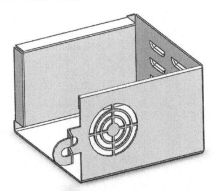

Adding Sheet Metal Gussets

1. To add gussets, click **Sheet Metal > Sheet Metal Gusset** on the CommandManager.
2. Click on the left side bend face of the base flange.

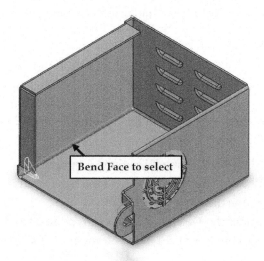

3. On the PropertyManager, under the **Position** section, set the **Offset** value to 30.
4. Under the **Profile** section, set the **Indent depth** to 12.
5. Click the **Rounded gusset** icon.
6. Under the **Dimensions** section, set the **Indent Width** value to 10.
7. Set **Indent Thickness** to **2**.
8. Turn ON the **Side face** icon.
9. Set **Side face draft** to 2.

10. Set **Inner corner fillet** and **Outer corner fillet** to 1 and 2, respectively.

11. Click **OK**.

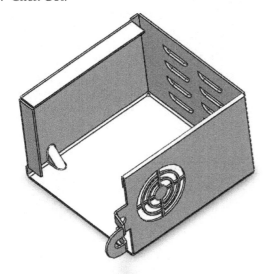

12. Make a linear pattern of the gusset.

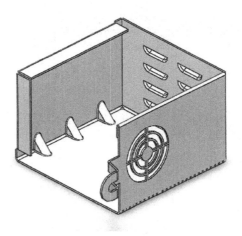

13. Mirror the gusset and the linear pattern about the right plane.

Making a Fill Pattern

1. Draw a sketch on the top face of the base flange.

162

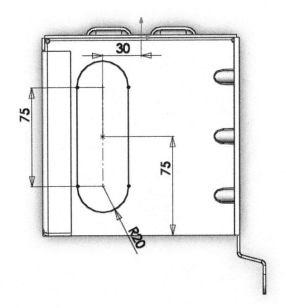

2. Click **Exit Sketch**.
3. To make a fill pattern, click **Features > Linear Pattern > Fill Pattern** on the CommandManager.
4. Select the sketch to define the fill boundary.
5. On the PropertyManager, under the **Features and Faces** section, select **Create seed cut** and select the **Polygon** icon.
6. Set the options in the **Features and Faces** section, as shown.

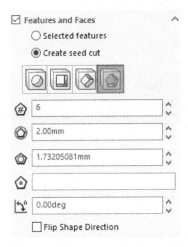

7. Under the **Pattern Layout** section, select the **Perforation** button.
8. Type-in 8 in the **Instance Spacing** box.
9. Set **Stagger Angle** to 46.
10. Set **Margins** to 1.

11. Click **OK** to make the fill pattern.

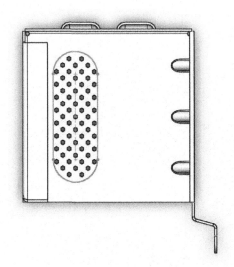

12. Mirror the fill pattern about the right plane.

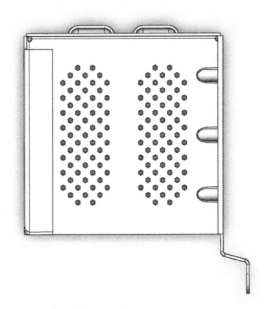

View the Flat Pattern

1. To view the flat pattern, click **Sheet Metal > Flatten** on the CommandManager.

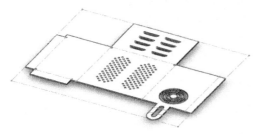

2. Again, click the **Flatten** button to switch back to the model view.

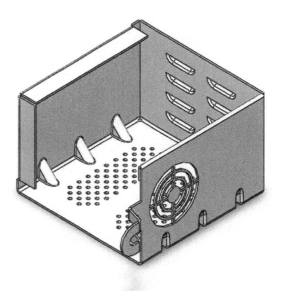

3. Save the sheet metal part.

TUTORIAL 2

In this tutorial, you will apply corner relief to 3 Bend corner.

1. Download and open the 3_Bend_Corner part file from the companion website.
2. On the CommandManager, click **Sheet Metal > Corners drop-down > Corner relief**.
3. Select **3 Bend Corner** on the PropertyManager.
4. Click the **Collect All Corners** button in the **Corners** section.

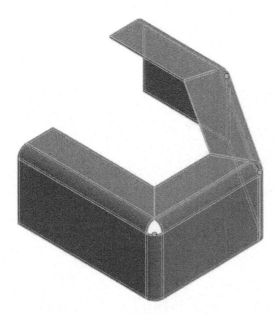

5. On the PropertyManager, under the **Relief type** section, select **Circular** .
6. Type 4 in the **Slot Width** box available in the **Relief type** section.
7. Click **OK** on the PropertyManager.

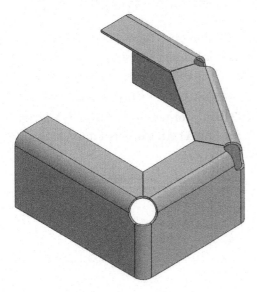

TUTORIAL 3

In this tutorial, you will create a normal cut.

1. Open a new part file.
2. On the CommandManager, click the **Sheet Metal** tab > **Base Flange/Tab** .
3. Click on the Front Plane.
4. Create the sketch, as shown.

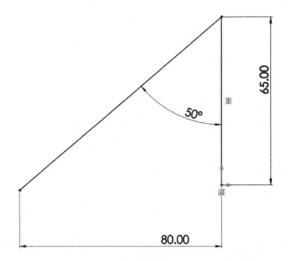

5. Click **Exit Sketch** on the CommandManager.
6. On the PropertyManager, expand the **Direction 1** section.
7. Select **Mid Plane** from the **End Condition** drop-down.
8. Type **80** in the **Depth** box.
9. Click **OK**.

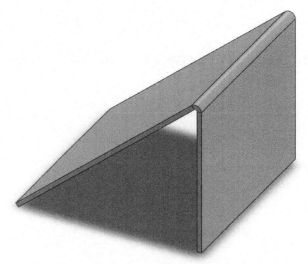

10. On the CommandManager, click the **Sheet metal** tab > **Extruded Cut**.
11. Click on the vertical face of the flange.
12. Create a rectangle and add dimensions to it, as shown.

SOLIDWORKS 2019 Learn by Doing

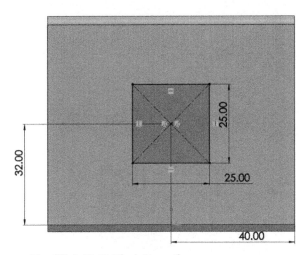

13. Click **Exit Sketch** on the CommandManager.
14. On the **Cut-Extrude** PropertyManager, click **Direction 1 > Through All**.
15. Check the **Normal cut** option.
16. Click **OK**.

17. In the FeatureManager Design Tree, click on the **Cut-Extrude1** feature, and then select **Edit Feature**.
18. On the **Cut-Extrude1** PropertyManager, uncheck the **Normal cut** option.
19. Click **OK**; the side faces of the cut feature are not normal to the sheet metal face.

To make the cut faces normal to the sheet metal face, SOLIDWORKS provides you with the **Normal Cut** tool.

20. On the Menu bar, click **Insert > Sheet Metal > Normal Cut**.
21. Select anyone of the side faces of the cut feature; all the side faces of the cut feature are selected automatically.

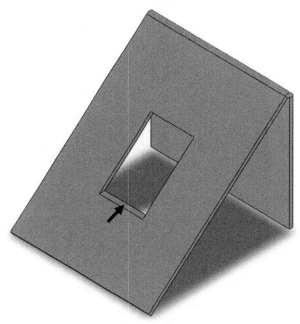

22. Click **OK** on the PropertyManager; the faces are made normal to the cut feature.

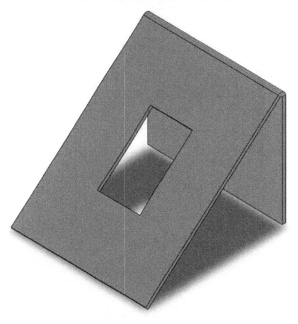

23. Save and close the file.

SOLIDWORKS 2019 Learn by Doing

TUTORIAL 4

In this tutorial, you will create a tab and slot feature. The **Tab and Slot** tool helps you to create tabs on one body and slots on another. A typical Tab and slot feature is displayed, as shown.

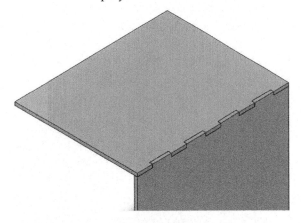

1. Open a new SOLIDWORKS part file.
2. Create a rectangular sketch on the Front plane, as shown.

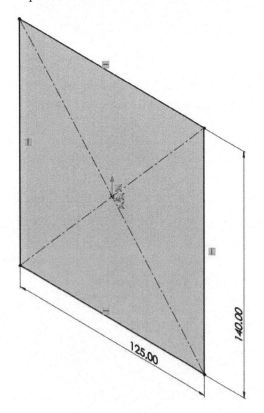

3. Activate the **Base Flange/Tab** tool, and then create a tab, as shown.

4. Create a line on the tab feature, as shown.

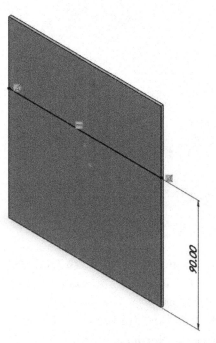

5. Activate the **Base Flange/Tab** tool, and then create a flange of 50 mm distance.

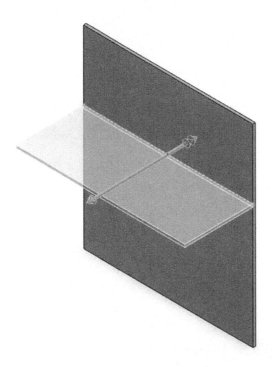

6. On the Menu bar, click **Insert > Sheet Metal > Tab and Slot**.
7. Click on the linear edge, as shown; the tab edge is defined.

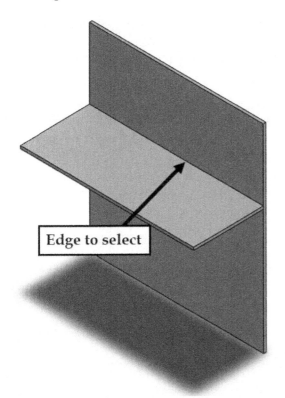

8. Rotate the model, and then select the back face of the first tab, as shown; the slot face is defined.

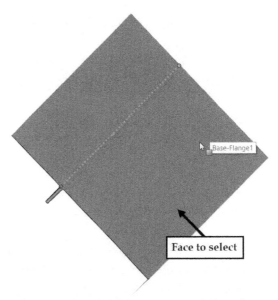

Notice that the **Start Reference Point** and **End Reference Point** are selected, automatically. If you want to change the reference points, then click in the corresponding selection boxes on the PropertyManager. Next, select the opposite end point of the linear edge.

Check the **Offset** option, if you want to offset the tabs and slots from the start and end reference points. Next, you need to type in a value in the **Offset distance from start reference point** and **Offset distance from end reference point** boxes.

9. In the **Spacing** section, click the **Equal Spacing** option.
10. Type **5** in the **Number of Instances** box.

You can also select the **Spacing Length** option, and then type a value in the **Spacing** box.

11. Type 12 in the **Length** box in the **Tabs** section.
12. Next, select **Up To Surface** from the **Height** drop-down. This option extends the tab height up to the slot surface.

You can also define the height of the tab by using the **Blind** or **Offset From Surface** option.

The **Blind** option is used to specify the tab height entering a value in the **Tab Height Value** box.

The **Offset From Surface** option offsets the tab from the slot surface by the value that you enter in the **Tab Offset Value** box. Check the **Reverse Direction** option to reverse the offset direction.

13. Click the **Chamfer Edge** option from the **Edges Type** section.
14. Type 1 in the **Chamfer Edge Treatment Value** box.
15. Leave the default value in the **Slot Clearance** box under the **Slot** section.
16. Click **OK** to create the tab and slot feature.

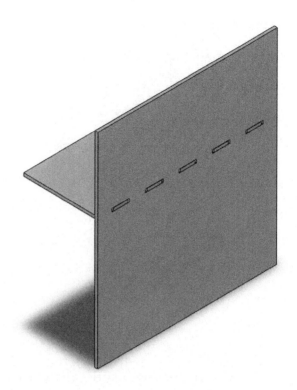

17. Save and close part file.

TUTORIAL 5

In this tutorial, you will create a **Swept Flange** feature. The **Swept Flange** tool allows you to create a sheet metal feature by sweeping a profile along the path.

1. Open a new SOLIDWORKS part file.
2. On the CommandManager, click **Sketch** tab > **Sketch**.
3. Click on the top plane.
4. On the CommandManager, click **Sketch** tab > **Arc** drop-down > **Centerpoint Arc**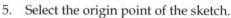
5. Select the origin point of the sketch.
6. Move the pointer downwards, and then specify the start point of the arc, as shown.

SOLIDWORKS 2019 Learn by Doing

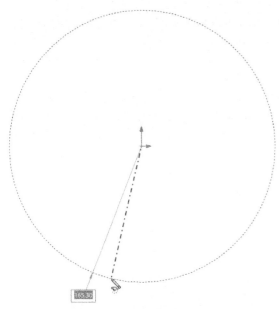

7. Move the pointer in the anti-clockwise, and then click to define the end point of the arc, as shown.

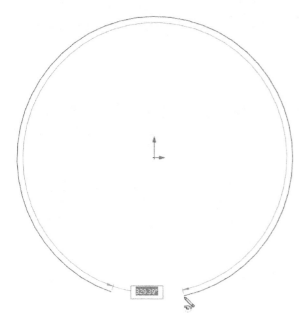

8. Create a vertical centerline, as shown.

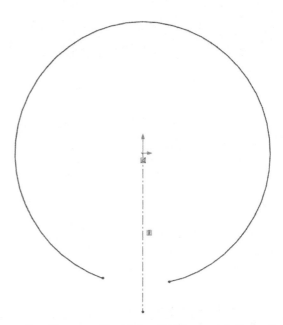

9. Press and hold the Ctrl key, and then click on the two end points of the arc and the centerline.
10. On the PropertyManager, click the **Symmetric** icon.
11. Click **OK**.

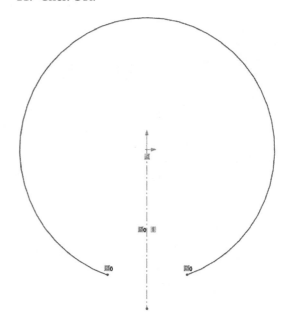

12. Add dimensions to the sketch, as shown.

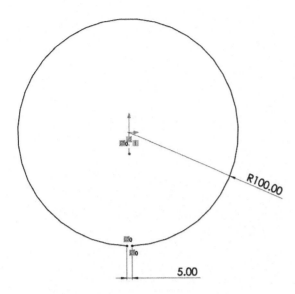

13. Click **Exit Sketch** on the CommandManager.
14. Change the **View Orientation** to **Isometric**.
15. On CommandManager, click the **Features** tab > **Reference Geometry** drop-down > **Plane**.
16. Select the arc and anyone of its endpoints.
17. Click **OK** on the **Plane** PropertyManager.
18. Start a new sketch on the newly created plane.
19. Draw the sketch profile, as shown.

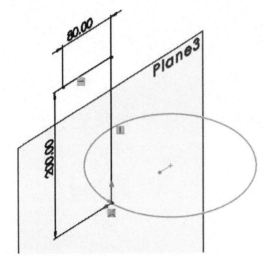

20. Click **Exit Sketch** on the CommandManager.

Next, you need to activate the Swept Flange tool and create the swept flange. By default, the **Swept Flange** tool is not displayed on the CommandManager. To add this command to the CommandManager, right click on the CommandManager, and then select **Customize**. On the **Customize** dialog, click the **Commands** tab, and then select **Sheet Metal** from the **Categories** list. Next, click and drag the **Swept Flange** button from the Buttons area, and then release it on the CommandManager; the **Swept Flange** button is added to the CommandManger.

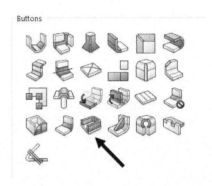

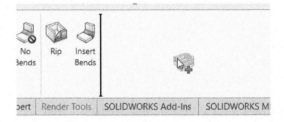

21. On the Menu bar, click **Insert > Sheet Metal > Swept Flange**.
22. Select the profile and path from the graphics window.
23. Click **OK** to create the swept flange.

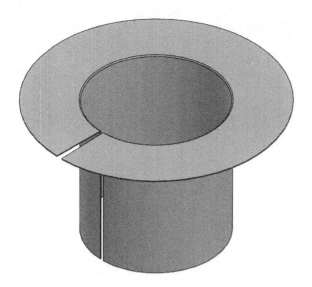

24. Save and close the part file.

TUTORIAL 6

In this tutorial, you will create a **Corner Trim** feature.

1. Download and open the Corner_trim part file from the companion website.

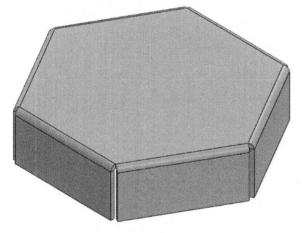

2. On the CommandManager, click **Sheet Metal > Flatten**.

3. On the CommandManager, click **Sheet Metal** tab > **Corner** drop-down > **Corner-Trim**.
4. Select the corner edges one-by-one (or) click the **Collect all corners** button.
5. Select **Circular** from the **Relief type** drop-down.
6. Change the View Orientation to Top.
7. Zoom-in to anyone of the corners and notice preview of the corner trim. By default, the center of the relief is located on corner.

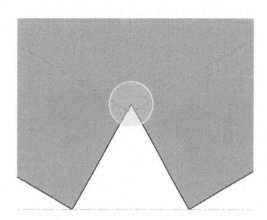

8. Check the **Centered on bend lines** option to move the center to the intersection of the bend lines.

SOLIDWORKS 2019 Learn by Doing

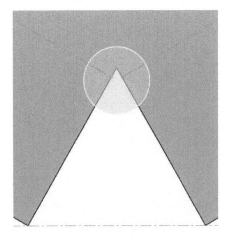

9. Change the **Radius** value to 5.

Notice the **Ratio to thickness** option below the **Radius** box. This option allows you to specify the relief size by entering the ratio value to the sheet metal thickness.

10. Select **Square** from the **Relief type** drop-down.

Notice that the relief is changed to square.

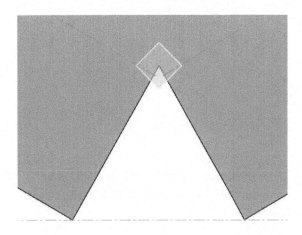

11. Check the **Add filleted corners** option.
12. Type 1 in the **Fillet radius** box.

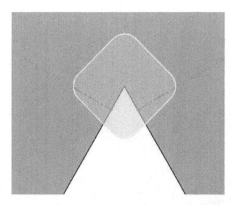

13. Click in the **Corner Edges** selection box under the **Break Corner Options** section.
14. Select the sheet metal corners to break (or) click the **Collect all corners** button to select all the corners.
15. Select the **Chamfer** icon from the **Break type** section.
16. Type 5 in the **Distance** box.

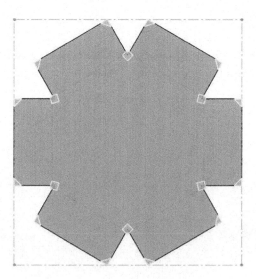

17. Click **OK** on the PropertyManager.
18. Click the **Flatten** icon on the CommandManager to exit the flatten state.

Notice that the corner trims are visible only in the Flattened state.

TUTORIAL 7

In this tutorial, you will convert an imported solid body into a sheet metal part.

173

1. Download the Tutorial_7. STEP file from the companion website.
2. On the SOLIDWORKS window, click the **Open** icon on the Quick Access Toolbar.
3. Browse to the location of the downloaded file, and then double-click on it.
4. Click **Yes** on the **SOLIDWORKS** message box.

5. Click **OK** on the **Import Diagnostics** PropertyManager.
6. On the CommandManager, click the **Sheet Metal** tab > **Convert to Sheet Metal**.
7. Click on the horizontal sheet metal face, as shown; the fixed face is defined.

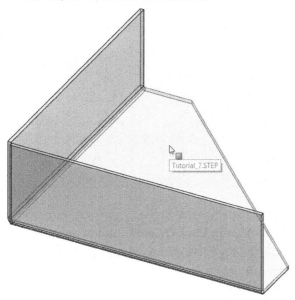

8. Set **Sheet thickness** to 2
9. Set **Default radius of bends** to 2.
10. Click the **Collect all Bends** button in the **Bend Edges** section.
11. Click **OK**.

Notice that the **Flatten** icon on the CommandManager is now available. You can flatten the sheet metal model and create drawings.

TUTORIAL 8

In this tutorial, you will create a multibody sheet metal part.

1. Start a new SOLIDWORKS part file.
2. Create a new Base tab feature, as shown. The sheet metal thickness is 2 mm.

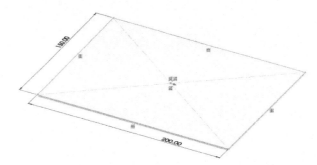

3. Create edge flanges of 40 mm length, as shown.

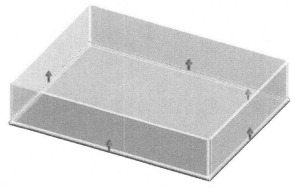

4. Activate the **Base Flange/Tab** tool, and then click on the outer face of the edge flange.

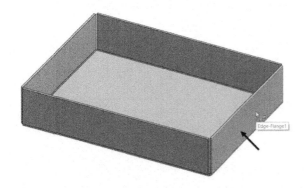

5. Change the view orientation to right plane.

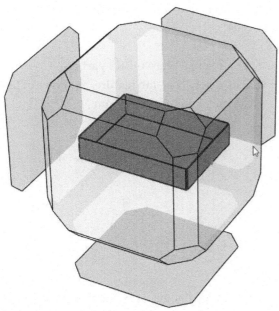

6. Create a rectangle, as shown.

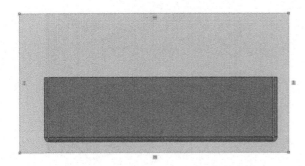

7. Press and hold Ctrl key, and then select the bottom edge and the bottom horizontal line of the rectangle.

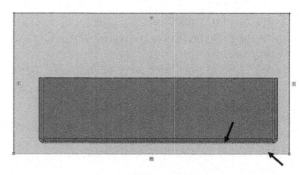

8. Click the **Collinear** icon the PropertyManager; the line is made collinear with the horizontal edge of the bend.
9. Likewise, make the vertical line collinear with the side edges, as shown.

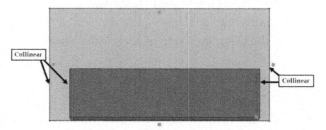

10. Add dimension to the vertical line, as shown.

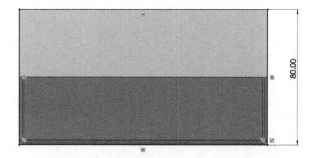

11. Click **Exit Sketch** on the CommandManager.
12. Change the **View Orientation** to **Isometric**.
13. On the PropertyManager, uncheck the **Merge result** option.
14. Check the **Reverse Direction** option.
15. Click **OK**; the tab feature is created as a separate body.

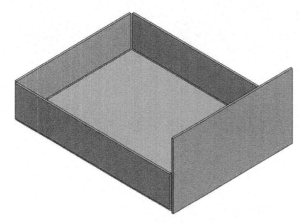

16. Expand the **Cut list** and **Sheet Metal** folders.

Notice two sheet metal bodies inside the Cut list and Sheet Metal folders.

17. Change the View Orientation to Left.

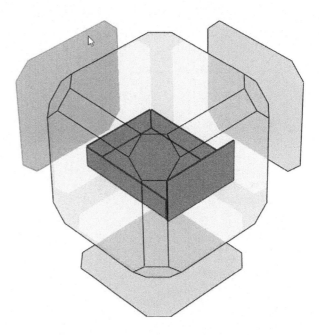

18. Activate the **Base Flange/Tab** tool.
19. Click on the edge flange face.

20. Activate the **Corner Rectangle** tool.
21. Click on the first and second corners, as shown.

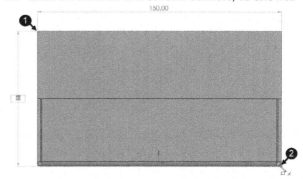

22. Click **Exit Sketch** on the CommandManager.
23. On the PropertyManager, uncheck the **Merge result** option.
24. Check the **Reverse direction** option.
25. Click **OK**.

Notice three sheet metal bodies inside the Sheet Metal folder in the FeatureManager Design Tree.

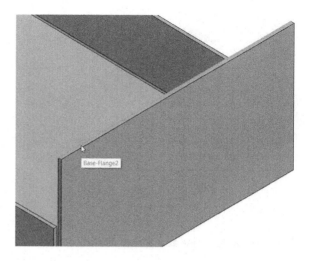

30. Click the **Inside** icon under the **Flange Position** section.
31. Click **OK** on the PropertyManager.

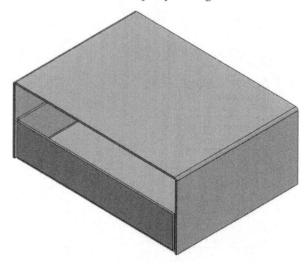

26. Activate the **Edge Flange** tool.
27. Click on the edge of the third sheet metal body, as shown.

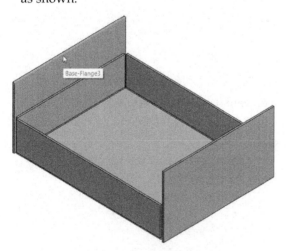

32. Activate the **Edge Flange** tool.
33. Click on the edge of the previously created edge flange, as shown.

28. On the PropertyManager, under the **Flange Length** section, select **Up To Edge And Merge** option from the **Length End Condition** drop-down.
29. Select the edge of the second tab feature, as shown.

177

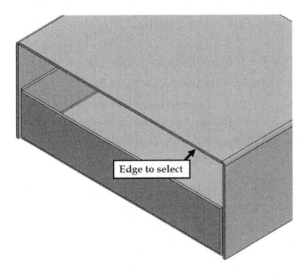

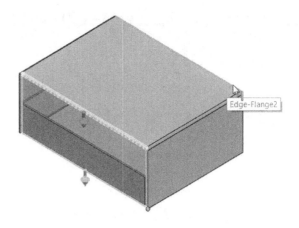

34. On the PropertyManager, select **Flange Length > Up To Vertex**.
35. Zoom to the bottom portion of the sheet metal part, and then select the vertex of the tab, as shown.

37. Click the **Bend Outside** icon in the **Flange Position** section.
38. Click **OK**.

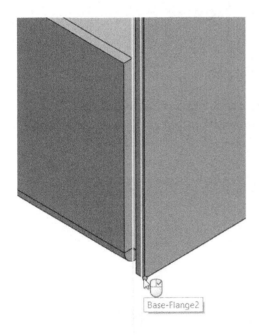

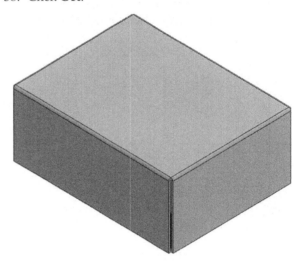

36. Click in the Selection box in the **Flange Parameters** section, and then select the edge on the back side, as shown.

Chapter 8: Top-Down Assembly

In this chapter, you will learn to

- Create a top-down assembly
- Insert fasteners using Toolbox
- Create advanced mates

TUTORIAL 1

In this tutorial, you will create the model shown in figure. You use top-down assembly approach to create this model.

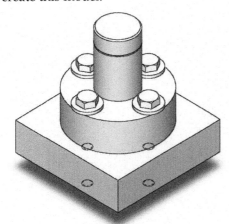

Creating a New Assembly File

1. Click the **New** icon on the Quick Access Toolbar, select the **Assembly** icon, and click **OK**.

2. Click **Cancel** ✕ on the **Begin Assembly** PropertyManager.

Creating a component in the Assembly

In a top-down assembly approach, you create components of an assembly directly in the assembly by using the **New Part** tool.

1. On the CommandManager, click **Assembly > Insert Components > New Part**.
2. In the FeatureManager Design Tree, click the Front plane. A new part is created and the **Edit Component** mode is activated.
3. Click **Exit Sketch**.
4. Click **Sketch > Sketch** on the CommandManager and select the Top plane from the FeatureManager Design Tree.
5. Create the sketch as shown below.

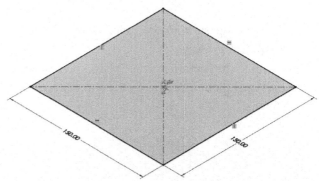

6. Click **Exit Sketch**.
7. Click **Features > Extruded Boss/Base** on the CommandManager and extrude the sketch up to 40 mm.

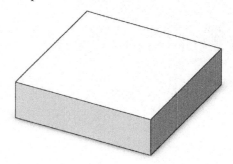

8. Start a sketch on the top face and draw a circle of **50 mm** diameter.

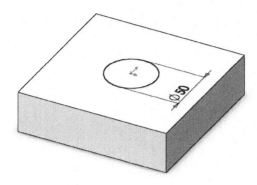

9. Click **Exit Sketch**
10. Extrude the sketch up to 95 mm distance.

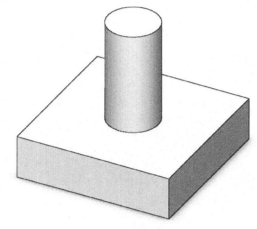

11. On the CommandManager, click **Features > Hole Wizard** .
12. On the PropertyManager, click the **Legacy Hole** icon.
13. On the PropertyManager, select **Type > Counterbored**.
14. In the **Section Dimensions** section, modify the dimensions as shown.

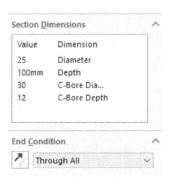

15. Set the **End Condition** to **Through All**.
16. Click the **Positions** tab and click on the top face of the second feature.
17. Select the origin point of the 3D sketch.

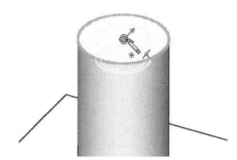

18. Click **OK**.

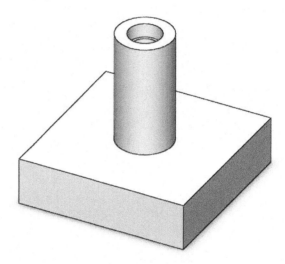

19. Create a through hole of 12 mm diameter on the first feature.

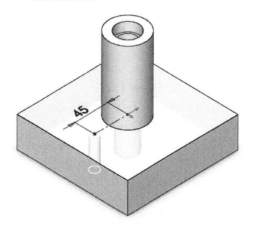

SOLIDWORKS 2019 Learn by Doing

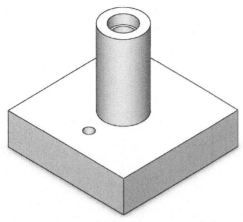

20. Create a circular pattern of the hole (refer to Chapter 6 > Tutorial 4 to know about Circular pattern).

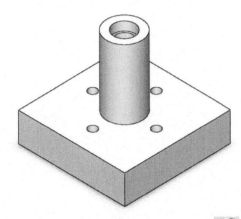

21. Deactivate the **Edit Component** icon on the CommandManager.

Creating the Second Component of the Assembly

1. On the CommandManager, click **Assembly > Insert Components > New Part** .
2. Select the Front plane of the assembly from the FeatureManager Design Tree.
3. Click **Exit Sketch** on the CommandManager.
4. Click **Sketch > Sketch** on the CommandManager.
5. Select top face of the Base.

6. On the ribbon, click **Sketch > Convert Entities** and select the circular edges of the Base.

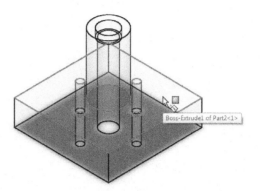

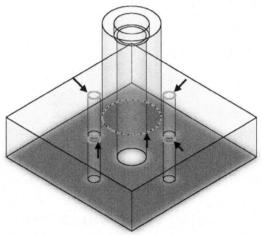

7. Click **OK** on the PropertyManager.
8. Draw a circle of 120 mm diameter.

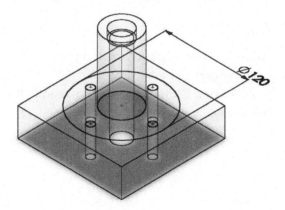

9. Click **Exit Sketch**.
10. Click the outer circle, right-click, click the down-arrows located at the bottom of the shortcut menu, and select **Contour Select Tool**.

181

11. Click in the region enclosed by the sketch.

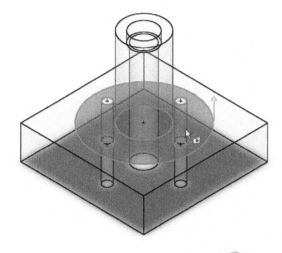

12. Activate the **Extruded Boss/Base** tool and extrude the sketch up to 40.

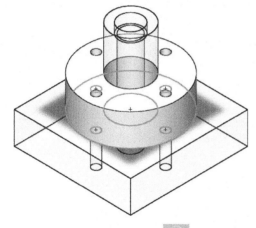

13. Exit the **Edit Component** Mode.

Creating the third Component of the Assembly

1. On the CommandManager, click **Assembly > Insert Components > New Part**.

2. Select the Front plane of the assembly from the FeatureManager Design Tree.
3. Draw a sketch, as shown in figure.

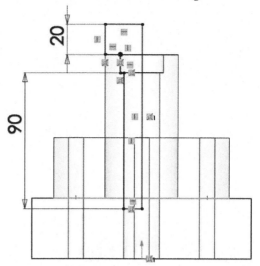

4. Click **Exit Sketch**.
5. Activate the **Revolved Base/Boss** tool and revolve the sketch. (refer to **Chapter 2 > Tutorial 2** to learn about the Revolved Base/Boss tool)

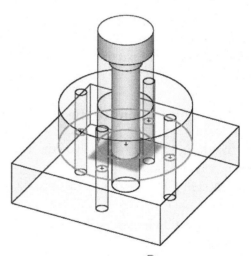

6. Activate the **Chamfer** tool (on the CommandManager, click **Features > Fillet drop-down > Chamfer**) and chamfer the edges, as shown in figure.

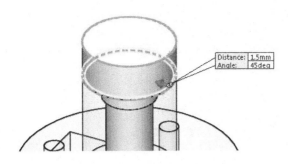

7. Activate the **Fillet** tool and round the edges, as shown in figure.

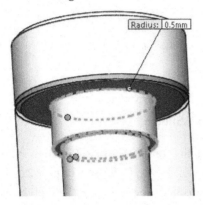

8. Click **Edit Component** on the CommandManager to exit the edit component mode.

Adding Bolt Connections to the assembly

1. Click the **Design Library** tab on the left side of the graphics window.
2. On the **Design Library** tab, select **Toolbox** and click **Add in now**.
3. On the **Design Library** tab, click **Toolbox > ANSI Metric**.
4. Under the **ANSI Metric** folder, click **Bolts and Screws > Hex Head**.
5. Click **Heavy Hex Bolt-ANSI B18.2.3.6M** and drag it into the graphics window.

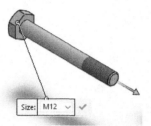

6. On the **Configure Component** PropertyManager, set the bolt properties as shown.

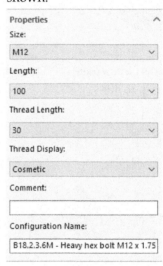

7. Click the **Add** button in the **Part Number** section and click **OK**.
8. Click **OK** on the PropertyManager. Another instance of the bolt is attached to the pointer.

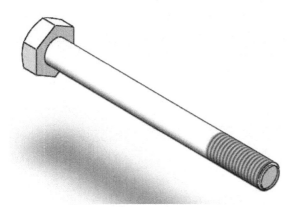

9. Click **Cancel** to stop inserting more bolts.
10. On the **Design Library** tab, click **Washer > Plain Washers**.
11. The **Regular Flat Washer** and drag it into the graphics window.
12. Set the washer size to **M12** and click the **Add** button under the **Part Numbers** section of the PropertyManager.
13. Click **OK** on the **Part Number** dialog.
14. Click **OK** and **Cancel**.

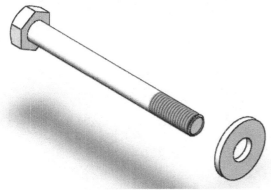

15. On the **Design Library** tab, under **ANSI Metric**, click **Nuts > Hex Nuts**.
16. Click and drag **Hex Heavy Nut** into the graphics window.
17. On the **Configure Component** PropertyManager, set the nut properties as shown.

18. Click the **Add** button under the **Part Numbers** section of the PropertyManager.
19. Click **OK** on the **Part Number** dialog.
20. Click **OK** and **Cancel**.

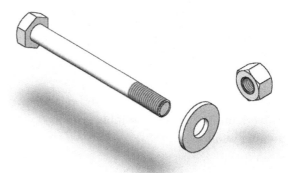

21. On the CommandManager, click **Assembly > Insert Components > New Assembly**. A new sub-assembly is inserted into the assembly.
22. In the FeatureManager Design Tree, click and drag the bolt, nut and washer into the sub-assembly.

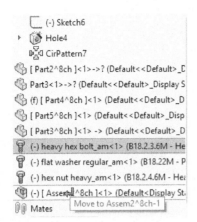

23. Right click on the sub-assembly and select **Open Subassembly**. The Sub-assembly is opened in another window.

24. On the CommandManager, click **Assembly > Mate**.
25. Click the **Multiple mate mode** icon on the PropertyManager.
26. Click on the cylindrical face of the bolt, and then click the cylindrical faces of the washer and nut. The bolt face is selected as a common mate entity.

27. Click **Add/Finish Mate**.
28. Click in the **Entities to mate**.
29. Select the flat face of the bolt.
30. Select the flat face of washer.

31. Click **Flip Mate Alignment**, and then click **OK** on the SOLIDWORKS dialog.
32. Click **Add/Finish Mate**.

33. Likewise, align the end faces of the bolt and nut, and click **OK** on the PropertyManager.

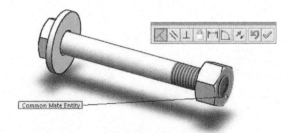

34. Save and close the sub-assembly.
35. On the CommandManager, click **Assembly > Mate**.
36. Click on the flat face for the washer and the part with holes.

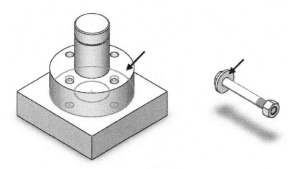

2. Select the sub-assembly from the FeatureManager Design Tree.
3. On the **Pattern Driven** PropertyManager, click in the **Driving Feature or Component** box.
4. Select the CircularPattern of the first component from the FeatureManager Design Tree.
5. Click **OK** on the PropertyManager.

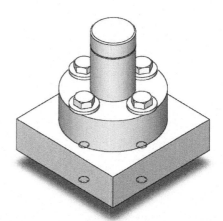

37. Click the **Coincident** icon, and click **Add/Finish Mate**.
38. Click the Cylindrical face of the bolt and circular edge of the hole as shown.

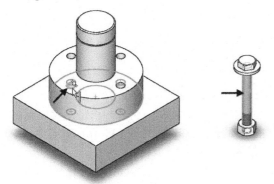

Sectioning an Assembly with Transparency

1. On the View Heads Up Toolbar, click the **Section View** icon.
2. On the PropertyManager, select **Zonal** from the **Section Method** section.
3. On the PropertyManager, select Front Plane from the **Section 1** section.

39. Click the **Concentric** icon, check the **Lock Rotation** option, and click **Add/Finish Mate**.
40. Click **OK** on the PropertyManager.

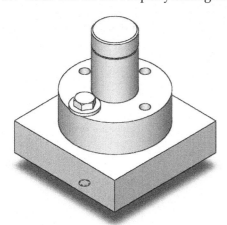

Patterning components in an assembly

1. On the CommandManager, click **Assembly > Linear Component Pattern > Pattern Driven Component Pattern**.

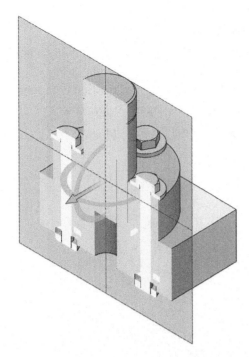

4. On the PropertyManager, check the **Transparency Section Components** section.
5. Select the components to turn transparent, as shown.

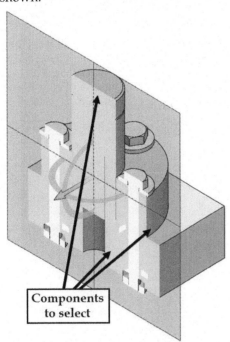

Components to select

6. Adjust the **Section Transparency** in the **Transparency Section Components** section.
7. Click **OK**.

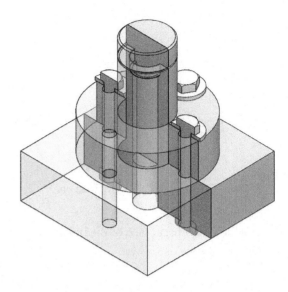

8. Click the **Section View** icon on the View Heads Up Toolbar.
9. Click the **Save** icon on the Quick Access Toolbar.
10. Click **Save All** on the **Save Modified Documents** dialog.
11. Type Ch8_tutorial1 in the **File name** box and click **Save**.
12. Select **Save internally (inside the assembly)**, and then click **OK**.

TUTORIAL 2

In this tutorial, you create a slider crank mechanism by applying advanced mates.

SOLIDWORKS 2019 Learn by Doing

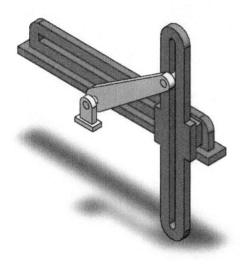

1. Create **Slider Crank Assembly** folder.
2. Download the part files of the assembly from the companion website. Next, save the files in the **Slider Crank Assembly** folder.
3. Start a new assembly file.
4. Click the pin icon on the **Begin Assembly** PropertyManager. This keeps the PropertyManager active.
5. Click the **Browse** button on the PropertyManager.
6. Browse to the **Slider Crank Assembly** folder, select all the components, and click **Open**.
7. On the PropertyManager, in the **Part/Assembly to Insert** section, click **Base**.
8. Click in the assembly window to position the Base component.
9. Likewise, position the other components in the assembly window.
10. Click **OK** on the PropertyManager.

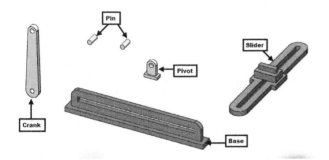

Creating Smart Mates

1. Press the Alt key and click on the face of the slider, as shown.

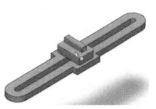

2. Keep the Alt key pressed and drag the component onto the face of the Base as shown.

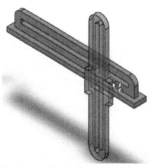

3. Release the left mouse button and notice that the Mates toolbar appears with the **Coincident** icon selected.
4. Click **Add/Finish Mate** to create the **Coincident** mate between the two faces.
5. Drag the slider up and rotate the view as shown.

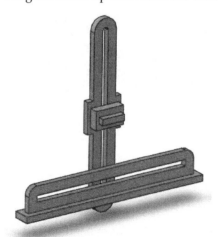

6. Click the face of the slider.

7. Press the Alt key and drag the slider onto the face of the Base as shown.

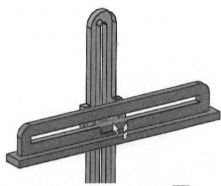

8. Click the **Flip Mate Alignment** icon.
9. Click **Add/Finish Mate**.
10. Click and drag the slider and notice that it can intersect with the base.

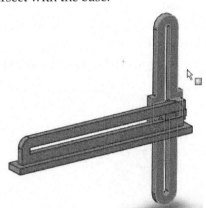

Creating the Limit Mate

1. On the CommandManager, click **Assembly > Mate**.
2. On the PropertyManager, expand the **Advanced Mates** section and click the **Distance** icon.
3. Select the end face of the Base as shown.

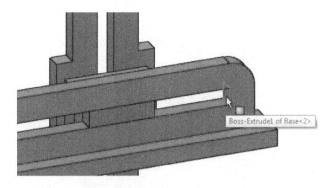

4. Rotate the view and select the end face of the slider as shown.

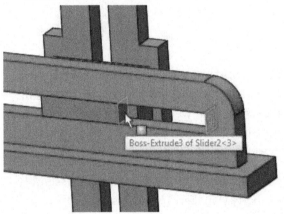

5. Set the **Distance** value to 1 mm.
6. Set the **Maximum Value** and **Minimum Value** to 459 and 1, respectively.

7. Click **OK** twice on the PropertyManager.
8. Click and drag the slider and notice that it is constrained between the end faces of the slot.

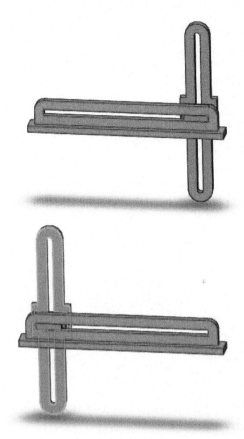

Creating the Slot Mate

1. On the CommandManager, click **Assembly > Mate**.
2. On the PropertyManager, expand the **Mechanical Mates** section and click the **Slot** icon.
3. Set the **Constraint** to **Free**.
4. Select the cylindrical face of the pin and flat face of the slider slot as shown.

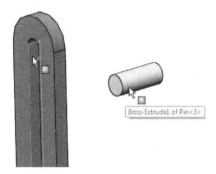

5. Click **OK** on the PropertyManager.
6. Expand the **Standard Mates** section and click the **Coincident** icon.
7. Select the flat faces of the pin and slider as shown.

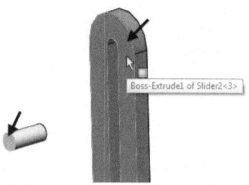

8. Click **Add/Finish Mate**, and then click **OK**.
9. Click and drag the pin and notice that it is constrained along the length of the slot.

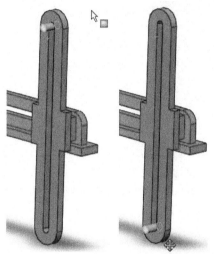

10. Press the Alt key, click and drag the upper hole of the crank.

11. Release the pointer onto the cylindrical of the pin.

12. Click **Add/Finish Mate** to add the **Concentric** mate between the hole and pin.
13. Use the **Mate** command to add the **Coincident** mate between the end face of the pin and flat face of the crank.

14. Assemble the other instance of the pin with the crank.

15. Assemble the pivot with the pin.

16. Make the bottom faces of the pivot and base coincident to each other.

17. Make the Right planes of the pivot and base coincident.

18. Click and drag the crank and notice that the slider moves along the slot.
19. Save and close the assembly and its parts.

Chapter 9: Dimensions and Annotations

In this chapter, you will learn to

- Create Centerlines and Center Marks
- Edit Hatch Pattern
- Apply Dimensions
- Place Hole callouts
- Place Datum Feature
- Place Feature control frame
- Place Surface symbol

TUTORIAL 1

In this tutorial, you create the drawing shown below.

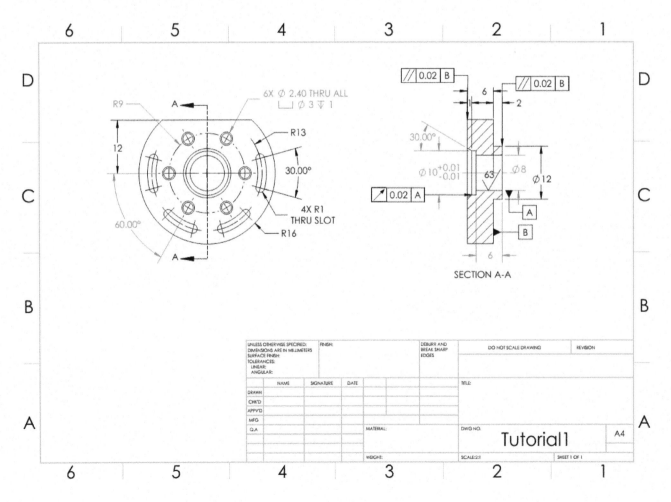

1. Download the Adapter Plate file from the Companion website.
2. Open a new drawing file using the **Sample** template.
3. Click **Cancel** on the **Model View** PropertyManager.
4. In the FeatureManager Design Tree, click the right mouse on Sheet1 and select **Properties**.
5. On the **Sheet Properties** dialog, select **Sheet/Format Size > A4 (ANSI) Landscape**, and then click **Apply Changes**.

Creating a Model View with Center Marks

1. On the **Quick Access Toolbar**, click the **Options** icon.
2. Click the **Document Properties** tab on the dialog and select **Detailing** from the tree.
3. Check the options in the **Auto insert on view creation** section, as shown.

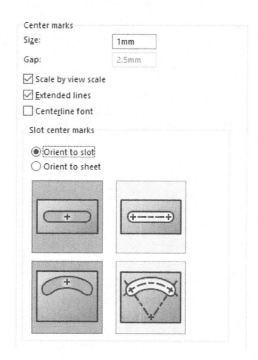

4. Select **Centerlines/Center Marks** in the tree.
5. Under the **Slot center marks** section, select **Orient to slot** and click the icons, as shown.
6. Type-in 1 in the **Size** box.
7. Check the **Scale by view scale** option to change the gap in the centreline with the view scale.
8. Click **OK**.
9. Click **View Layout > Model View** on the CommandManager.
10. Click **Browse** button on the PropertyManager.
11. Browse to the location of the Adapter Plate and double-click on it.
12. Set the **Scale** to **Use sheet scale**.
13. Set the **Orientation** to **Front**.
14. Set the **Display Style** to **Hidden Line Removed**.
15. Place the front view on the left-side on the drawing sheet.
16. Click **OK**.

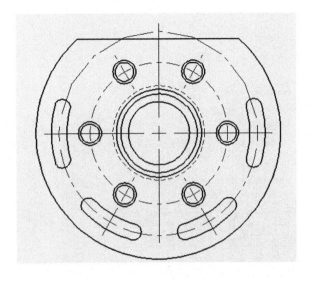

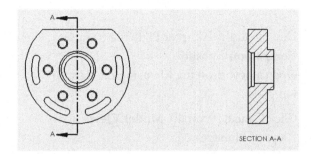

Creating Centerlines and Center Marks

1. Click **Annotation > Centerline** on the CommandManager.
2. Select the parallel lines on the section view, as shown below. The centerline is created.

17. Select the view and press **Delete**.
18. Click **Yes** on the **Confirm Delete** dialog.
19. On the **Quick Access Toolbar**, click the **Options** icon.
20. Click the **Document Properties** tab on the dialog and select **Detailing** from the tree.
21. Uncheck the options in the **Auto insert on view creation** section and click **OK**.
22. Create the front view and notice the difference.

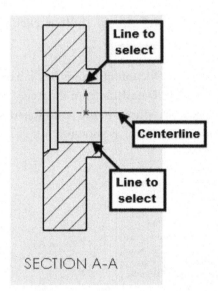

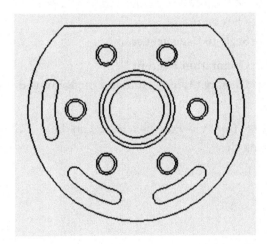

3. Click **OK** on the PropertyManager.
4. Click **Annotation > Center Mark** on the CommandManager.
5. On the PropertyManager, under **Manual Insert Options** section, click the **Circular Center Mark** icon.
6. Select the outer circles of the counterbore holes

23. Click **View Layout > Section View** on the CommandManager.
24. Select the center point of the front view.
25. Click **OK**.
26. Place the section view on the left side.

195

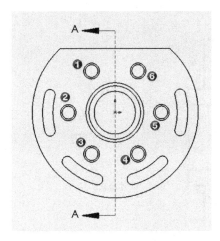

7. Click **OK** on the PropertyManager.

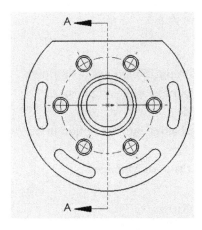

8. Activate the **Center Mark** command.
9. On the PropertyManager, under the **Auto Insert** section, check **For all slots**.
10. Select the front view.
11. Check the **Circular lines** option and uncheck all other options.
12. Click the **Arc Slot Ends** icon under the **Manual Insert Options** section of the PropertyManager.
13. Activate the **Slot Ends** icon.
14. Click **OK**.

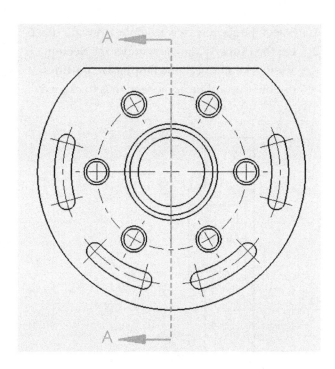

Editing the Hatch Pattern

1. Click on the hatch pattern of the section view. The **Area Hatch/Fill** PropertyManager appears.

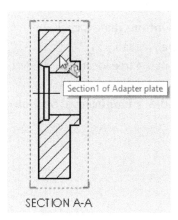

2. Uncheck the **Material crosshatch** option.

You can select the required hatch pattern from the **Hatch Pattern** drop-down. You can adjust the hatch scale and angle.

3. Click **OK**.

Emphasizing the Outline of the Section View

1. Select the section view from the drawing sheet.
2. On the PropertyManager, under the **Section View** section, check the **Emphasize outline** option: the outline of the section is thickened.

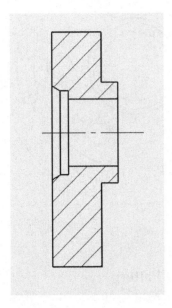

3. Click on the **Options** icon on the Quick Access Toolbar.
4. On the **System Options** dialog, click the **Document Properties** tab.
5. Click **Line Font** in the tree located at the left side.
6. Select **Type of Edge > Emphasized Section Outline**.

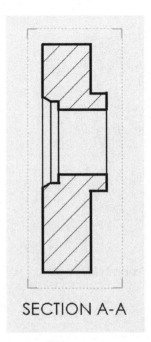

SECTION A-A

7. Select 0.5 mm from the **Thickness** drop-down.
8. Click **OK**; the thickness of the emphasized outline is changed.
9. Uncheck the **Emphasize outline** option in the **Section View** section.
10. Click **OK** on the PropertyManager.

Applying Dimensions

11. Click **Annotation > Model Items** on the CommandManager.
12. Select **Source > Entire model** and uncheck the **Import items into all views** option on the PropertyManager.
13. Click on the front view.
14. Click **OK**.
15. Drag and arrange the dimensions as shown.

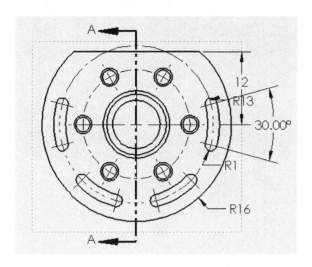

16. On the CommandManager, click **Annotation > Hole Callout** ⌴⌀.
17. Select the counterbore hole and position the hole callout as shown.

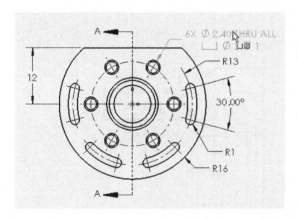

18. On the CommandManager, click **Annotation > Smart Dimension**.
19. Select the center marks of the holes.
20. Move the pointer in the region between the holes and click to position the dimension.

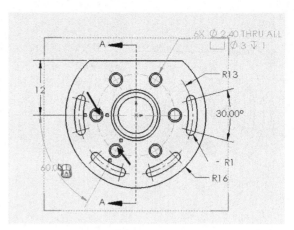

21. Select the R1 dimension and type-in the text in the **Dimension Text** box on the PropertyManager.

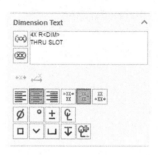

22. Click **Close Dialog** on the PropertyManager and position the dimension properly.

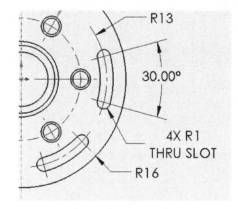

23. Dimension the pitch circle diameter of the counterbore holes as shown.

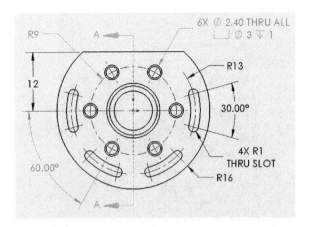
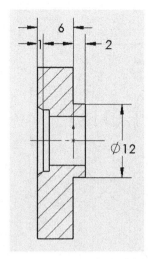

24. On the CommandManager, click **Annotation > Model Items**.
25. Select **Source > Entire model** and uncheck the **Import items into all views** option on the PropertyManager.
26. Click on the section view. Click **OK**.

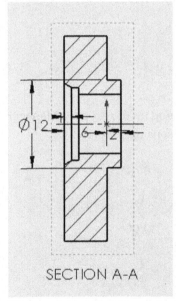

27. Click and drag the dimensions as shown.

28. Select the 2 mm dimension and notice the highlighted origins.
29. Click and drag the endpoints to the new locations as shown.

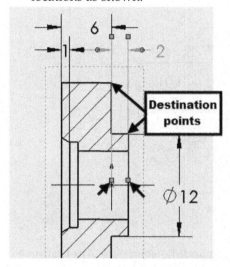

30. Likewise, modify the origins of other dimensions as shown.

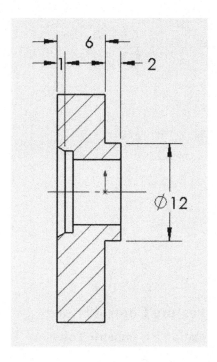

31. Activate the **Smart Dimension** command.
32. Select the lines, as shown.
33. Move the pointer toward right and click to place the dimension.

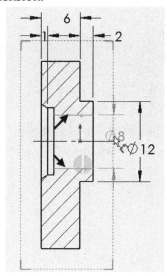

34. Likewise, add the counterbore dimension.

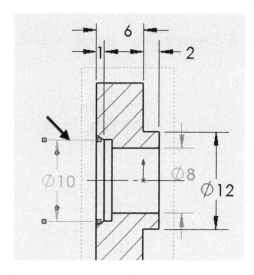

35. Select the counterbore dimension.
36. On the PropertyManager, under the **Tolerance/Precision** section, set the **Tolerance Type** to **Bilateral**.
37. Set the tolerance parameters as shown.

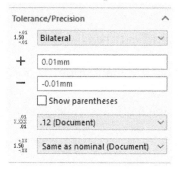

38. Click **Close Dialog**.

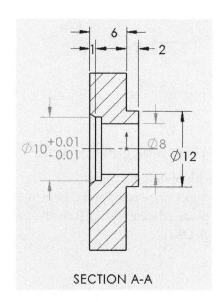

39. Likewise, apply the other dimensions, as shown below.

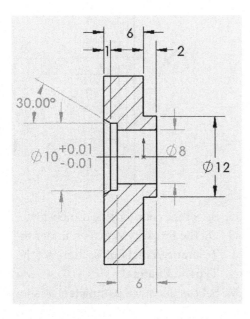

Placing the Datum Feature

1. Click **Annotation > Datum Feature** on the CommandManager.
2. Select the extension line of the dimension, as shown below.

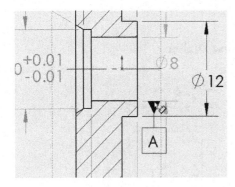

3. On the PropertyManager, click the **Filled Triangle with Shoulder** icon.
4. Move the cursor downward and click.
5. Likewise, place a datum feature B, as shown below. Click **OK**.

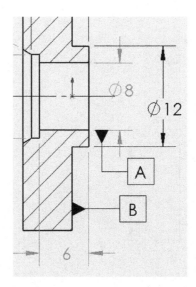

Placing the Feature Control Frame

1. Click **Annotation > Geometric Tolerance** on the CommandManager.
2. On the dialog, select **Circular Runout** from the **Symbol** drop-down.

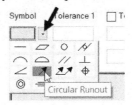

3. Type-in **0.02** and **A** in the **Tolerance 1** and **Primary** boxes.
4. Select a point on the line, as shown.
5. Move the cursor horizontally toward right and click.
6. Click **OK**.

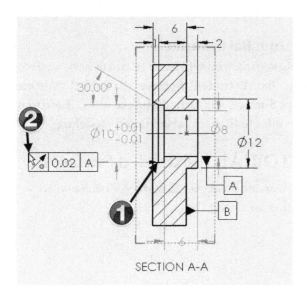

7. Activate the **Geometric Tolerance** command.
8. On the dialog, select **Parallel** from the **Symbol** drop-down.
9. Type-in **0.02** and **B** in the **Tolerance 1** and **Primary** boxes.
10. Select the endpoint of the edge as shown.
11. Move the pointer vertically up and click to position the feature control frame.

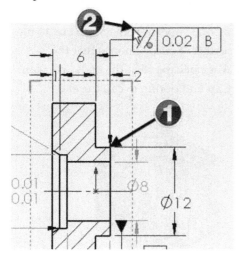

12. Likewise, add another feature control frame and click **OK**.

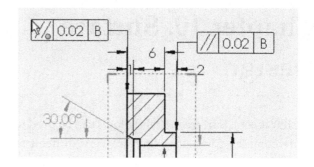

Placing the Surface Texture Symbols

1. Click **Annotation > Surface Finish** on the CommandManager.
2. Set the **Maximum Roughness** value to 63 on the PropertyManager.

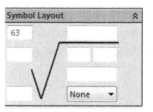

3. Click on the inner cylindrical face of the hole, as shown below.

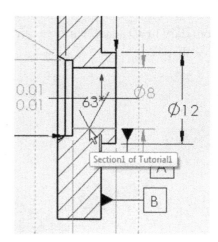

4. Click **OK**.
5. Save and close the file.

Chapter 10: Surface Design

SOLIDWORKS Surface modeling tools can be used to create complex geometries that are very difficult to create using solid modeling tools. In addition, you can also use these tools to fix broken imported parts. In this chapter, you will learn the basics of surfacing tools that are mostly used. The surfacing tools are available on the **Surfaces** Command Manager. You can also find these tools on the menu bar (click **Insert > Surface** on the Menu bar).

If the **Surfaces** CommandManager is not displayed by default, you can customize it. Right-click on any of the tabs of the CommandManager and select **Surface** from the shortcut menu.

SOLIDWORKS offers a robust set of surface design tools. A surface is an infinitely thin piece of geometry. For example, consider a box shown in Figure. It has six faces. Each of these faces is a surface, an infinitely thin piece of geometry that acts as a boundary in 3D space. Surfaces can be simple or complex shapes.

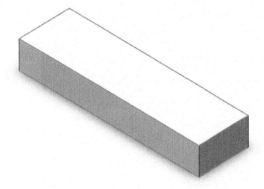

In solid modeling, when you create solid features such as an Extruded Boss or a Revolved Boss, SOLIDWORKS creates a set of surfaces forming a closed volume. This airtight closed volume is considered as a solid body. Although, you can design a geometry using solid modeling tools, but the surface modeling tools give you more flexibility.

Creating Basic Surfaces

In this section, you will learn to create basic surfaces using the **Extruded Surface**, **Revolved Surface**, **Swept Surface**, and **Lofted Surface** tools. These tools are similar to that available in solid modeling.

TUTORIAL 1 (Extruded Surfaces)

1. To create an extruded surface, first create an open or closed sketch.

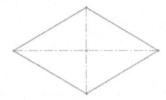

2. Click the **Extruded Surface** button on the **Surfaces** Command Manager.
3. Select the sketch. The **Surface-Extrude** Property Manager appears and is similar to the **Boss-Extruded** Property Manager.
4. Enter a value in the **Depth** box available in the **Direction 1** section.
5. Click **OK** ✓ on Property Manager to create the extruded surface. You will notice that the extrusion was not capped at the ends. You can check the **Cap end** option to cap the ends

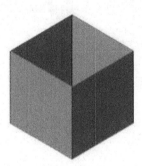

TUTORIAL 2 (Revolved Surfaces)

1. To create a revolved surface, first create an open or closed profile and the axis of revolution.

SOLIDWORKS 2019 Learn by doing

2. Click the **Revolved Surface** button on the **Surfaces** Command Manager.
3. Select the sketch. The preview of the revolved surface appears.
4. Enter the angle of revolution in the **Direction 1 Angle** box and click **OK**.

Even if you create an enclosed surface, SOLIDWORKS will not recognize it as a solid body. You will notice that the **Mass Properties** button is not available in the **Evaluate** Command Manager. This means that there exists no solid body. You will learn to convert a surface body into a solid later in this chapter.

TUTORIAL 3 (Swept Surfaces)

1. To create a swept surface, create a sweep profile and a path.

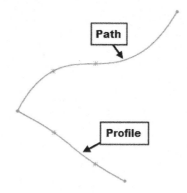

2. Click the **Swept Surface** button on the **Surfaces** Command Manager (or) click **Insert > Surface > Sweep**.
3. Select the sweep profile and then the path from the graphics window.
4. Click **OK** on the Property Manager.

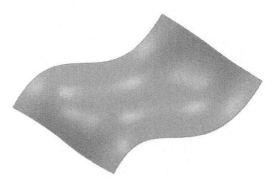

Various ways of creating swept surfaces are given next.

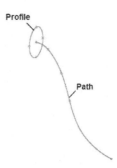

SOLIDWORKS 2019 Learn by doing

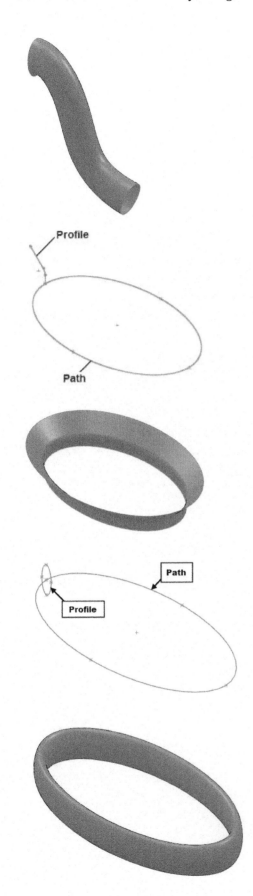

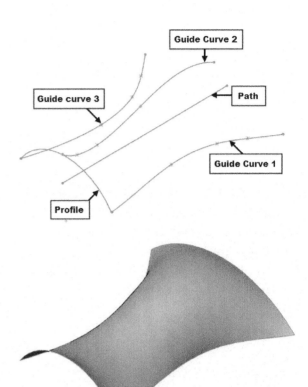

TUTORIAL 4 (Lofted Surfaces)

1. To create a swept surface, create two or more profiles.

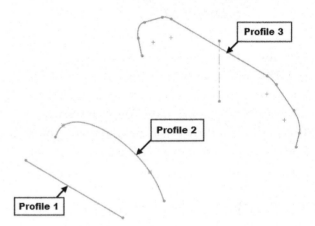

2. Click the **Lofted Surface** button on the **Surfaces** Command Manager (or) click **Insert > Surface > Loft** on the Menu bar.
3. Select the loft profiles from the graphics window.
4. Click **OK** on the Property Manager.

SOLIDWORKS 2019 Learn by doing

Various ways of creating lofted surfaces are given next.

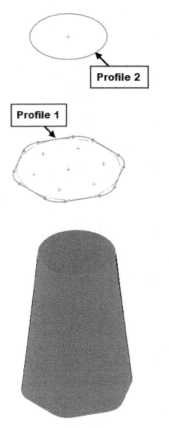

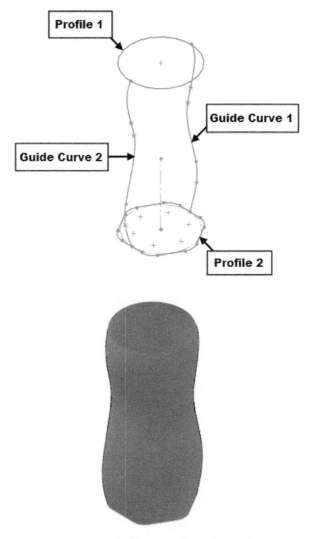

TUTORIAL 5 (Planar Surfaces)

1. To create a planar surface, click the **Planar Surface** button on the **Surfaces** Command Manager (or) click **Insert > Surface > Planar**.

The PropertyManager prompts you to select the bounding entities. You can select a closed sketch or closed loop of edges.

SOLIDWORKS 2019 Learn by doing

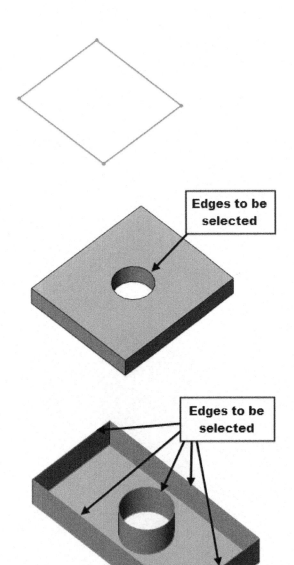

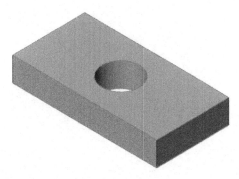

Creating Ruled Surfaces

The **Ruled Surface** tool allows you to create surfaces attached to the edges of an existing surface. You can find the **Ruled Surface** tool on the **Surfaces** Command Manager. You can also activate this tool from the menu bar by clicking **Insert > Surface > Ruled Surface**.

You can create five types of ruled surfaces using the options in the Property Manager. These five types of ruled surfaces are discussed next.

TUTORIAL 6 (Creating a Ruled Surface using the Tangent to Surface option)

1. To create a planar surface, click the **Ruled Surface** button on the **Surfaces** Command Manager (or) click **Insert > Surface > Ruled Surface**.
2. To create this type of ruled surface, select the **Tangent to Surface** option from the **Type** group of the **Ruled Surface** Property Manager.
3. Select an edge from the model.

2. Select a closed sketch or a closed loop of edges.
3. Click **OK** on the Property Manager. The planar surface will be created.

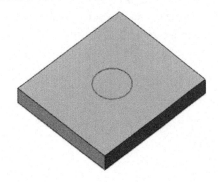

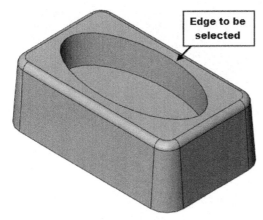

Notice the preview of the ruled surface. The resultant surface will be tangent to the selected edge. In this case, the selected edge is associated with two reference surfaces (the vertical and the top surfaces). As a result, there will be two solutions created from the selected edge. Click the **Alternate Face** button from the **Edge Selection** group to view the alternate solution.

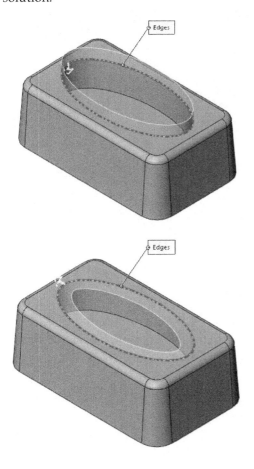

4. Enter a distance value in the **Distance** box of the **Distance/Direction** group.

You will notice two options- **Trim and Knit** and **Connecting surface** options available in the **Options** group. These options are useful while creating multiple ruled surfaces at a time. The **Trim and Knit** option, if enabled trims and knits the continuous ruled surfaces. The **Connecting surface** option creates a connecting surface at the sharp corners of the ruled surfaces.

5. Click **OK** to create the ruled surface.

TUTORIAL 7 (Creating a Ruled Surface using the Normal to Surface option)

1. To create this type of ruled surface, select the **Normal to Surface** option from the **Type** group of the **Ruled Surface** Property Manager.
2. Select an edge from the model.

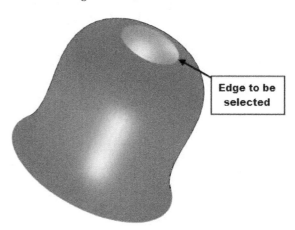

3. Enter a distance value in the **Distance** box of the **Distance/Direction** group.
4. Click the **Reverse Direction** button in the **Distance/Direction** group to reverse the direction, if required.
5. Click **OK** to create the ruled surface normal to the surface on which the selected edge lies.

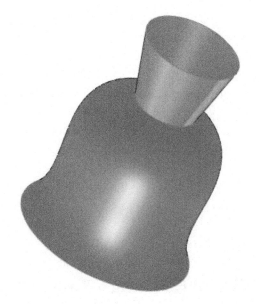

TUTORIAL 8 (Creating a Ruled Surface using the Tapered to Vector option)

1. To create this type of ruled surface, activate the Ruled Surface command (On the CommandManager, **Surfaces > Ruled surface**) and select the **Tapered to Vector** option from the **Type** group of the **Ruled Surface** Property Manager; some additional options appear in the **Distance/Direction** section.

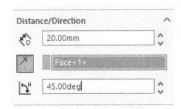

2. Select an edge from the model.
3. Click on the **Reference Vector** box available in the **Distance/Direction** group.
4. Select a face from the model to define the reference vector.

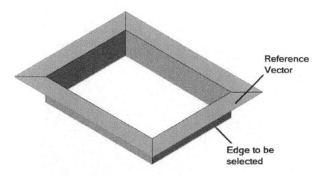

5. Specify the distance of the ruled surface in the **Distance** box.
6. Specify the taper angle of the ruled surface in **Angle** box available in the **Distance/ Direction** group.
7. Click the **Reverse Direction** button, if required.
8. Click **OK**.

The following figure shows the ruled surface created at a taper angle of 60 degrees.

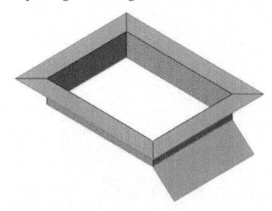

TUTORIAL 9 (Creating a Ruled Surface using the Perpendicular to Vector option)

1. To create this type of ruled surface, select the **Perpendicular to Vector** option from the **Type** group of the **Ruled Surface** Property Manager.
2. Select a face or an edge to define the reference vector.
3. Select an edge from the model.

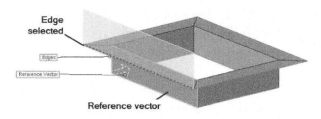

4. Specify the distance of the ruled surface in the **Distance** box.
5. Click the **Reverse Direction** button, if required.
6. Click **OK**.

TUTORIAL 10 (Creating a Ruled Surface using the Sweep option)

This option creates a ruled surface by sweeping the selected edge along a reference vector.

1. To create this type of ruled surface, select the **Sweep** option from the **Type** group of the **Ruled Surface** Property Manager.
2. On the **Ruled Surface** PropertyManager, click in the **Edge Selection** box.
3. Select an edge or loop of edges from the model.

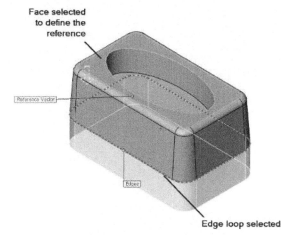

4. Specify the distance of the ruled surface in the **Distance** edit box.
5. Click in the **Reference Vector** selection box available in the **Distance/Direction** section.
6. Select a face or an edge to define the reference vector.

You can also use the **Coordinate input** option available in the **Distance/Direction** section to define the reference vector.

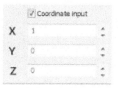

7. Click the **Reverse Direction** button, if required.
8. Click **OK**.

TUTORIAL 11 (Offset Surface)

1. To create a planar surface, click the **Offset Surface** button on the **Surfaces** Command Manager (or) click **Insert > Surface > Offset**.
2. Select the faces to offset.

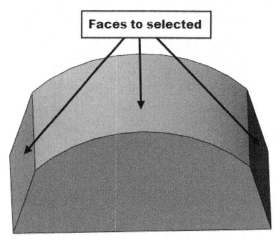

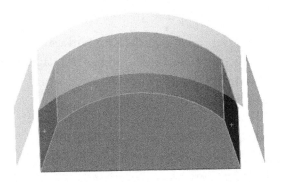

3. Specify the offset distance in the **Offset Distance** edit box.

SOLIDWORKS 2019 Learn by doing

4. Click **OK** on the Property Manager. The offset surface is created.

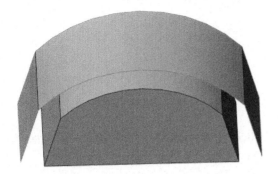

TUTORIAL 12 (Knitting Surfaces)

The surfaces which you create act as individual surfaces unless they are knitted together. The **Knit Surface** tool lets you to combine two or more surfaces to form a single surface.

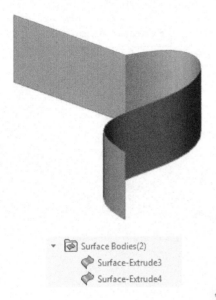

1. To knit surfaces, click the **Knit Surface** button on the **Surfaces** CommandManager (or) click **Insert > Surface > Knit**.
2. Select the surfaces to knit.

The **Merge entities** option available in the **Selections** section is used to merge the overlapping or redundant surfaces.

The options in the **Gap Control** group are used to knit the surfaces with small gaps. The **Knitting tolerance** box is used to define a tolerance value for the gaps. The gaps within the specified tolerance value will be knitted. You can also specify the gap range by using the sliders in the **Gap Control** group.

3. After specifying the required options, click the **OK** button to knit the surfaces.

In some cases, you may need to extract the surfaces of the solid body. You can use the **Knit Surface** tool to extract the surfaces of the solid body. Hide the solid body to see the extracted surfaces.

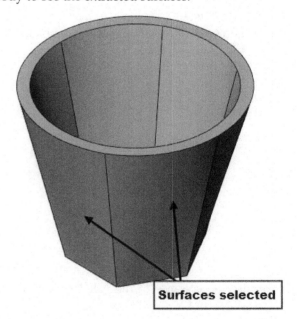

Creating a Solid by Knitting Surfaces

You can convert surfaces forming a closed enclosure into solid using the **Knit Surface** tool. Create surfaces forming a closed enclosure. Activate the **Knit Surface** tool and select the surfaces. On the PropertyManager, check the **Create Solid** option, and then click **OK**.

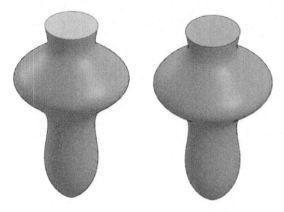

TUTORIAL 13 (Trimming Surfaces)

You can trim surfaces using the **Trim Surface** tool. The surfaces are trimmed using a trimming tool. The trimming tool can be a surface, plane or a sketched entity.

1. To trim a surface, click the **Trim Surface** button on the **Surfaces** Command Manager (or) click **Insert > Surface > Trim**; the **Trim Surface** Property Manager appears.

You can trim a surface using the **Standard** and **Mutual** options available in the **Trim Type** group. The two trimming methods are discussed next.

Trimming a Surface using the Standard option

2. To trim a surface using this option, click the **Standard** option in the **Trim Types** group.
3. Select **Keep selections** on the PropertyManager.
4. Select the trim tool and surface to keep.

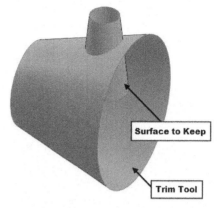

If you select the **Remove selections** option in the **Selections** group, you need to select the surface to remove.

5. Click **OK** to trim the surface.

You can also trim a surface using a sketch.

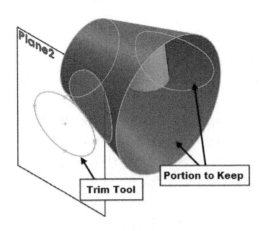

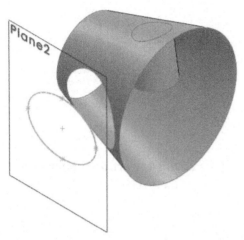

You can also use a surface as a trim tool that does not extend completely along the surface to be trimmed.

In this case, the **Surface Split Options** will be useful. If you use the **Natural** option, the split will occur following the natural extension of the trim tool.

If you select the **Linear** option, split will be a straight line to the nearest edge.

If you select the **Split All** option, multiple split lines will appear. You can decide which portion of the surface to keep or remove.

Trimming Surfaces using the Mutual option

The **Mutual** option is used to trim multiple surfaces at a time. For example, you can use this option for the following case.

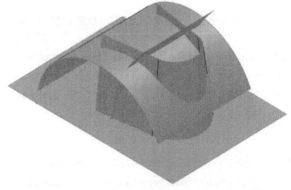

1. To trim surfaces using this option, select the **Mutual** option from the **Trim Type** group.
2. Select the required surfaces from the model (All surfaces in this case).
3. After selecting the required surfaces, select the **Keep selections** or **Remove selections** option.

SOLIDWORKS 2019 Learn by doing

If you select the **Keep selections** option, you need to select the surfaces to be kept. If you select the **Remove selections** option, you need to select the surfaces to be removed. In this case, you select the **Keep selection** option.

4. Click in the next selection box of the PropertyManager.
5. Select the surfaces to be kept.

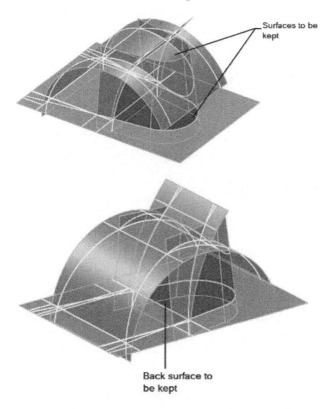

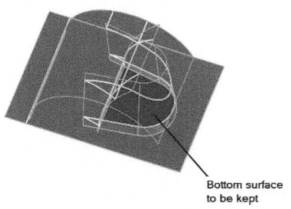

6. Click OK to trim the surfaces.

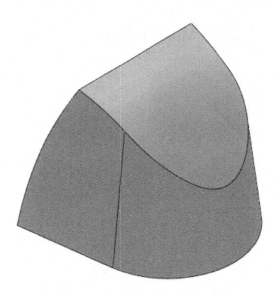

TUTORIAL 14 (Extending Surfaces)

During the design process, you may sometimes need to extend a surface. You can extend a surface using the **Extend Surface** tool.

1. To invoke this tool, click the **Extend Surface** button on the **Surfaces** Command Manager (or) click **Insert > Surface > Extend**.

The parameters used to define an extended surface are available on this PropertyManager. You can select an edge, multiple edges or an entire surface to extend.

Single Edge

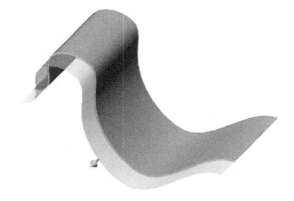

Multiple Edges

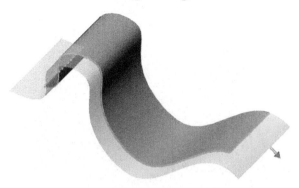

Entire Surface

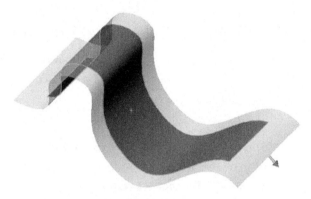

Same Surface Extension

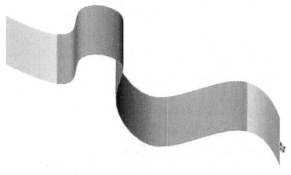

Linear Extension

4. Click **OK**.

TUTORIAL 15 (Offset on Surface)

You can offset the edges of a surface using the **Offset on Surface** tool.

1. On the ribbon, click **Sketch > Offset On Surface**.

Tip: If the Offset On Surface tool is unavailable on the CommandManager, right click on the Sketch tab of the CommandManager, and then select Customize CommandManager.

2. Select an edge from the surface body.
3. Select the **Distance** option and type a value in the **Distance** box. If you select the **Up to point** option, you can define the distance by selecting a vertex or point. The **Up to surface** option is used to define the distance by selecting a surface.

When the surface you have selected is not planar, you can decide the type of extension by using the **Extension Type** options. Use the **Same Surface** option to extend the surface by maintaining the curvature of the original surface. If you select the **Linear** option, the extended surface will be created tangent to the original surface.

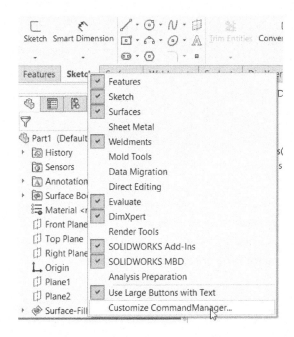

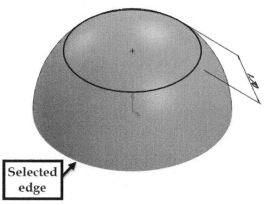

The **Euclidean Offset** option creates an offset curve by measuring the offset distance in the linear direction. This results in the longer offset distance.

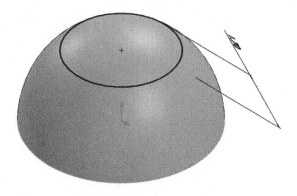

*On the **Customize** dialog, click the **Commands** tab and select **Sketch** from the **Categories** list. Next, click and drag the **Offset On Surface** command. Keep the left mouse button pressed, move the cursor onto the CommandManager, and then release the mouse button; the **Offset On Surface** command is available on the CommandManager.*

2. Click on the surface.

4. On the PropertyManager, type in a value in the **Offset Distance** box.
5. Click **OK**.

3. On the PropertyManager, select the **Offset type** (**Geodesic Offset** or **Euclidean Offset**).

The **Geodesic Offset** option creates an offset curve with the shortest distance between the selected edge and the curve. The offset distance is measured along the supporting surface.

A 3D Sketch is created on the selected surface body.

6. Press Ctrl+Z on your keyboard to undo the **Offset On Surface** operation.
7. On the CommandManager, click **Sketch > Offset On Surface**.
8. Type 5 in the **Offset Distance** box of the PropertyManager.
9. Select the edges of the surface, as shown.

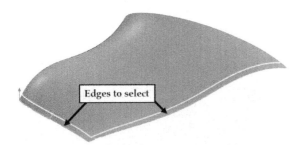

10. Click **OK** on the PropertyManager.
11. Click the **Exit Sketch** icon located at the top right corner of the graphics window.

TUTORIAL 16 (Untrimming a Surface)

You can untrim a trimmed surface using the **Untrim Surface** tool.

1. Click the **Untrim Surface** button on the **Surfaces** Command Manager (or) click **Insert > Surface > Untrim**.
2. Select the edges to be untrimmed.

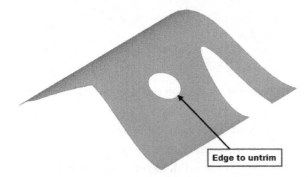

3. Click **OK**.

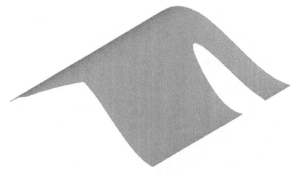

If you select the edge, which is intersecting the boundary of the surface, the untrim surface is created within the boundary. Make sure that the **Edge untrim type** is set to **Extend edges**.

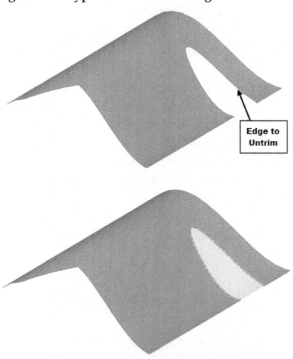

If you check the **Merge to original** option available in the **Options** group, the untrim surface will be merged with the original surface. If you uncheck this option, the untrim surface will be created as an individual surface.

When you untrim the external edges, you have control over the surface created. You can extend the untrim surface beyond the boundary of the surface by entering the extension percentage on the PropertyManager.

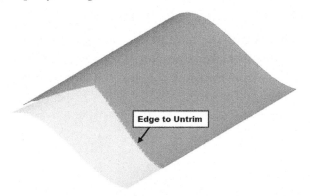

If you select the external edges adjacent to each other, the untrim surface will be bound by the selected edges.

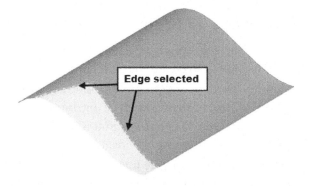

If you select the **Connect endpoints** option available in the **Options** group, only the portion necessary to connect the two endpoints is created.

You can use the **Untrim Surface** tool to untrim an entire surface. In addition, the PropertyManager has options to untrim the internal, external, or all the edges of the surface.

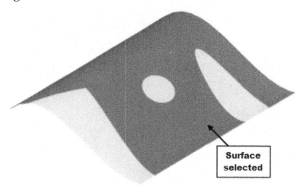

TUTORIAL 17 (Deleting Holes)

1. To delete a hole, select it from the model and press the **Delete** key. The **Choose Option** dialog appears.

2. Select the **Delete Hole(s)** option and click **OK**.

SOLIDWORKS 2019 Learn by doing

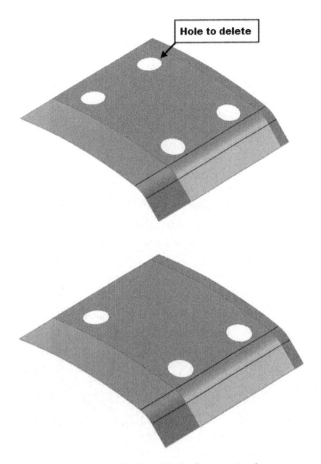

You will notice the **Delete Hole** feature in the FeatureManager Design Tree.

If you want the hole to be back, you can delete the **Delete Hole** feature from the FeatureManager Design Tree. You can also edit the **Delete Hole** feature. Click on the **Delete Hole** feature and click **Edit Feature**.

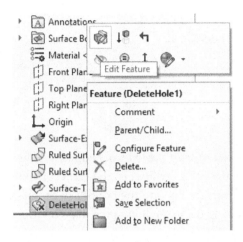

The PropertyManager shows the list of holes that were deleted. You can add more holes to the list by selecting them from the model. You can also remove the hole from the list. Make sure that there is at least one hole in the list.

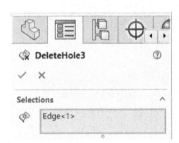

TUTORIAL 18 (Filled Surface)

The **Filled Surface** tool can be used either to patch holes in models or to create complex surfaces. While patching surfaces, the **Filled Surface** tool gives you more options than deleting holes or untrimming. It provides more control over the definition of the resultant patch. For example, consider the model shown in figure. You can see that a face is missing. In a case like this, both the **Delete Hole** and **Untrim Surface** tools fail to fill this gap. The **Filled Surface** tool will be used in this case.

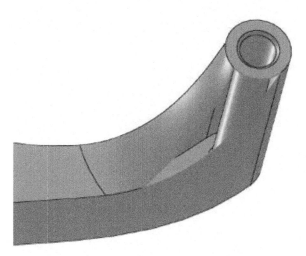

1. To create a filled surface, click the **Filled Surface** button on the **Surfaces** Command Manager (or) click **Insert > Surface > Fill** on the menu bar.
2. To select the patch boundaries, right-click on one of the gap edges and select the **Select Open Loop** option from the shortcut menu. All the gap edges are selected.

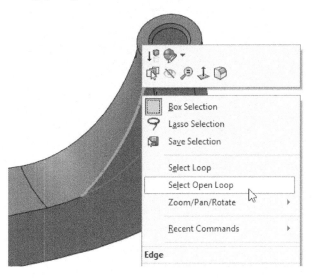

3. Select an option from the **Curvature Control** drop-down. This defines the curvature continuity of the fill surface.

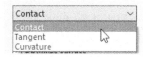

The options in this drop-down are **Contact**, **Tangent**, and **Curvature**. Most of the gap edges should be tangent to the surrounding faces.

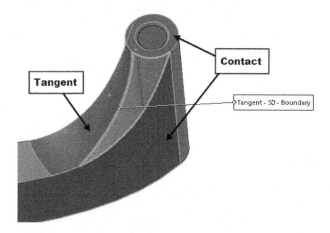

The **Apply to all edges** option is used to apply the curvature setting to all edges.

4. Click **OK** to create the filled surface.

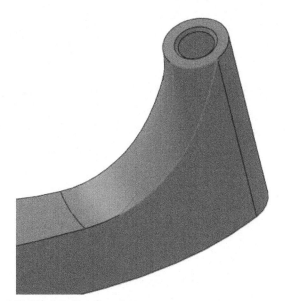

TUTORIAL 19

You can also use the **Filled Surface** tool for creating a new surface.

SOLIDWORKS 2019 Learn by doing

1. Activate the **Filled Surface** tool and select the patch boundary.
2. Click in the **Constraint Curves** selection box and then select the constraint curves.

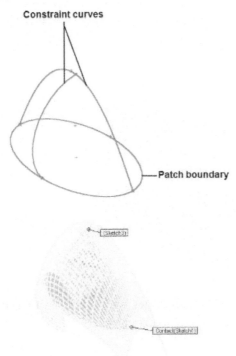

TUTORIAL 20 (Converting a Surface to Solid)

Creating a solid from a surface can be accomplished by simply thickening a surface. You can also create a solid if a volume is enclosed by the surface. For example, consider the surface shown in figure. It encloses a volume. However, there is only one surface body listed in the FeatureManager Design Tree.

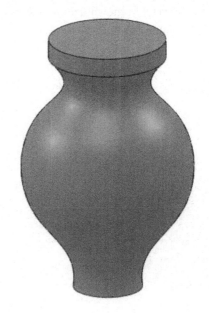

3. Specify the curvature setting (**Contact**, **Tangent**, or **Curvature**).

The **Optimize Surface** option available in the **Patch Boundary** group will create a simple surface very quickly. If you uncheck this option, the **Resolution Control** slider will appear. You can use this slider to define the resulting surface. You can remove wrinkles or other imperfections from the surface. However, the surface will be created very slowly. It is recommended that you use the **Optimize Surface** option for quick results.

4. After specifying the required settings, click **OK** to create the filled surface.

SOLIDWORKS 2019 Learn by doing

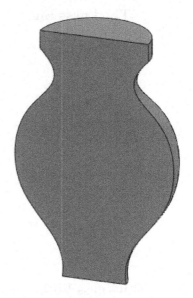

1. To make this surface into a solid, click the **Thicken** button on the **Surfaces** Command Manager.
2. Select the enclosed surface.

You will notice that the **Create solid from enclosed volume** option is enabled. This option is available only when you select an enclosed surface.

3. Check the **Create solid from enclosed volume** option.
4. Click **OK** to create a solid.

You can use the **Mass Properties** tool (On the CommandManager, click **Evaluate > Mass Properties**) to check whether the surface is converted into a solid or not. You can also use the **Section View** tool available on the View Heads-Up Toolbar.

TUTORIAL 21 (Thickening the Surface)

The **Thicken** tool can also be used to add a thickness to the surface. If the geometry contains more than one surface, than make sure that they are knit together using the **Knit Surface** tool.

1. Activate the **Thicken** command and select the surface to thicken.
2. Type-in the thickness value on the PropertyManager.
3. Define the thickness side using the **Thickness** buttons. Select the **Thicken Side1** button to add thickness outside the surface. The **Thicken Side2** button is used to add thickness inside the surface. The **Thicken Both Sides** button is used to add thickness to both sides of the surface.
4. Click **OK**.

Thickness Side1

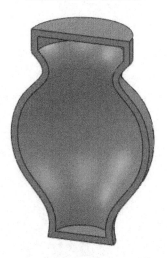

Thickness Both Sides

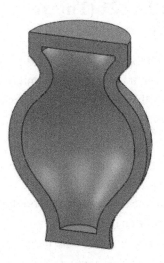

Thickness Sides2

TUTORIAL 22 (Deleting Faces)

You can delete unwanted faces from a model. In case of a solid, you can delete a face and make it a surface model.

1. To delete a face, click the **Delete Face** button from the **Surfaces** Command Manager.
2. Make sure that the **Delete** option is selected in the **Options** group.
3. Select the face to be deleted.

4. Click **OK** to delete the face.

You can also use the **Delete and Patch** option available in the **Options** group. This option will be useful for the following type of cases.

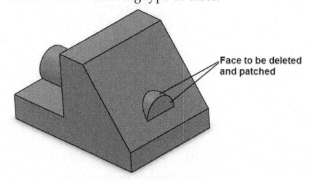

1. Select this option from the **Options** group and then select the faces to be deleted.

2. Click **OK**.

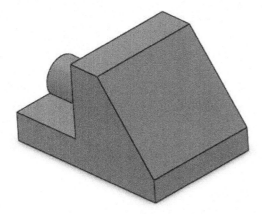

The **Delete and Fill** option is used for the following type of cases.

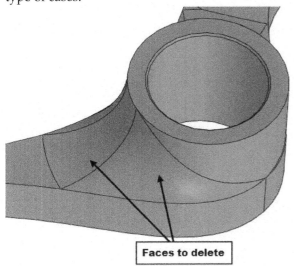

Resulting face is shown next.

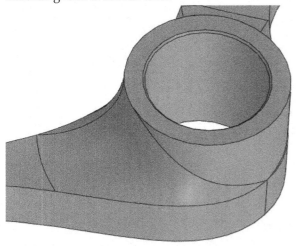

TUTORIAL 23 (Replacing Faces)

The **Replace Face** tool replaces a face or group of faces with another face or group of faces.

1. To replace a face, click the **Replace Face** button on the Command Manager (or) click **Insert > Face > Replace** on the Menu bar.
2. Select the target faces for replacement.
3. Click in the **Replacement Surface** selection box and select the replacement surface.

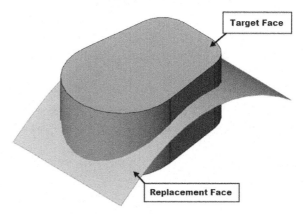

4. Click **OK** to replace the surface.

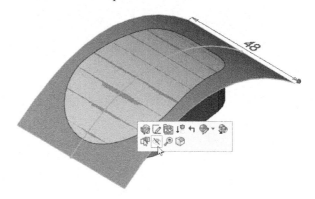

SOLIDWORKS 2019 Learn by doing

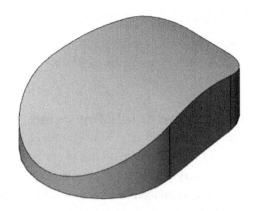

TUTORIAL 24 (Cutting with Surfaces)

You can cut a solid with a surface using the **Cut with Surface** tool. For example, you can cut the solid shown in figure using a surface, and create a complex face on the top.

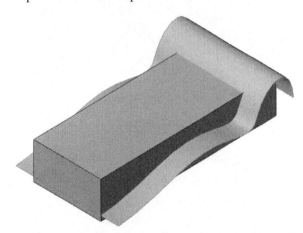

1. To cut a solid using a surface, click the **Cut with Surface** button on the **Surfaces** Command Manager (or) click **Insert > Cut > With Surface** from the Menu bar.
2. Select the cutting surface.

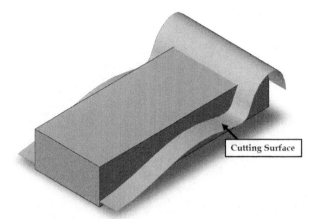

3. Specify the direction of the cut using the arrow that appears on the surface.
4. Click **OK**. Hide the extruded surface to view the result.

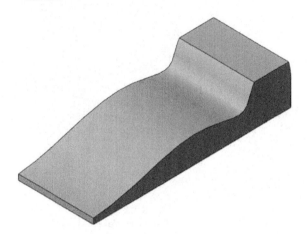

The **Bodies to Keep** dialog appears if the cut results in more than one body. Select the **All bodies** option (or) the **Selected Bodies** option and select the bodies to keep from the list. Click **OK** to cut the solid.

TUTORIAL 25 (Thickened Cut)

You can also use the **Thickened Cut** tool to cut a solid with the surface.

1. Click the **Thickened Cut** button on the **Surfaces** CommandManager (or) click **Insert > Cut > Thicken**.
2. Select the cutting surface.

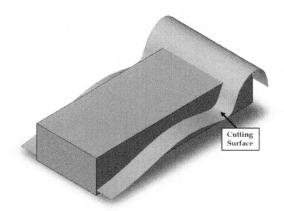

3. Specify the thickness side by clicking anyone of the icons in the **Thickness** section of the PropertyManager.

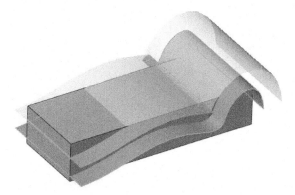

4. Specify the thickness value in the **Thickness** box available on the PropertyManager.
5. Click **OK**.

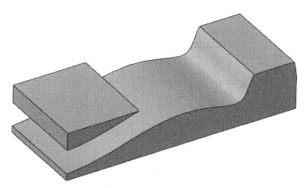

TUTORIAL 26 (Freeform Surfaces)

The **Freeform** tool is a powerful tool that is used to create ergonomic shapes. This tool allows you to push and pull a surface to create complex shapes easily. A freeform shape can be created using a face of the solid body or surface.

1. To create a freeform surface, click the **Freeform** button on the **Surfaces** Command Manager (or) click **Insert > Surface > Freeform** on the Menu bar.
2. Select a face to modify. A mesh appears on the selected surface.

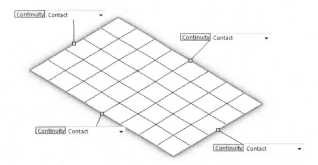

In addition, **Continuity** callouts are attached to the surface boundaries. These callouts are used to control the boundaries of the face. The options in the callouts are **Contact**, **Tangent**, **Curvature**, **Moveable**, and **Moveable/Tangent**.

3. Select **Moveable** from the **Continuity** drop-down. The boundary acts as a control curve.
4. On the PropertyManager, click the **Add Points** button in the **Control Points** group and add control points to the boundary.

SOLIDWORKS 2019 Learn by doing

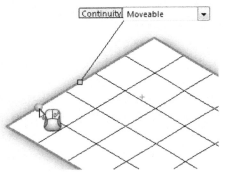

5. Click the **Add Points** button again or press ESC.
6. Select a control point on the boundary. A reference triad appears, as shown.

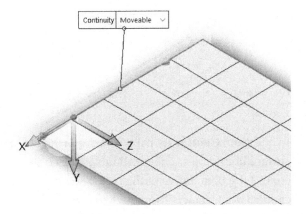

7. Click and drag the Y-axis of the triad and notice the surface. You can use the scale to move the control point precisely.

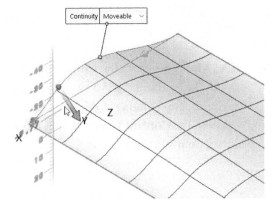

8. Likewise, drag the Z and X axes to modify the surface.

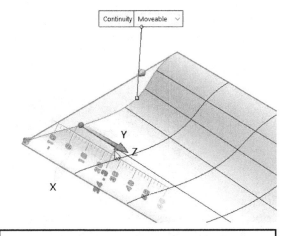

Moving the Control Point in Z-direction

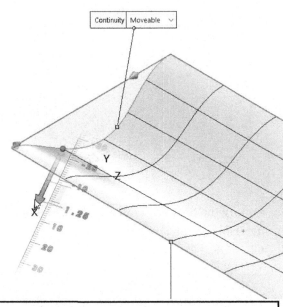

Moving the Control Point in X-direction

9. Click and drag the origin of the triad.

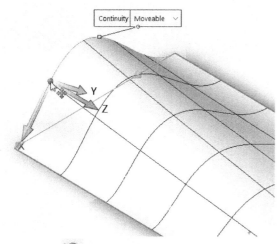

Click **Undo** on the PropertyManager, if you want to return to the previous state of the surface. The behaviour of the triad can also be controlled using the options in the Property Manager.

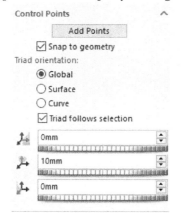

You can change the orientation of the triad using the **Global**, **Surface**, and **Curve** options. The **Triad follows selection** option will move the triad along the control point.

10. Select the control curve and notice the tangency control arrows.

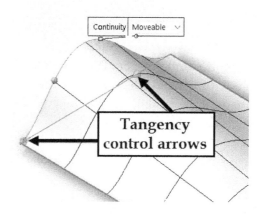

11. Drag the tangency control arrows to modify the curvature.

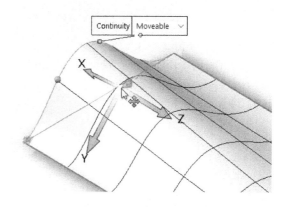

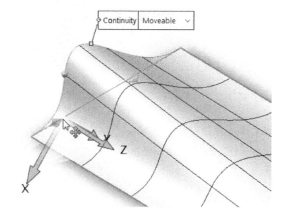

After modifying the surface, if you have by mistake changed the option in the **Continuity** callout, the modifications will be lost.

12. Click the **Add Curves** button in the **Control**

Curves group to add control curves on the surface.

You can create two types of control curves- **Through points** and **Control polygon**. The **Through Points** curve is formed joining the various points. The **Control polygon** is similar to that used while creating a spline.

13. Select the required curve type (**Through points** or **Control polygon**).

14. Move the pointer on the surface. You will notice that a green curve appears on the surface. If you click the **Flip Direction** button in the Property Manager (or) press Tab on your keyboard, the curve will appear in the other direction.

15. Move the pointer and click to specify the location of the control curves. You can create as many curves as possible by clicking at the required locations.

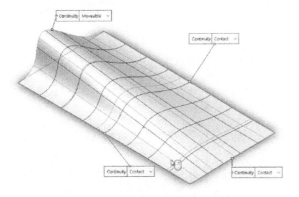

16. Click the **Add Curves** button again or press ESC.
17. Add control points on the control curves by using the **Add Points** button.

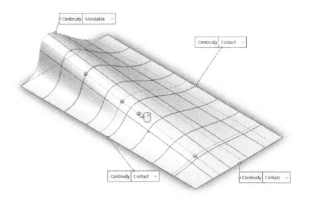

18. Click the **Add Points** button again or press ESC.
19. Select the required control curve; the control points appear on it. Push and pull the control points to modify the surface.

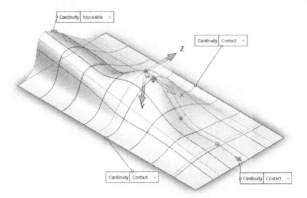

While modifying the surface if you want to change the control curve type (for this example **Though points**), you can select the required option from the **Control Curves** section. The control curve type will be changed.

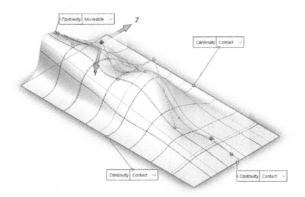

The **Display** section in the Property Manager can be used to modify the display.

20. Drag the **Face transparency** slider to change the transparency of the surface.
21. Drag the **Mesh density** slider to refine the mesh.

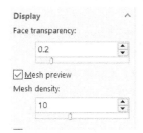

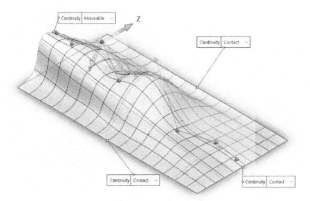

22. Display zebra stripes by checking the **Zebra stripes** option.

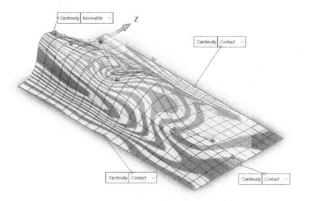

23. Uncheck the **Zebra stripes** option.
24. Check the **Curvature combs** and **Direction 1** options. The curvature combs appear in the first direction.

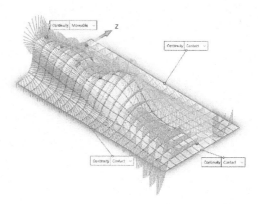

You can set the curvature type, scale and density of the curvature combs

25. Click **OK** on the Property Manager.

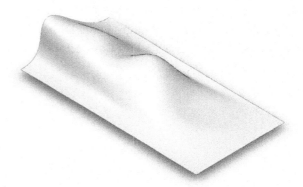

TUTORIAL 27 (Boundary Surfaces)

The **Boundary Surface** tool is very similar to the **Lofted Surface** tool but allows you to create surfaces that can be tangent, or curvature, continuous in both the directions.

1. To create a boundary surface, click the **Boundary Surface** button on the **Surfaces** Command Manager (or) click **Insert > Surface > Boundary Surface** on the Menu bar.
2. Select the curves or edges to define the **Direction 1** of the boundary surface.

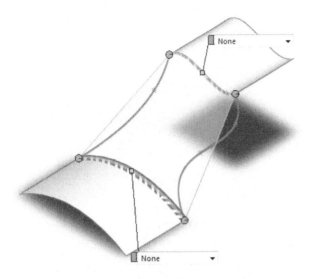

To avoid the twist, make sure that you click on the same side of the two curves. If a twist is created, right-click on anyone of the edges in the **Direction 1** selection box and choose the **Flip Connectors** option.

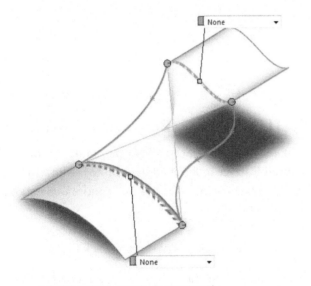

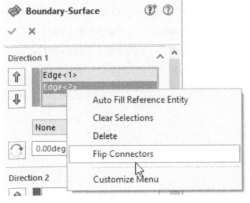

You can specify the way the boundary surface will be connected to the selected edges. To do so, select the required edge from the **Direction 1** selection box. Next, select the **Tangent type** option.

3. Select the **Edge 1** from the **Direction 1** selection box.
4. Select **Tangency To Face** option from the **Tangent type** drop-down (for this example).
5. Specify the tangent length in the **Tangent Length** box or by dragging the arrow displayed on the curve.

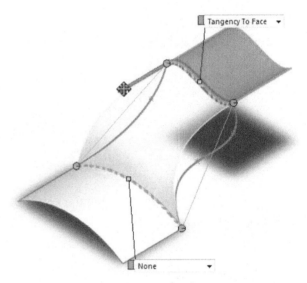

6. Select the **Edge 2** from the **Direction 1** selection box.
7. Select **Curvature To Face** option from the **Tangent type** drop-down (for this example).

SOLIDWORKS 2019 Learn by doing

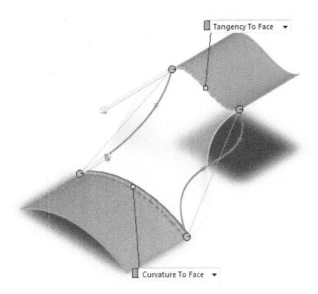

8. Click in the **Direction 2** selection box.
9. Select the guide curves.

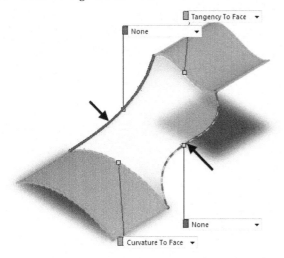

You will notice that the **Tangent type** drop-down is replaced by the **Tangent influence** option in the **Direction 1** group. This is just another way to specify the tangent value.

In addition, the **Curve Influence Type** drop-down appears under both the **Direction 1** and **Direction 2** groups. Select the required option from this drop-down.

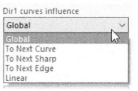

10. Click **OK** to create the boundary surface.

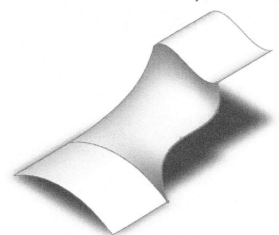

TUTORIAL 28 (Flatten Surface)

The **Flatten Surface** tool is flattens the surface model.

1. On the **Surface** CommandManager, click the **Surface Flatten**  tool.
2. Select the faces from the surface model, as shown.

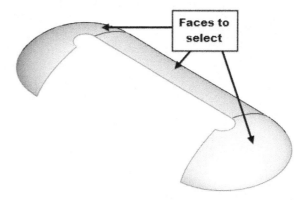

3. Click in the reference selection box.
4. Select the horizontal edge.

232

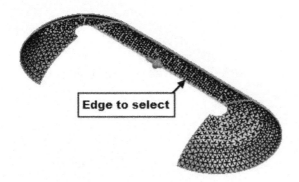

5. Click **OK**.

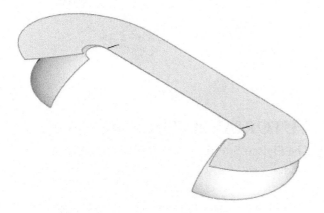

6. Right click on the flatten surface and select **Export to DXF / DWG**.
7. Select **Dxf** from the **Save as type**.
8. Type a name in the **File name** box and click **Save**.

SOLIDWORKS 2019 Learn by doing

Chapter 11: Mold Tools

In this chapter, you will learn the basics of mold tools in SOLIDWORKS. The process of a creating mold is very complex but the in-built mold tools in SOLIDWORKS make it easy for you.

In SOLIDWORKS, mold tools are located in the **Mold Tools** CommandManager. You need to customize the Command manager to display this CommandManager. Click the right mouse button on any of the tab in the CommandManager and select **Mold Tools** to display the mold tools.

TUTORIAL 1

In this tutorial, you will design a mold for the part, as shown.

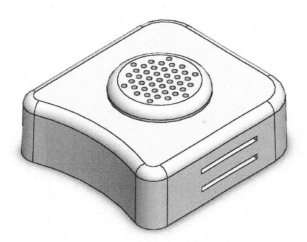

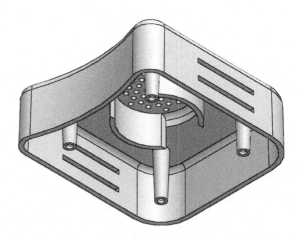

Performing Draft Analysis

1. Download the plastic part from the companion website and open it in SOLIDWORKS.
2. Click the **Draft Analysis** button on the **Mold Tools** CommandManager.
3. Select the Top plane from the FeatureManager Design Tree to specify the Direction of Pull.
4. Set **Draft Angle** to 1 degree.
5. Click **OK**.

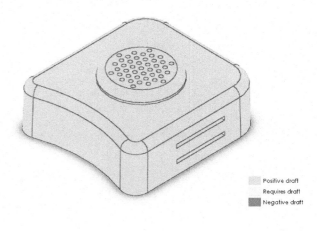

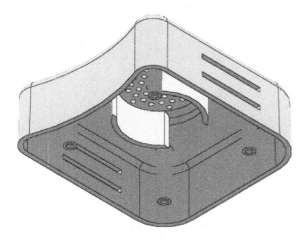

The faces displayed in green color are having a positive draft. Whereas, the faces highlighted in red color are having negative draft.

6. Place the pointer on the outer faces of the part and notice the positive draft angle.

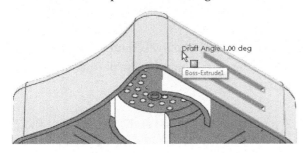

7. Place the pointer on the faces highlighted in yellow color. Notice that the draft angle is zero. You need to apply draft to these faces.

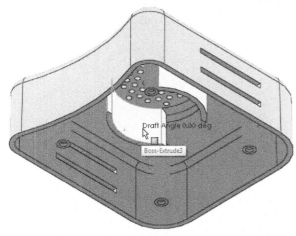

8. On the CommandManager, click **Mold Tools > Draft**.

9. Select the bottom face of the model to define the Direction of Pull.
10. Select the faces highlighted with yellow color.
11. Type 1 in the **Draft Angle** box.
12. Click **OK** on the PropertyManager.

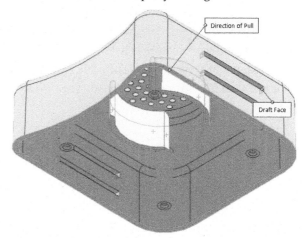

Notice that all the inner faces are red color and outer faces are green.

13. Turn OFF the **Draft Analysis** button on the CommandManager.

Applying Shrinkage allowance

Molded parts will shrink after they are removed from the mold and allowed to cool. To compensate for the shrinkage, you can scale the model to make it slightly larger.

1. To apply a scale feature, click the **Scale** button on the **Mold Tools** CommandManager.

In the **Scale about** drop-down available on the PropertyManager, you can specify the scale factor about the centroid, origin, or coordinate system of the model.

2. For this tutorial, set **Scale about** to **Centroid**.
3. Check **Uniform scaling**.

Note
You can scale the model uniformly or non-uniformly. To scale the model uniformly, check **Uniform scaling**. To scale non-uniformly, uncheck

Uniform scaling and enter scale factors in the X, Y and Z directions. The non-uniform scaling will result in a deformed shape of the model.

4. Enter 1.02 as **Scale Factor**.
5. Click **OK** to scale the model.

Notice that the scale feature is listed in the FeatureManager Design Tree. The scale feature will not affect the size of previously existing features or sketches.

Inserting Mold Folders

SOLIDWORKS adds mold folders to the FeatureManager Design Tree after creating the mold. However, it is recommended that you add the mold folders before creating the mold.

1. On the CommandManager, click **Mold Tools > Insert Mold Folders**.

Creating a Parting Line

A parting line acts as the boundary between the positively and negatively drafted faces of a part. It divides the model into a core and cavity. In addition, the two halves of the mold come into contact at the parting line.

1. To create a parting line, click the **Parting Lines** button on the **Mold Tools** CommandManager.

The parting line uses the draft analysis tool to determine the positively and negatively drafted faces. In order to create a parting line, you need to specify the direction of pull.

2. Select the Top plane from the FeatureManager Design Tree to define the direction of pull.

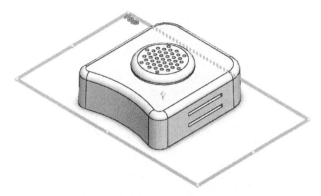

3. Set **Draft Angle** to 1 degree.
4. Make sure that the **Use for Core/Cavity Split** and **Split faces** options are checked.

The **Use for Core/Cavity Split** option is checked to use the parting line to create the core and cavity. Note that if there are multiple parting lines created, the **Use for Core/Cavity Split** option identifies parting line to be used for splitting the mold.

5. Click the **Draft Analysis** button on the **Parting Line** PropertyManager. The parting line appears on the model.

The parting line is created at the point where the positively and negatively drafted faces come together.

6. Click **OK** on the PropertyManager. The parting line is created and is displayed in the FeatureManager Design Tree.

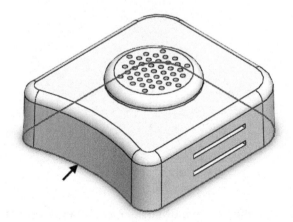

Next, you need to create the shut-off surfaces

Creating Shut-off Surfaces

Shut-off surfaces are necessary when the part being molded has openings on it. To create the opening in the model, the two halves of mold called core and cavity will have to touch each other. A shut-off surface is needed to define the face where the core and cavity will touch.

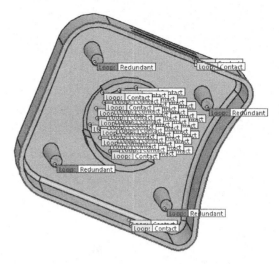

1. To create shut-off surfaces, click the **Shut-off Surfaces** button on the **Mold Tools** CommandManager. The openings on the model are detected automatically.

The inner edges of the openings are automatically selected. These are used to create a shut-off surface.

2. Select **All Tangent** from the **Reset All Patch Types** group.
3. Make sure that the **Knit** option is checked.

Note that the core and cavity surfaces are automatically created along with the shut-off surfaces. The core surface acts as the boundary between the core and the part. The cavity surface acts as the boundary between the cavity and the part.

The **Knit** option combines or knits the shut-off surfaces to the core and cavity surfaces.

4. Rotate the model and notice the redundant loops on the mounting boss holes.

5. Press the Shift key, zoom in, and click on the loops highlighted as redundant. The redundant loops are deselected.
6. Click **OK** to create the shut-off surfaces.
7. To display the results, click the right mouse button on the **Solid Bodies** folder in the FeatureManager Design Tree.

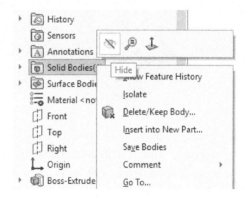

7. Click **Hide** on the Pop-up menu displayed; the core and cavity surfaces are displayed.
8. Expand the **Surface Bodies** folder in the Feature Manager and hide any one of the surfaces to see the other surface.

Core Surface

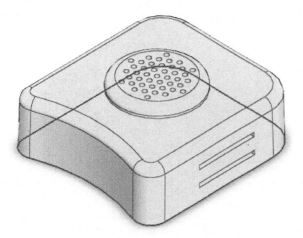

Cavity Surface

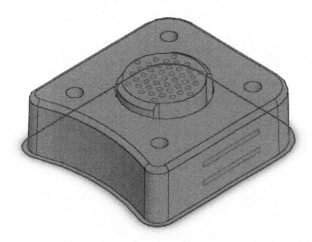

Next, you need to create parting surfaces. In order to do so, you need to hide the core and cavity surfaces and show the solid body.

Creating Parting Surfaces

The parting surfaces extend away from the part and act as contact surface between the core and the cavity blocks.

1. Click on the **Solid Bodies** folder and select **Show**.
2. To create parting surfaces, click the **Parting Surfaces** button the **Mold Tools** CommandManager.

Now, you need to define the method to create the parting surface.

3. Select the **Perpendicular to pull** option. Notice that the parting line is selected, automatically.
4. Select the **Smooth** icon from the **Parting Surface** group.
5. Type-in 40 in the **Distance** box located at the top in the **Parting Surface** section.
6. In the **Options** section, check the **Manual mode** option. Notice the dotted handles on the parting surface.

You can drag these handles to adjust the parting surface.

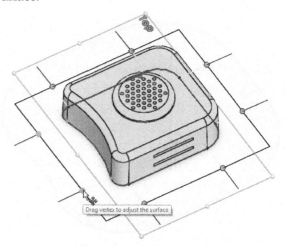

7. Click **OK** to create the parting surface.

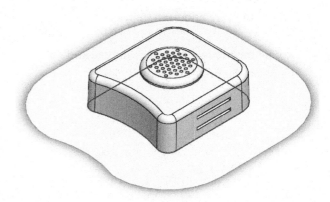

Next, you need to create the mold.

Creating the Tooling Split

First, you need to create a plane that will represent the interface between a core and cavity blocks.

1. Click the **Tooling Split** button on the **Mold Tools** CommandManager and select the parting surface.
2. Create the sketch as shown in figure. You have to make sure that the sketsch covers the part completely.

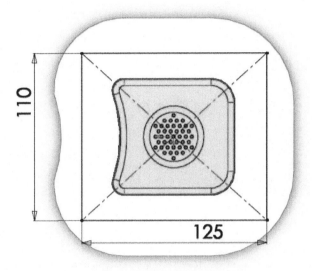

9. Exit the sketch.
10. Specify the **Depth in Direction 1** as 40 in the **Block Size** group.
11. Specify the **Depth in Direction 2** as 10 in the **Block Size** group.
12. Click **OK** to create the mold.

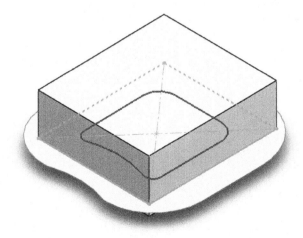

13. Hide the part body, parting surface, core surface, and cavity surface.

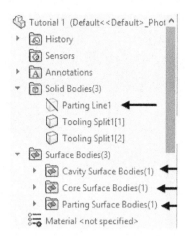

14. Click the **Section View** icon the View Heads Up toolbar.
15. Click the **Right** icon on the PropertyManager.
16. Drag the arrow and notice the gap in the mold. The gap will be filled with material to create the geometry.

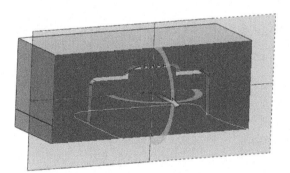

17. Click the **Top** icon on the PropertyManager and drag the arrow. Notice the gap inside the mold.

SOLIDWORKS 2019 Learn by doing

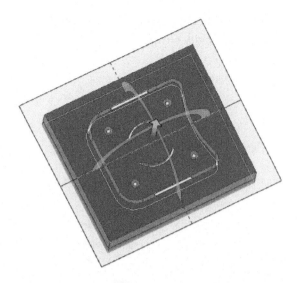

18. Click **Cancel** × on the PropertyManager.
19. In the FeatureManager Design Tree, expand the **Solid Bodies** folder, click the right mouse button on the tooling split and select **Change Transparency**.
20. Likewise, change the transparency of the other tooling split.

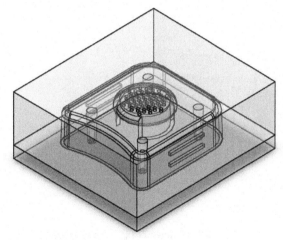

21. Click the right mouse button on any feature of the part body and select **Show**.

Performing the Undercut analysis

The undercut analysis is performed to detect the portions of the part that cannot be molded using the primary direction of pull.

1. Hide the tooling splits.

2. To perform undercut analysis, click the **Undercut Analysis** button on the **Mold Tools** CommandManager.

Note that the direction of pull is already specified and you do not need to specify it in this case.

Notice the colors displayed on the geometry. Refer to the **Undercut Faces** section on the PropertyManager to get a good understanding of these colors.

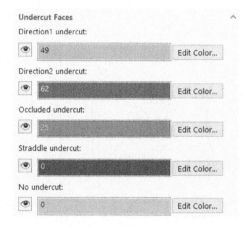

The **Direction1 undercut** faces are one which are not visible from the first pull direction. A single arrow in the graphics window indicates the first pull direction.

The **Direction2 undercut** faces are one, which are not visible from the second pull direction. A double arrow in the graphics window indicates the second pull direction.

Notice the red faces of the model. These are defined as occluded undercuts, which are not visible from either pull directions.

3. Click **OK** on the PropertyManager.

SOLIDWORKS 2019 Learn by doing

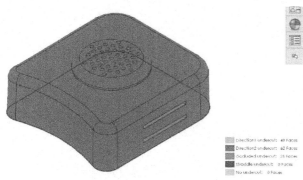

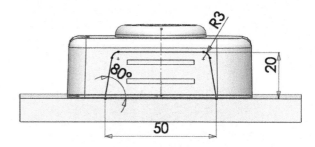

Next, you need to create side cores.

Creating side cores

1. Turn OFF the **Undercut Analysis** button on the CommandManager.
2. To create a side core, click the **Core** button on the **Mold Tools** CommandManager.
3. Select the inner face of the model, which is having openings.

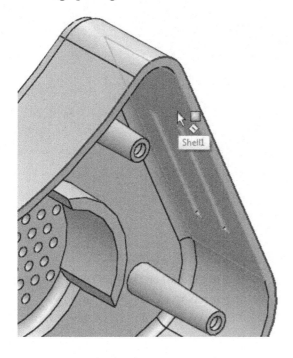

4. Show the lower tooling split.
5. Create the sketch as shown in figure.

6. Exit the sketch.
7. Click in the **Core/Cavity body** field.

8. Select the upper tooling split from the **Solid Bodies** folder in the **FeatureManager Design** tree.

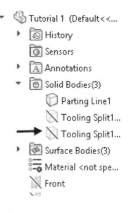

9. Type-in 4 in the **Draft Angle** box.
10. Check the **Draft outward** option.
11. Select **Through All** from the second drop-down in the **Parameters** group.
12. Uncheck the **Cap ends** option.
13. Click **OK** to create the side core.
14. Hide the other bodies and display the side core body.

242

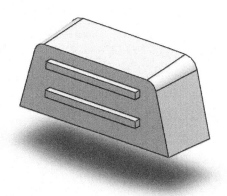

14. Likewise, create another side core for the other openings.

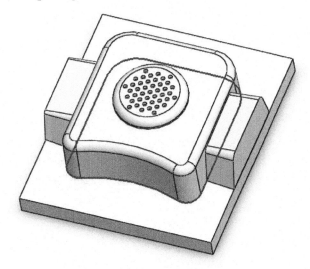

15. Show all the solid bodies.
16. On the CommandManager, click **Direct Editing > Move Copy Bodies** .
17. Select the upper tooling split and click the **Translate/Rotate** button on the PropertyManager.
18. Uncheck the **Copy** option.
19. Click and drag the Y-axis of the manipulator.

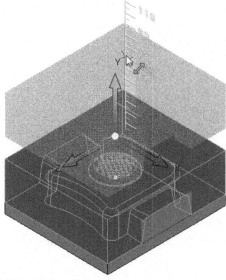

20. Click **OK**.
21. Likewise, move the bodies as shown.

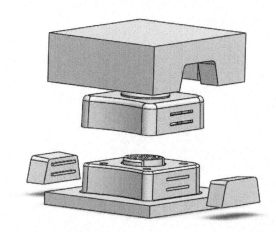

22. Save the part file.

Creating your own surfaces

1. In the **FeatureManager Design Tree**, click and drag the bar located at the bottom.
2. Release it above the tooling split. The tooling split and cores are suppressed.

3. Hide the part body and show all the surface bodies.
4. Draw a circle on the top face of the cavity surface, as shown.

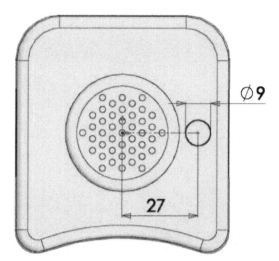

5. Create an extruded surface with the capped end and draft angle.

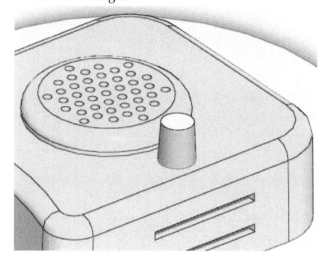

6. Hide the Core surface.
7. Trim the Cavity surface, as shown.

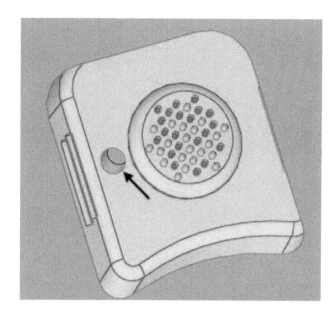

8. In the FeatureManager Design Tree, drag the bar and release it below the cores.
9. In the FeatureManager Design Tree, click on the Tooling Split and select the **Edit Feature**.

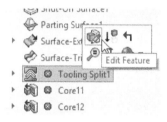

10. On the PropertyManager, click in the Cavity selection box and select the extruded surface.

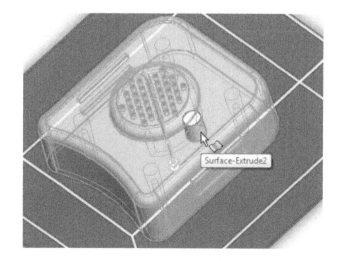

11. Click **OK**.

12. Show the cavity solid body and notice the difference.

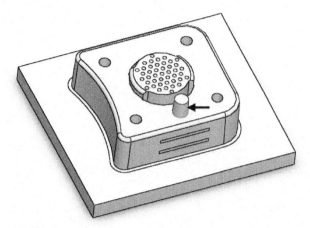

13. Save and close the file.

Chapter 12: Weldments

SOLIDWORKS provides a set of tools for creating welded frames and structures. In addition to creating welded frames and structures, you can use these tools for different applications. In this chapter, you will learn all of the tools used to create weldments. You will also learn to create custom weldment profiles and add them to your Library.

The weldment tools are located in the **Weldments** Command Manager. You need to customize the CommandManager to display this CommandManager. Click the right mouse button on anyone of the tabs on the CommandManager, and select **Weldments** from the shortcut menu.

TUTORIAL 1

In this tutorial, you create a simple weldment, as shown in figure below.

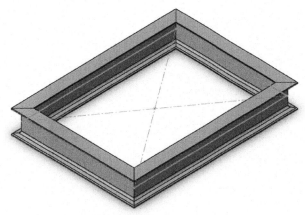

1. Start a new part file.
2. Click the **Options** button on the Quick access toolbar.
3. Click the **Document Properties** tab on the **Options** dialog.
4. Click the **Units** node.
5. Select the **MMGS (millimeter, gram, second)** option.
6. Click the **OK** button to close the dialog.

7. Create a layout sketch on the top plane, as shown.

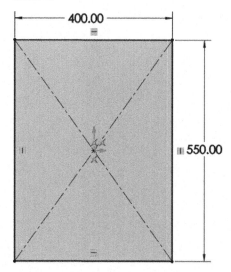

8. Exit the sketch.
9. Click the **Weldments** tab on the Command Manager.
10. Click the **Structural Member** button the **Weldments** tab.

In this **Structural Member** PropertyManager, you need to define the parameters of the structural member.

11. Select **iso** from the **Standard** drop-down.
12. Select **sb beam** from the **Type** drop-down.
13. Select **80X6** from the **Size** drop-down. Next, you need to define the position of the structural members.
14. Select the left vertical line and bottom horizontal line of the layout sketch. A structural member is created on the selected sketch segment.

You will notice that **Group1** is listed in the **Groups** selection box. In addition, the selected segments are listed in the **Path segments** selection box of the **Settings** section.

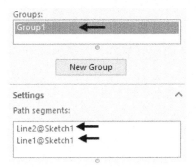

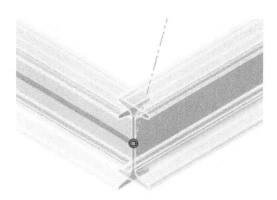

If you click the **New Group** button, a new group will be created. If you select the line segments from the layout sketch, they will be listed under the second group. Note that the size and parameter settings will be applied to all the groups. If you change the size of the structural member, it will be applied to members of all the groups.

You can change the type of corner treatment by using the icons available below the **Apply corner treatment** option.

15. Select the other two segments of the layout sketch.

By using these icons, the corner treatment can be applied to all the structural members. If you select the **End miter** button, the **Merge miter trimmed bodies** option will be available. This option is used to merge the trimmed bodies into a single body.

If you select the **End butt1** or **End butt2** button, the **Simple cut** and **Coped cut** buttons will be available. The **Simple cut** button is used to create a simple cut between the structural members. The **Coped cut** button creates a cut, which takes the shape of the cutting surface.

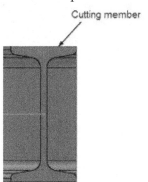

You can control the end condition of the structural members by using the **Apply corner treatment** option in the **Settings** section. By default, this option is checked. As result, the corner treatment is applied between the structural members. If you uncheck this option, the corner treatment will not be applied.

Simple Cut

Coped Cut

The **Gap distance** box is used to specify gaps at the corners of the structural members.

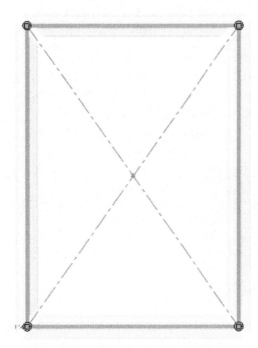

If you want to apply the corner treatment individually, click on the corner point that you want to change.

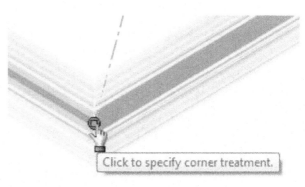

The **Corner Treatment** window appears.

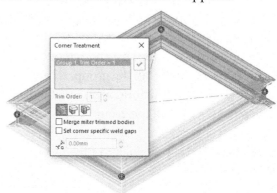

You can select the required options from the **Corner Treatment** window and click the green check on the window; the corner treatment will be applied to the selected corner.

The **Alignment** option in the **Settings** section is used to specify the alignment of the structural member about the line segment. Click in the **Alignment** selection box and select the horizontal line; the **Align horizontal axis** and **Align vertical axis** options get active.

The **Align horizontal axis** option aligns the horizontal axis of the beam cross-section with the line segment.

The **Align vertical axis** option aligns the vertical axis of the beam cross-section with the line segment.

The **Rotation Angle** box allows you to align the structural member at an angle to the line segment.

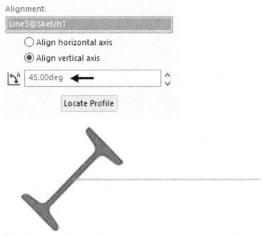

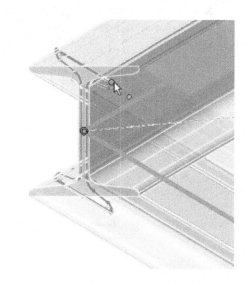

The **Locate Profile** button allows you to locate the profile of the beam cross-section in the graphics window.

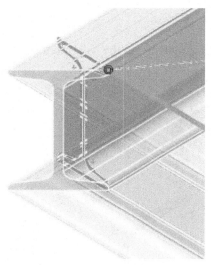

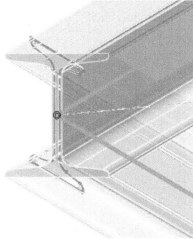

You can change the position of the profile by clicking any another point on the profile.

You can also use the **Mirror Profile** option and mirror the profile about the **Horizontal axis** or **Vertical axis**.

16. After specifying all the settings, click **OK** on the **PropertyManager**.

Notice the two features: **Cut list** and **Weldment** are listed in the **FeatureManager Design Tree**.

250

SOLIDWORKS 2019 Learn by doing

17. Save and close the document.

TUTORIAL 2

In this tutorial, you will create the weldment model as shown.

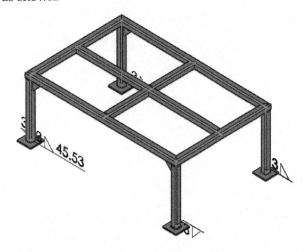

1. Start a new part document.
2. Create the layout sketch as shown.

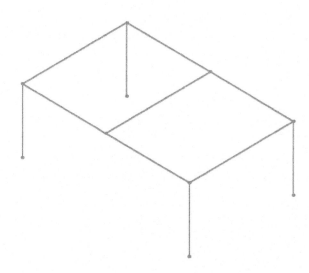

This layout sketch can be created as a 3D sketch or a combination of 2D and 3D sketches.

You can follow the steps given next to create the layout sketch.

3. On the CommandManager, click **Weldments > 3D Sketch**.
4. On the CommandManager, click **Sketch > Line**.
5. Select the origin point, move the pointer up along the dotted lines, and click.

6. On the CommandManager, click **Sketch > Rectangle drop-down > Corner Rectangle**.
7. Select the end point of the line to define the first corner of the rectangle.
8. Press the Tab key until the rectangle is oriented, as shown.

SOLIDWORKS 2019 Learn by doing

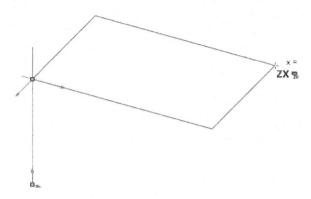

9. Move the pointer and click to create the rectangle.
10. On the CommandManager, click **Sketch > Line**.
11. Select the corner point of the rectangle, as shown.
12. Press the Tab key to switch to the XY plane.
13. Move the pointer the downward and click.
14. Press Esc to deactivate the tool.

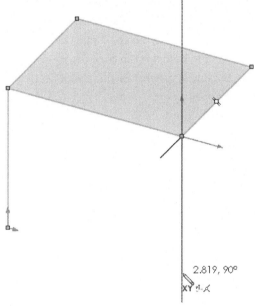

15. Likewise, create other lines as shown.

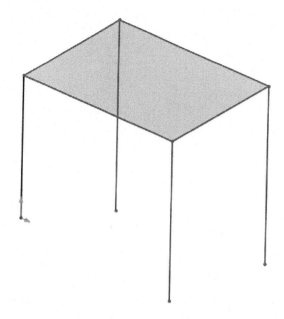

16. Activate the **Line** tool and select the midpoint of the horizontal line, as shown.

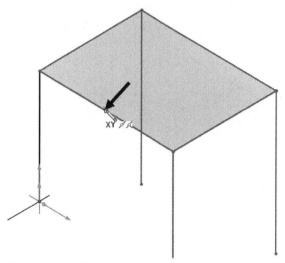

17. Press the Tab key to switch to the YZ plane.
18. Select the midpoint of the other horizontal line and press Esc.

SOLIDWORKS 2019 Learn by doing

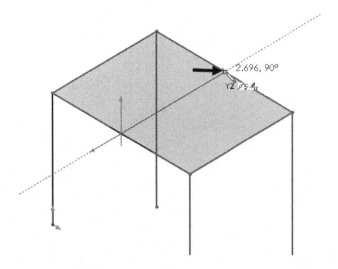

19. Press the Ctrl key and select all the vertical lines.
20. Click the **Equal** = icon on the PropertyManager.
21. Click **OK** on the PropertyManager.
22. Add 300 mm dimension to anyone of the vertical lines.
23. Press the Ctrl key and click on the corner points of the rectangle, as shown.

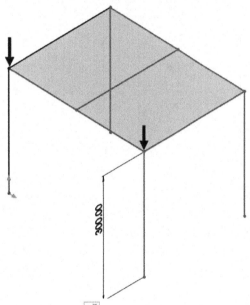

24. Click **Along X** icon on the PropertyManager.
25. Click **OK** on the PropertyManager.
26. Add dimensions to the length and width of the rectangle. The sketch is fully defined and turned into black.
27. Exit the sketch.

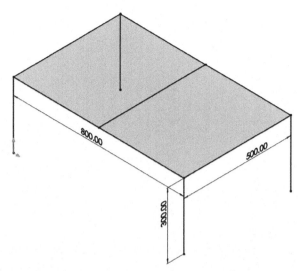

After creating the layout sketch, you need to create the structural members.

Adding Structural members

1. Click the **Structural Member** button on the **Weldment** CommandManager.
2. Select **iso** from the **Standard** drop-down.
3. Select **square tube** from the **Type** drop-down.
4. Select **30X30X2.6** from the **Size** drop-down.
5. Select the line segments of the sketch in the sequence given next.

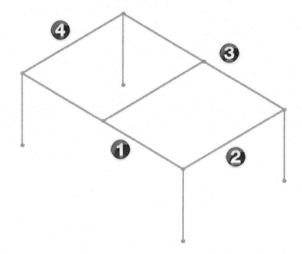

Note that you can select either the continuous or parallel line segments. If you try to select the non-continuous or parallel segment, you will be not allowed to do so.

253

SOLIDWORKS 2019 Learn by doing

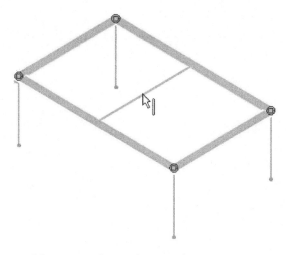

To add structural members to the non-continuous segments, you need to create a new group.

6. Click the **New Group** button below the **Groups** selection box and select the line segments.

Group 2

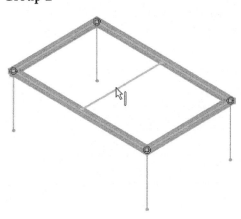

Group 3

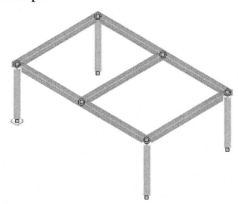

Note that the order in which the structural members are created defines the members that will be trimmed. The structural members that are crossing already created members will be trimmed.

7. Click the **OK** button on the **PropertyManager** to accept the selection.
8. In the FeatureManager Design Tree, click on the **3DSketch** and select **Edit Sketch**.
9. Draw a line connecting the midpoints of the horizontal lines, as shown.

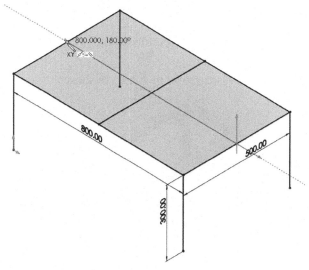

10. Exit the sketch.
11. Activate the **Structural Member** tool.
12. Select **iso** from the **Standard** drop-down.
13. Select **square tube** from the **Type** drop-down.
14. Select **30X30X2.6** from the **Size** drop-down.
15. Select the line segment and create a structural member, as shown.

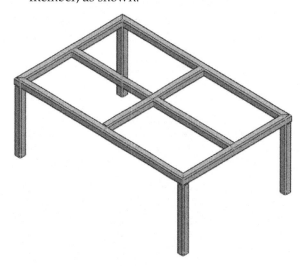

Trimming the Structural Members

The structural members will be trimmed automatically if you have created them as a single instance. However, if you have created the structural members by activating the **Structural Member** tool several times, they will not be trimmed automatically. You need to trim those members by using the **Trim/Extend** tool.

1. To trim the structural members, click the **Trim/Extend** button on the **Weldments** CommandManager.
2. Select the structural member, as shown.

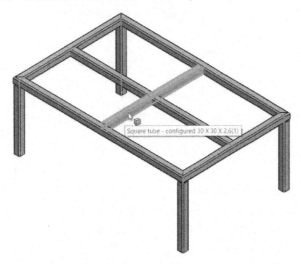

3. Select the **Bodies** option from the **Trimming Boundary** section.
4. Click in the **Trimming Boundary** selection box and select the horizontal member, as shown.

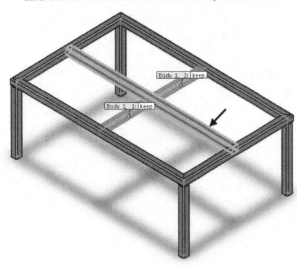

5. Click the **Simple cut between bodies** button.
6. Click **OK**. The structural member will be trimmed.

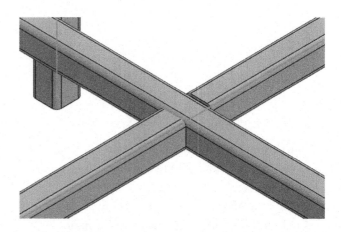

7. Again, activate the **Trim/Extend** tool.
8. Select the body to be trimmed, as shown.
9. Click in the selection box in the **Trimming Boundary** section.
10. Select the structural member intersecting the first body.

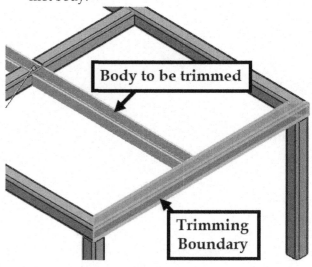

11. Click the **End Miter** icon on the PropertyManager. The two structural members will be trimmed to form a mitered corner.

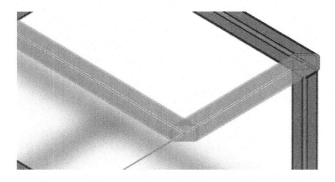

12. Click the **End Butt1** icon.

13. Click the **End Butt2** icon.

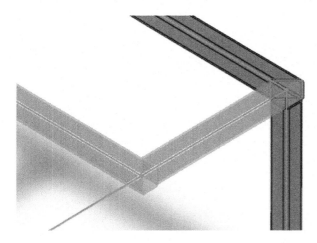

14. Click the **End Trim** icon on the PropertyManager and select the **Face/plane** option.
15. Select the side faces of the intersecting structural members.

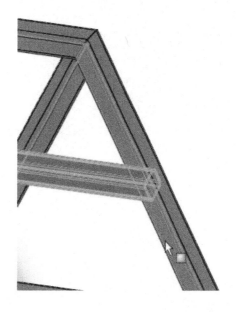

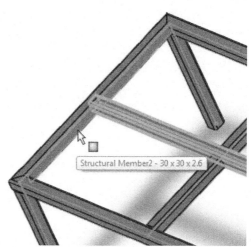

16. Click **OK** to trim the structural member.

Creating Gussets

Gussets are plates used to reinforce corners. Gussets can be created between any two faces that intersect at an angle between 0 and 180 degrees.

1. To create a gusset, click the **Gusset** button on the **Weldments** CommandManager.
2. Select the two faces to join with a gusset, as shown.

SOLIDWORKS 2019 Learn by doing

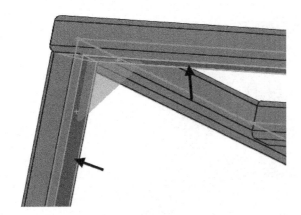

The gusset can be created in a triangular or polygonal shape.

3. Select the **Triangular Profile** icon from the **Profile** section.

The size of the gusset can be controlled by the options available in the **Profile** section. Each option corresponds to the dimension shown on the profile button.

4. Enter the values as shown.

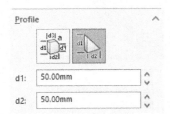

The **Chamfer** button in the **Profile** section allows you to add a chamfer to the inside edge of the gusset.

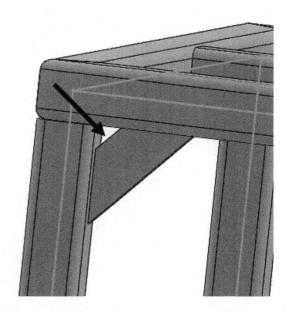

The thickness of the gusset can be specified using the thickness buttons and the **Gusset Thickness** edit box.

5. Click the **Both Sides** icon and enter 6 in the **Gusset Thickness** box.

The location of the gussets can be defined by using the options in the **Location** section.

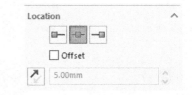

If you want to define the gusset at an offset from the location, check the **Offset** option and enter the offset value in the **Offset Value** box.

6. Click the **Mid Point** button in the **Location** section.
7. Click **OK** to create the gusset.

257

SOLIDWORKS 2019 Learn by doing

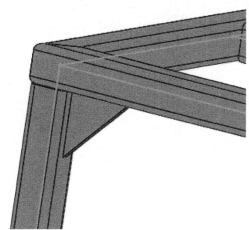

You can also use the **Extruded Boss/Base** tool to create gussets with custom shapes and sizes.

Creating Base Plates

1. On the CommandManager, click **Weldments > Extruded Boss/Base**.
2. Zoom and rotate the model to display the bottom face of the front left column.
3. Select the bottom face of the column.

4. On the **Sketch** tab, click **Rectangle drop-down > Center Rectangle**.
5. Select the origin point and create a centered rectangle.

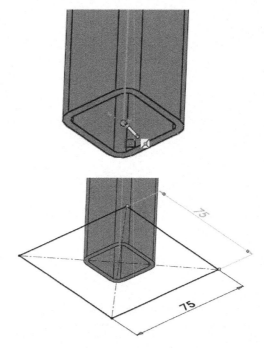

6. Exit the sketch.
7. Leave the **Merge result** option unchecked.
8. Type-in 5 in the **Depth** box and extrude the sketch downwards.

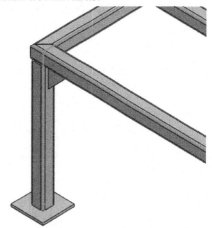

Mirroring Gussets and Base plates

1. On the CommandManager, click **Weldments > Reference Geometry > Plane**.
2. Select the Top plane from the FeatureManager Design Tree.
3. Select the two points from the layout sketch, as shown.

SOLIDWORKS 2019 Learn by doing

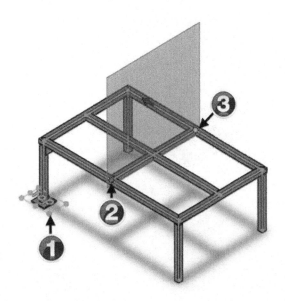

4. Click **OK** on the PropertyManager.
5. On the CommandManager, click **Features > Mirror**.
6. Select the new plane to define the mirror plane.
7. On the PropertyManager, expand the **Bodies to Mirror** section.
8. Select the gusset and base plate, and then click **OK**.

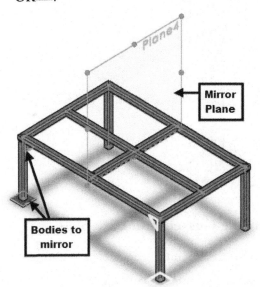

9. Hide the plane.

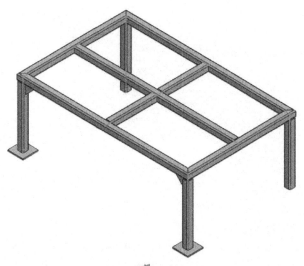

10. Activate the **Plane** tool, and select the Front plane and the point, as shown.

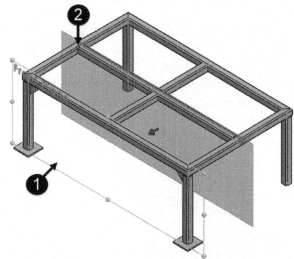

11. Mirror all the base plates and gusset bodies about the new plane.

259

SOLIDWORKS 2019 Learn by doing

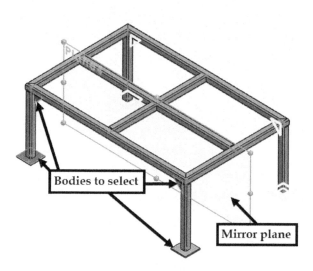

Creating Fillet Beads

You can create fillet beads to add weld information to the model. The **Fillet Bead** is the older SOLIDWORKS tool. The **Weld Bead** tool can be used instead of this tool for performance and new enhancements. However, this tool is explained to know its basic functionality.

1. To create a fillet bead, click **Insert > Weldments > Fillet Bead** from the Menu bar.

You can create three types of fillet beads: **Full Length**, **Intermittent** and **Staggered**.

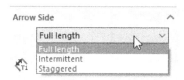

2. Select **Full Length** from the drop-down available in the **Arrow Side** section.
3. Enter **3** in the **Fillet size** box.

Next, you need to select intersecting faces to create a fillet weld between then.

4. Zoom to the base plate of the front right column.
5. Select the top face of the base plate.
6. Click in the **Face set 2** selection box and select a face of the column, as shown.

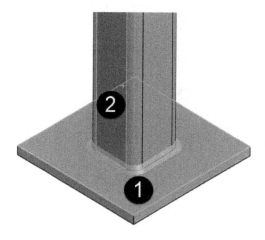

7. Make sure that the **Tangent Propagation** option is checked. You will notice that the bead is created around the structural member.
8. Leave the **Add weld symbol** option checked.
9. Click **OK** to create the fillet bead.

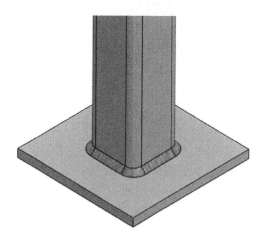

Creating Weld Beads

You can add weld beads to parts, assemblies or multi-body parts.

1. To add a weld bead, click the **Weld Bead** button on the **Weldments** CommandManager.
2. Zoom to the base plate of the front left column.
3. Select the top face of the base plate.
4. Select the faces of the column, as shown.

SOLIDWORKS 2019 Learn by doing

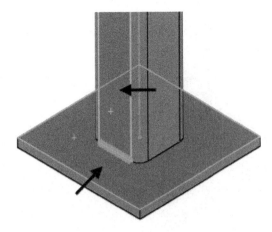

5. Check the **Tangent Propagation** option and notice that all the tangent edges are selected. The **All around** option also gives the same result.

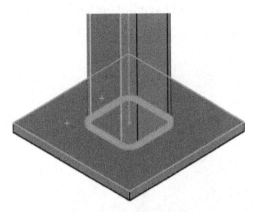

6. Uncheck the **Tangent Propagation** option and select the **Both sides** option. The opposite edge also is selected.

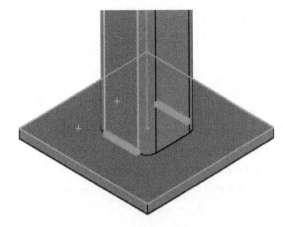

The **Both sides** option will be more useful while adding a weld to the gussets or plates.

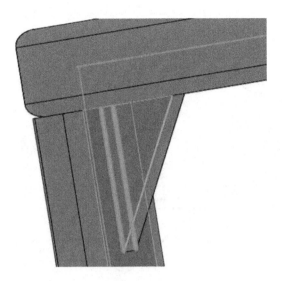

7. Select the **Selection** option and select faces, as shown.

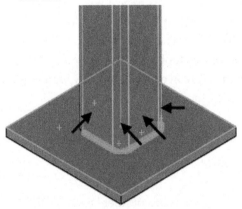

8. Check the **Form/To Length** option on the PropertyManager. Notice two arrows at the start and ends of the weld path.

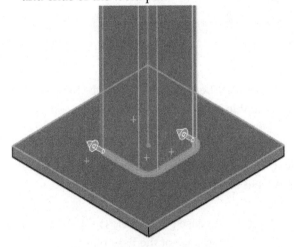

9. Type-in 10 in the **Start point** box and notice that the start point is offset by 10 mm. In addition,

the weld length is updated, automatically.

10. Click the **Reverse Direction** icon next to the **Start point** box. The start and ends of the weld are reversed.

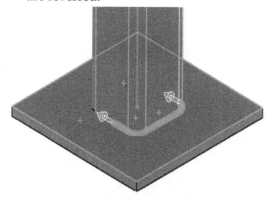

You can also check the **Intermittent Weld** option to create gaps along the weld.

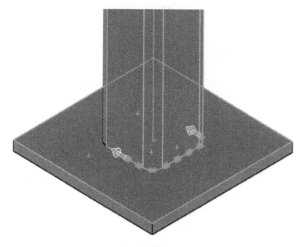

You can create an intermittent weld by specifying the **Gap and weld length** or **Pitch and weld length**.

11. Enter 3 in the **Bead Size** box
12. Click the **Define Weld Symbol** button in the **Settings** section.

13. Click the **Weld Symbol** button on the top of the leader.
14. Select the **Fillet** symbol from the flyout.

You can also click **More Symbols** on the flyout to open the **Symbol library** dialog. You can select symbols from a wide range of categories. Click **OK** after selecting the desired symbol.

15. Click **OK** on the dialog. Notice the weld symbol.

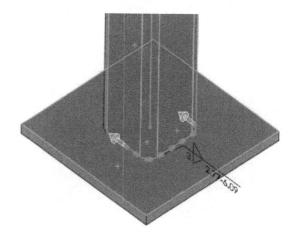

You can create multiple weld paths in a single instance.

16. Click the **New Weld Path** button in the **Weld Path** section.

Now, you need to define the weld path. You can define the weld path by selecting faces from the model or using the **Smart Weld Selection Tool**.

17. Click **Smart Weld Selection Tool** in the **Weld Path** section.
18. Click and drag the pointer crossing the edges, as shown. The edges are selected as soon as you release the pointer.

SOLIDWORKS 2019 Learn by doing

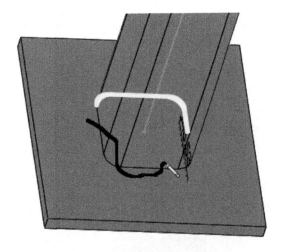

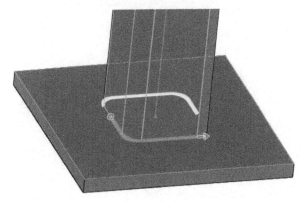

Notice that the offset is applied to the new weld path as well. You can uncheck the **From/To Length** option to remove the offset for the selected weld path.

19. Click **OK** on the Property Manager. The weld is added to the model.

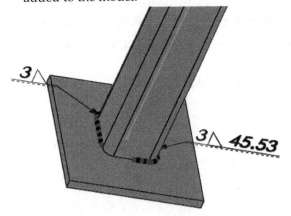

20. Activate the **Weld Bead** tool.
21. Zoom to the base plate of the back right column.

22. On the PropertyManager, select the **Weld Path** option.
23. Click the right mouse button on the horizontal edge of the column and select **Select Tangency**. All the tangentially connected edges are selected.

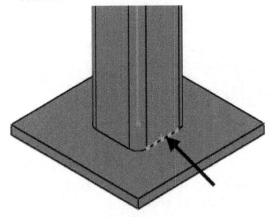

24. Leave the settings on the PropertyManager and click **OK**.

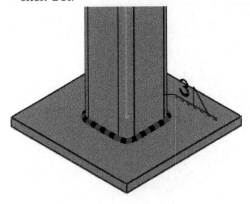

25. Likewise, add the weld bead to the other column.

Notice that there is a **Weld Folder** in the FeatureManager Design Tree. It is added to the FeatureManager Design Tree as you create weld beads.

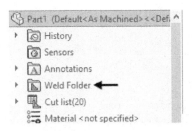

SOLIDWORKS 2019 Learn by doing

On expanding this folder, you can see the welds that are created.

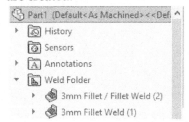

You can edit the properties of the weld by right clicking on it and selecting **Properties**.

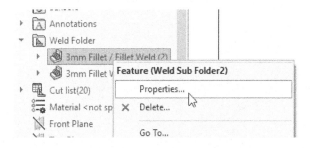

The **Weld Bead Properties** dialog appears.

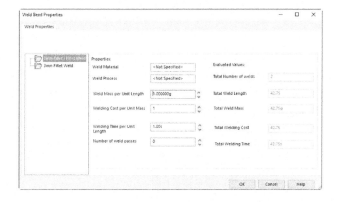

You can change the properties of the weld bead in this dialog. Note that weld beads are for representation same as cosmetic thread. They do not have any mass properties. When you have calculated the total mass of the model, the mass of the weld bead is excluded from model. You can add the **Total Weld Mass** value to the total mass of the model.

To edit a weld bead, right click on it and select **Edit Feature**.

TUTORIAL 3 (Creating End Caps)

End caps are used to close the open ends of the structural members. Note that you can only apply end caps to structural members having linear edges. You cannot apply them to round tubes.

1. Start a new part document and create the model, as shown.

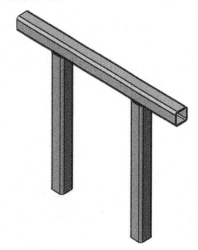

2. To create an end cap, click the **End Cap** button on the **Weldments** Command Manager.
3. Select the end face of the structural member, as shown.

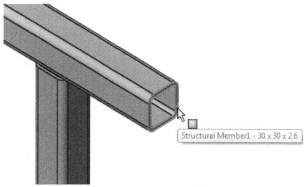

4. Click the **Outward** icon under the **Thickness**

264

direction section. The preview of the end cap appears on the outer face.

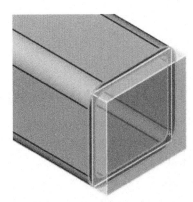

5. Click the **Inward** icon under the **Thickness direction** section. The preview of the end cap appears inside the structural member. However, it will be created on the end face of the member. The inward end cap means that it will be created inside the original length of the structural member.

 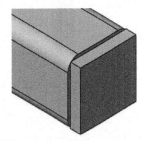

6. Click the **Internal** icon under the **Thickness direction** section. The preview of the end cap appears inside the structural member. You can further inset the end cap by entering a value in the **Inset Distance** box.

 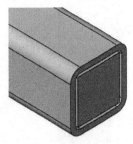

7. Click the **Outward** icon and specify the **Thickness** as **3**.

The size of the end cap can be defined using the options in the **Offset** section.

8. Select **Offset value** and enter 5 in the **Offset value** box. The size of the end cap is reduced by 5 mm. You can click the **Reverse Direction** icon to increase the end cap size.

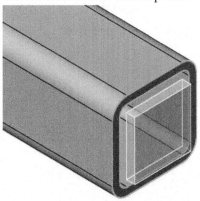

9. Select **Thickness Ratio** and enter 1 in the **Thickness Ratio** box.
10. Deselect the Reverse Direction icon. The size of the end cap is reduced by the weldment thickness value.

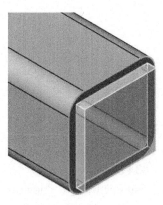

11. Change the **Thickness Ratio** to 0.5. The size of the weldment is reduced by the half of the weldment thickness value.

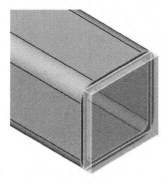

12. Check the **Corner Treatment** option to apply chamfer or fillet the end cap corners.
13. Select **Chamfer** and type-in 3 in the **Chamfer Distance** box.

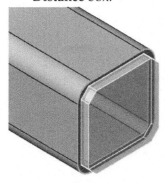

14. Select **Fillet** and type-in 3 in the **Fillet Radius** box.

15. Click **OK** to create the end cap.

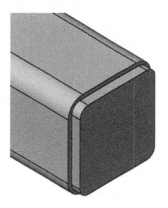

TUTORIAL 4 (Working with Cut lists)

1. Open the Tutorial 2 file.

Cut lists are used to document weldment designs. They contain the information about the type of structural members, the lengths of the individual members and any other information necessary to manufacture a weldment. SOLIDWORKS automatically creates a cut list as you design a weldment. As soon as a weldment is added, the **Cut list** folder is added to the FeatureManager Design Tree.

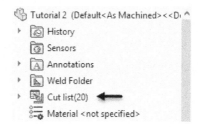

You will notice that the **Solid Bodies** folder is missing. When a structural member is added to the part, it creates a weldment and the **Solid Bodies** folder is replaced with the **Cut list** folder. As you continue to add weldment features, these features are listed individually within the **Cut list** folder.

SOLIDWORKS 2019 Learn by doing

The Cut list is generated and updated automatically as the **Update automatically** option is selected. You can click the right mouse button on the Cut list and deselect this option.

You can see that several subfolders are created within the **Cut list** folder. All the like items such as plates, end caps, and gussets are grouped into individual subfolders. Structural Members and weldment components are represented by the weld symbol. Other items are listed in normal folders. You can also reorder these folders by clicking and dragging them.

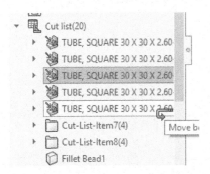

You can also exclude items from the **Cut list** by right-clicking on them and selecting **Exclude from cut list**.

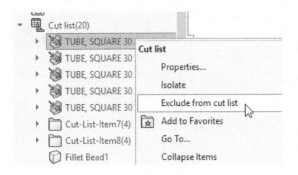

You can also include the excluded items by right-clicking and selecting **Include in cut list**. It is recommended that you make changes to the **Cut list** only after completing the weldment design. If you add any additional members to the model, you will lose all of the changes made to the Cut list order.

Adding Cut list to the Weldment Drawing

1. Create a drawing by selecting **New > Make Drawing from Part/Assembly**.

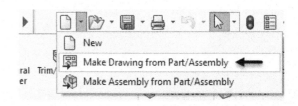

2. Select **A2 (ISO)** from the **Sheet Format/Size** section and click **OK**.
3. On the **View Layout** CommandManager, click the **Model View** tool.
4. Double-click on the Tutorial 2.
5. Place the Isometric view on the drawing sheet.

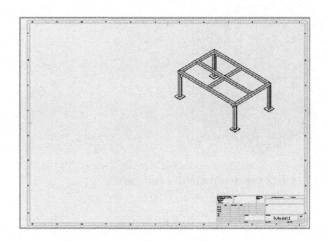

6. Click **Annotation > Tables > Weldment Cut List** on the CommandManager.

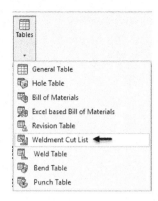

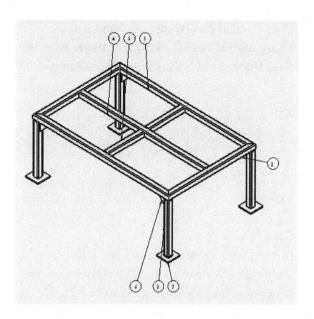

7. Select the view from the drawing sheet. The **Weldment Cut List** PropertyManager appears. The options in this PropertyManager are similar to the **Bill of Materials** one.
8. Click **OK** on the Property Manager and place the cut list table on the drawing sheet.

ITEM NO.	QTY.	DESCRIPTION	LENGTH
1	2	TUBE, SQUARE 30 X 30 X 2.60	830
2	2	TUBE, SQUARE 30 X 30 X 2.60	530
3	4	TUBE, SQUARE 30 X 30 X 2.60	265
4	1	TUBE, SQUARE 30 X 30 X 2.60	770
5	2	TUBE, SQUARE 30 X 30 X 2.60	220
6	4		
7	4		

The **Description** and **Length** may or may not be populated in the cut list. It depends on the type of weldment. The **Description** and **Length** of the structural members are automatically populated. Notice that the **Description** and **Length** of the members such as gussets, base plates, and end caps are not populated automatically. To know about the members that are not populated, you need to add balloons to the model view.

9. On the CommandManager, click **Annotation > Auto Balloon**.
10. Select the view and click **OK**. Notice that the gussets and base plate are annotated with the 6 and 7 number balloons.

You need to populate these properties manually. To do so, you need to switch to the part document and add properties to these members.

11. Open the part document of the weldment.
12. Expand the **Cut list** folder in the **FeatureManager Design Tree**.
13. Right-click on the **Cut-list-Item7** subfolder under the Cut list folder and select **Properties**; the **Cut List Properties** dialog appears.

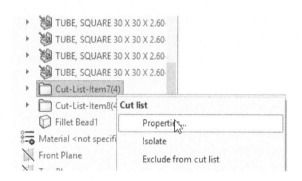

14. In the **Cut List Properties** dialog, enter **DESCRIPTION** in the **Property Value** field and **Gusset** in the **Value/Text Expression** field.

	Property Name	Type	Value / Text Expression
1	MATERIAL	Text	"SW-Material@@@Cut-List-Item7@Tutorial 2.SL
2	QUANTITY	Text	"QUANTITY@@@Cut-List-Item7@Tutorial 2.SLDP
3	Description	Text	Gusset
4	<Type a new proper		

SOLIDWORKS 2019 Learn by doing

15. Click the **Cut-list-Item8** folder and enter **DESCRIPTION** in the **Property Value** field and **Base Plate** in the **Value/Text Expression** field.

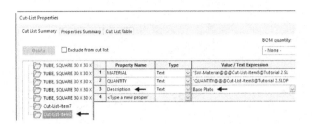

16. Click **OK**.
17. Switch to the Drawing document of the weldment. Notice that the **Description** column is populated in the Cut list table.

ITEM NO.	QTY.	DESCRIPTION	LENGTH
1	2	TUBE, SQUARE 30 X 30 X 2.60	830
2	2	TUBE, SQUARE 30 X 30 X 2.60	530
3	4	TUBE, SQUARE 30 X 30 X 2.60	285
4	1	TUBE, SQUARE 30 X 30 X 2.60	770
5	2	TUBE, SQUARE 30 X 30 X 2.60	220
6	4	Gusset	
7	4	Base Plate	

Adding Columns to the Cut list table

You can add more columns to the cut list table and save it as a template for the later use.

1. Place the pointer on the table and notice that row and column headers.
2. Click the right mouse button on the right most column and click **Insert > Column Right**.
3. On the PropertyManager, enter **Weight** in the **Title** box and click **OK**.
4. Open the part document of the weldment.
5. In the FeatureManager Design Tree, click the right mouse button on the **Gusset** folder and select **Properties**.
6. On the **Cut List Properties** dialog. enter **Weight** in the **Property Value** field and **48** in the **Value/Text Expression** field.

7. Click **OK**.
8. Switch to the drawing and notice that the value is not updated in the cut list table.
9. Click in the **Weight** column header.

D	
LENGTH	Weight
830	
530	
285	
770	
220	

10. On the PropertyManager, select **Cut list item property**.
11. Select **Weight** from the drop-down menu.
12. Click the green check to update the table.

ITEM NO.	QTY.	DESCRIPTION	LENGTH	Weight
1	2	TUBE, SQUARE 1.18 X 1.18 X 0.10	32.68	
2	2	TUBE, SQUARE 1.18 X 1.18 X 0.10	20.87	
3	4	TUBE, SQUARE 1.18 X 1.18 X 0.10	11.22	
4	1	TUBE, SQUARE 1.18 X 1.18 X 0.10	30.31	
5	2	TUBE, SQUARE 1.18 X 1.18 X 0.10	8.66	
6	4	Gusset		48
7	4	Base Plate		

13. To save the cut list table as a template, right-click on the table and select **Save As**.
14. Type **Custom_cutlist** and click **Save**.

Creating Bounding box

Bounding box is the smallest box around a weldment. It gives you an idea about the weldment dimensions. You can use the bounding box to add some properties to the Cut list, automatically.

1. Open the part document of the weldment model.
2. In the FeatureManager Design Tree, expand the **Cut list** folder.
3. Click the right mouse button on the **Gusset** folder and select **Create Bounding Box**.
4. Expand the **Gusset** folder and notice a 3D sketch inside it.

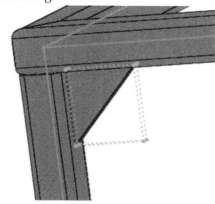

5. Click on the 3D sketch and notice a dotted box around the gusset.

6. Click the right mouse button on the **Gusset** folder and select **Properties**. Notice the thickness, width, length, and volume properties on the **Cut list Properties** dialog.
7. Click **OK** to close the dialog.

You can edit or delete the bounding box by simply clicking the right mouse button on the folder and selecting **Edit Bounding Box** or **Delete Bounding Box**.

Adding a Weld table to the Weldment Drawing

You can show the weld beads or fillet beads of a weldment in a drawing document. You can show them in the form of a Weld table in the drawing.

1. To add a weld table, click **Insert > Tables > Weld Table** on the Menu bar.

2. Select the Isometric view from the drawing.
3. Click **OK** on the Property Manager.
4. Place the weld table on the drawing sheet.

ITEM NO.	WELD SIZE	SYMBOL	WELD LENGTH	WELD MATERIAL	QTY.
1		△	23.36		1
2	3	△	2.77-5.54{23.36}		1
3		△	19.39		1
4	3	△	2.77-5.54{19.39}		1
5	3	△	111.07		2

You can also add weld symbols and other annotations to the model view on the drawing.

Adding a Weld Symbols

1. To add weld symbols or other annotations, click **Annotation > Model Items** on the Command Manager.
2. On the **Model Items** Property Manager, set the **Source** to **Entire model**.
3. Deselect the **Marked for drawing** icon.
4. Select the icons from the **Annotations** section, as shown.

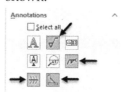

5. Click **OK**. The annotations are displayed on the model view.

SOLIDWORKS 2019 Learn by doing

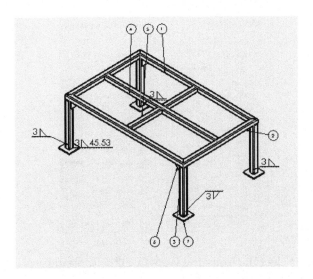

6. Save the Part document and the drawing document.

Creating Sub Weldments

You can break down a weldment into sub weldments to make it easy to manage them.

1. Open a Part document created in Tutorial 2.
2. Right-click on the Command Manager and select **Selection Filter**. The **Selection Filter** toolbar appears at the bottom.

3. Click the **Filter Solid bodies** button on the **Selection Filter** toolbar.

4. Press the Ctrl key and select the structural members as shown.

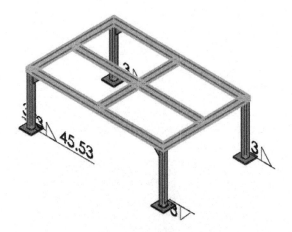

5. Right-click and select **Create Sub-Weldment**.
6. Expand the **Cut list** folder in the FeatureManager Design Tree.

You will notice a new folder under the cut list folder.

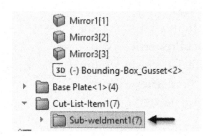

7. Open the drawing document of the weldments model. Place the cut list table on the drawing sheet.

ITEM NO.	QTY.	DESCRIPTION	LENGTH	Weight
1	1			
1	4	TUBE, SQUARE 1.18 X 1.18 X 0.10	11.22	
3	4			48
4	4	Base Plate		

You will notice that the **Description** and **Length** values are empty in the cut list. This is because sub weldments are not recognized as weldment parts. You need to save the sub weldments as a separate weldment part.

8. Switch to the part document.
9. Press the Ctrl key and select the structural members as shown.

SOLIDWORKS 2019 Learn by doing

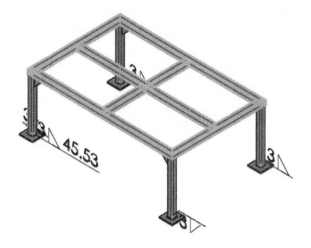

10. In in the FeatureManager, click the right mouse button and select **Insert into New Part**.
11. On the PropertyManager, check the **Cut list properties to** option and select **Cut list properties**. This option allows you to insert the cut list table into the drawing.
12. Click **OK** on the PropertyManager.
13. Save the file as Tutorial 2-Sub-weldment1.

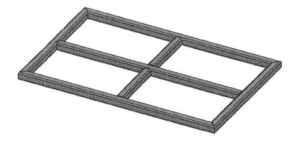

18. Create a drawing by selecting **New > Make Drawing from Part/Assembly**.

14. Insert the isometric view and cut list table into the drawing.

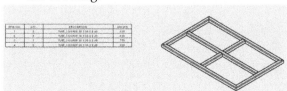

15. Save it as a separate part file.

TUTORIAL 5 (Creating Custom Profiles for structural members)

If you want to create a structural member using a profile that is not available in SOLIDWORKS, you can create a custom profile.

1. Close the SOLIDWORKS application, if opened.
2. Run SOLIDWORKS as administrator.
3. Open a new Part document.
4. Create a sketch on anyone of the planes, as shown in figure.

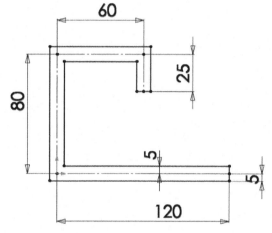

5. Exit the sketch.
6. On the Quick Access Toolbar, click the **Options** icon.
7. On the **System Options** dialog, click **File Locations** in the tree.
8. Select **Weldment Profiles** from the **Show folders for** drop-down.
9. View the location of the weldment profiles and click **OK**.
10. Select the sketch from the FeatureManager Design Tree.
11. Click **File > Save As** on the Menu bar; the **Save As** dialog appears.
12. On this dialog, set the **Save as type** as **Lib Feat Part (*.sldlfp)**.
13. Browse to the location of the weldment profiles.
14. Create the **Custom Profiles** folder.

15. Create a sub folder with the name **C-Shape** in the **Custom Profiles** folder.
16. Save the file in the **C-Shape** folder as **C120**.
17. Start a new Part document.
18. Create a sketch on the Top plane, as shown in figure.

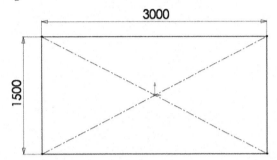

19. Exit the sketch.
20. Click **Weldments > Structural Member** on the Command Manager.
21. On the Property Manager, make the selections, as shown in figure.

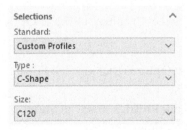

22. Select the line segments from the sketch. The structural members are created.

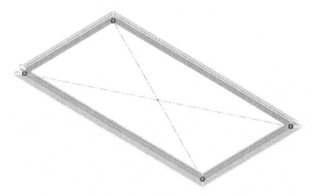

You can also click the **Locate Profile** button and change the position of the profile.

23. Click **OK**.

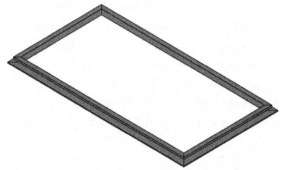

24. Save the file.

Chapter 13: MBD Dimensions

Geometric Dimensioning and Tolerancing

During the manufacturing process, the accuracy of a part is an important factor. However, it is impossible to manufacture a part with the exact dimensions. Therefore, while applying dimensions to a drawing you need to provide some dimensional tolerances, which lie within acceptable limits. The following figure shows an example of dimensional tolerances applied to the drawing.

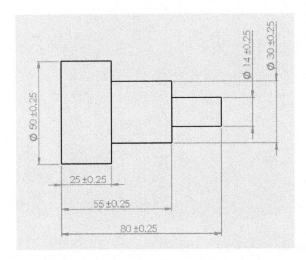

The dimensional tolerances help you to manufacture the component within a specific size range. However, the dimensional tolerances are not sufficient for manufacturing a component. You must give tolerance values to its shape, orientation and position as well. The following figure shows a note, which is used to explain the tolerance value given to the shape of the object.

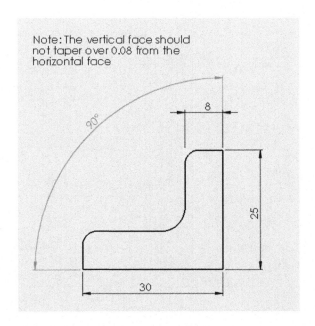

Providing a note in a drawing may be confusing. To avoid this, we use Geometric Dimensioning and Tolerancing (GD&T) symbols to specify the tolerance values to shape, orientation and position of a component. The following figure shows the same example represented by using the GD&T symbols. In this figure, the vertical face to which the tolerance frame is connected, must be within two parallel planes 0.08 apart and perpendicular to the datum reference (horizontal plane).

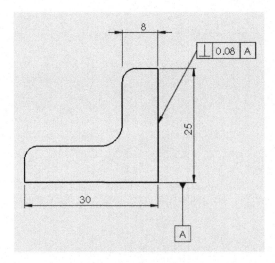

Providing GD&T in 2D drawings is common and well known method. However, you can provide GD&T information to 3D models as well. The DimXpert tools help you to add GD&T information to the 3D models based on the universal standards such as ASME Y14.41 – 2003 and ISO 16792: 2006. However, you can add GD&T information based on your custom standard as well.

In this chapter, you will learn to use **MBD Dimensions** tools to add GD&T information to parts. There are many ways to add GD&T information and full-define the parts and assemblies. There are few methods explained in this chapter but you need to use a method that suits your design.

The Model based dimensions tools are available on the **MBD Dimensions** Command Manager. If the **MBD Dimensions** CommandManager is not displayed by default, you can customize it. Right click on any of the tabs of the CommandManager and select **MBD Dimensions** from the shortcut menu.

TUTORIAL 1 (Auto Dimension Scheme)

This tutorial teaches you to apply tolerances using the **Auto Dimension Scheme** tool. This tool automates the process of adding dimensions and tolerances to the 3D model.

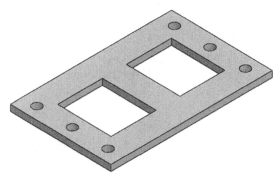

1. Download the DimXpert part files from the Companion website and open the Tutorial 1 file.
2. On the Quick Access Toolbar, click the **Options** icon to open the **System Options** dialog.
3. Click the **Document Properties** tab and select **Drafting Standard** from the tree.
4. Set the **Overall drafting standard** to ISO.

5. Click **OK**.
6. On the CommandManager, click **MBD Dimensions > Auto Dimension Scheme** .
7. On the PropertyManager, set the **Part type** to **Prismatic**. This option is selected for the parts that have planar faces. The **Turned** option can be used for cylindrical shaped parts.
8. Set the **Tolerance type** to **Plus and Minus**.

The **Tolerance type** defines the way in which the features such as holes and cuts are located with reference to datum feature.

The **Plus and Minus** option adds location dimensions with + and – tolerances.

The **Geometric** option uses Geometric Tolerance symbols to represent the positions of features such as holes and cuts. The type of GD&T symbols used will be based on the **Part type**. For example, if you set the **Part type** to **Prismatic**, the Position symbol will be used to locate a hole. However, if the **Part type** is set to **Turned**, the Circular Runout symbol will be used to position a hole.

Next, you need to define the datum features. A datum is used as a reference to measure the location, shape, and size of a feature. A datum can be a surface, point, or axis.

9. On the PropertyManager, click in the **Primary Datum** selection box and select the top face of the geometry.
10. Click in the **Secondary Datum** selection box and select the front face of the geometry.
11. Click in the **Tertiary Datum** selection box and select the right face.

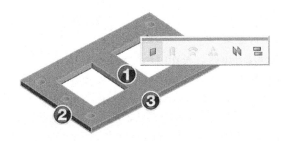
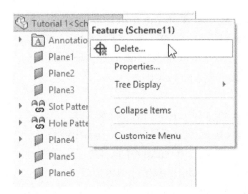

12. Under the **Scope** section, select **All features**.
13. Check all the options in the **Feature Filters** section and click **OK** ✓.

Notice the dimensions added to the 3D geometry. They all have + and – tolerances.

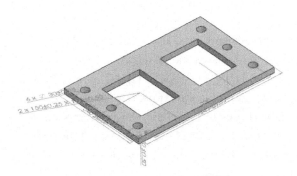

14. Click the **DimXpertManager** ⊕ tab on the left pane and notice the features listed in it. The **Auto Dimension Scheme** tool recognizes and lists the features to be manufactured, automatically.

Notice that the Extruded Cut feature is recognized as a Slot feature. The MBD Dimensions recognizes the features based on the manufacturing language.

15. Right click on the part in the DimXpertManager tree and select **Delete**.

16. Click **Yes** on the **SOLIDWORKS** message to delete all the dimensions and tolerances.
17. On the DimXpertManager tree, click the **Auto Dimension Scheme** ⊕ icon.
18. Set the **Tolerance type** to **Geometric**.
19. Select the primary, secondary, and tertiary datums. They are same, as previously selected.
20. Leave the default settings and click **OK**. Notice the dimensions and geometric tolerances added with reference to the datums.

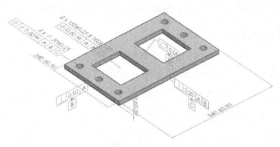

21. Right click on the part in the DimXpertManager tree and select **Delete**.
22. Click **Yes** on the **SOLIDWORKS** message to delete all the dimensions and tolerances.
23. Activate the **Auto Dimension Scheme** ⊕ tool.
24. Select the primary, secondary, and tertiary datums. They are same, as previously selected.
25. On the PropertyManager, set the **Scope** to **Selected features**.
26. Select anyone of the holes.
27. Select the **Pattern** icon from the Selection toolbar. The entire pattern is selected.
28. Likewise, select anyone of the faces of the extruded feature. The extrude features are selected as pattern.

SOLIDWORKS 2019 Learn by Doing

29. Rotate the model and select the bottom and side faces.

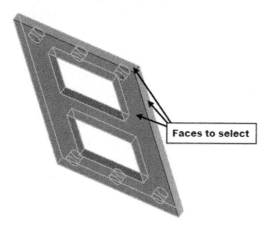

30. Select the **Plane** icon from the Selection toolbar.
31. Click **OK** to add dimensions and tolerance to the selected features only.

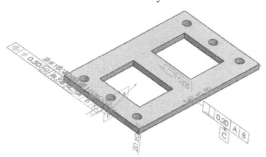

32. Save and close the file.

TUTORIAL 2 (Adding the GD&T Information Manually)

In this tutorial, you will add dimensions and tolerances manually.

1. Open the Tutorial 2 part file.
2. On the CommandManager, click **MBD Dimensions > Datum** .
3. On the PropertyManager, type **A** in the **Label** box under the **Label Settings** section.
4. Select the front face of the geometry.
5. Move the pointer and click to position the datum.

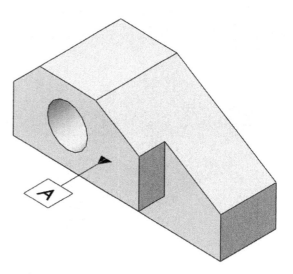

6. Likewise, define the datum B and C, and click **OK**.

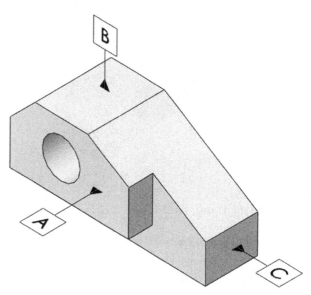

Notice the three plane features in the DimXpertManager tree.

- Tutorial 2-resource<Scheme2>
  - Annotations
  - Plane1
  - Plane2
  - Plane3

You can click and drag the datum or its origin point.

SOLIDWORKS 2019 Learn by Doing

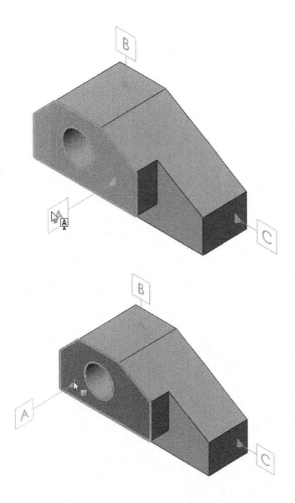

Adding Size Dimensions

You add size dimensions to the geometry to provide the manufacturing information. These dimensions do not control the geometry. Instead, they are controlled by the size of the geometry.

1. On the CommandManager, click **MBD Dimensions > Size Dimension**.
2. Select the hole and place the dimension.

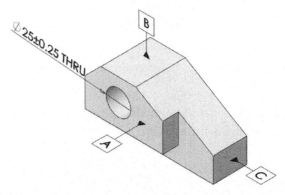

Notice the tolerance values added to the dimension. These are the default tolerance values set on the **System Options** dialog. You can change the tolerance value on the **System Options** dialog. You can also change the tolerance on the **Tolerance/Precision** section of the **DimXpert** PropertyManager.

In addition, if you select a single hole from the geometry, all the holes of same size will be selected, automatically and the hole count will be added to the dimension, as shown.

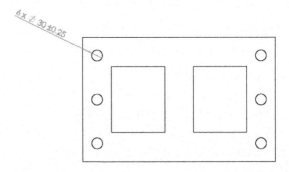

7. On the CommandManager, click the **Show Tolerance Status** icon. Notice that the datum faces are highlighted in green, which means that they are fully-defined.

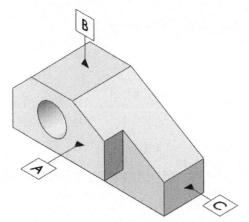

Now, you need to fully-define all other faces by adding dimensions and tolerances.

3. Click **OK** on the **DimXpert** PropertyManager.

4. Click the **Show Tolerance Status** icon on the DimXpertManager. Notice that the hole is highlighted in yellow, which means that it is under constrained.

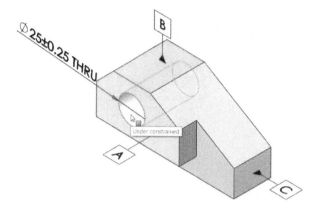

Adding Location Dimensions

You add location dimensions to a feature with reference to a datum.

1. On the CommandManager, click **MBD Dimensions > Location Dimension**.
2. Rotate the model and select its left vertical face.
3. Select the hole and position the dimension, as shown.

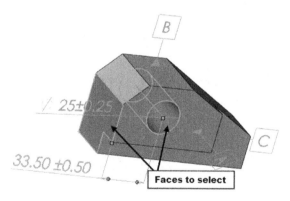

On the **DimXpert** PropertyManager, the **Tolerance Feature** and **Origin Feature** are displayed in the **Reference Features** section. You can swap these features by clicking the **Swap Features** icon.

You can also change the tolerance value in the **Tolerance/Precision** section.

4. Add a dimension between the bottom face and hole. Click OK on the PropertyManager.

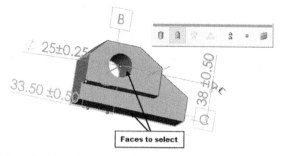

5. On the CommandManager, click **MBD Dimensions > Location Dimension**.
6. Select the lower horizontal edge of the geometry and notice the faces perpendicular to the edge are highlighted.
7. Position the dimension and click **OK** on the PropertyManager.

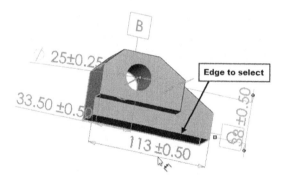

Adding Geometric Tolerances

1. On the CommandManager, click **MBD Dimensions > Geometric Tolerance**.
2. On the **Properties** dialog, select Position from the **Symbol** drop-down.
3. Type 0.02 in the **Tolerance 1** box and click the **Maximum Material Condition** icon.
4. Type A, B, and C in the **Primary**, **Secondary**, and **Tertiary** boxes, respectively.
5. Select the hole and position the tolerance frame. The **SOLIDWORKS** message appears showing that tolerance over constrains the part.
6. Click **OK** to add the tolerance.
7. Click **OK** on the **Properties** dialog and delete the location dimensions, as shown.

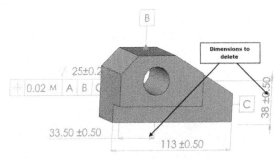

8. Add three tolerance frames to the faces, as shown.

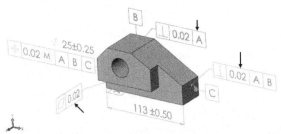

You can change the orientation of the annotation by clicking the right mouse button on it and selecting **Select Annotation View**. Select a new annotation view from the popup menu. If you select Front annotation view, the orientation of the datum will be changed to Front plane.

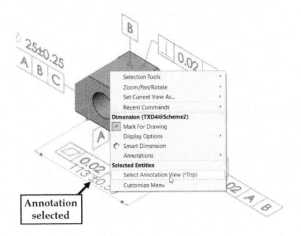

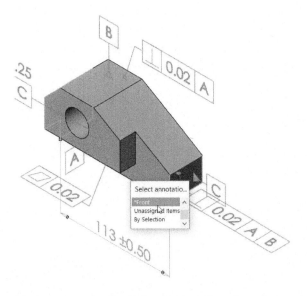

If you select the **By Selection** option, then datum is oriented to the selected plane.

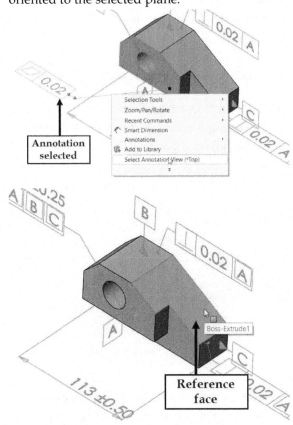

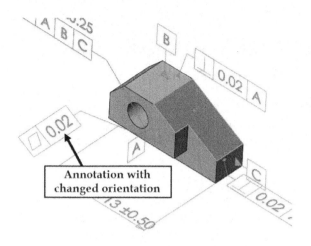

Adding other dimensions to Fully-define the part

1. On the CommandManager, click **Location Dimension** and add dimensions, as shown.

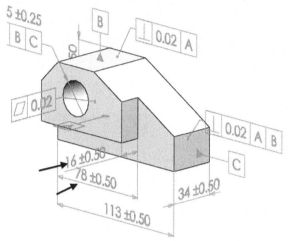

2. Activate the **Location Dimension** tool and click the left vertical face of the geometry.
3. Click the **Create Intersection Line** icon on the Selection toolbar.
4. Select the inclined face and click **OK** on the Selection toolbar.

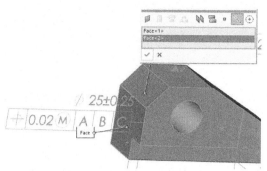

5. Select the top face of the geometry and position the dimension.
6. On the PropertyManager, click the **Swap Features** icon to change the origin feature.
7. Click **Close Dialog**.
8. Click the **Show Tolerance Status** icon and notice that the inclined face is highlighted in yellow.

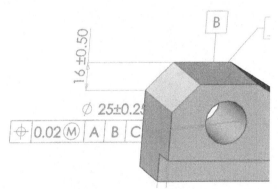

In addition, notice that the other inclined is not fully-defined. You need to add dimensions to fully-define these two faces.

9. Activate the **Location Dimension** tool and click the top face of the geometry.
10. Click the **Create Intersection Line** icon on the Selection toolbar.
11. Select the left inclined face and click **OK** on the Selection toolbar.
12. Select the C datum face and position the dimension.
13. On the PropertyManager, click the **Swap Features** icon to change the origin feature.

SOLIDWORKS 2019 Learn by Doing

14. Click **Close Dialog**.

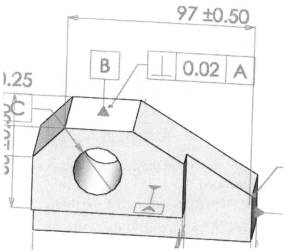

15. Likewise, add the angle and linear dimensions, as shown.

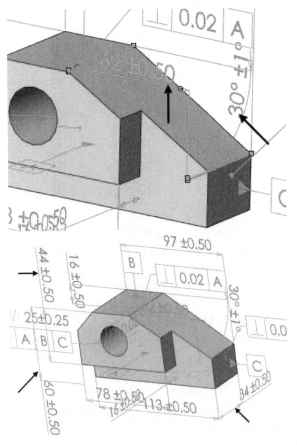

Notice that all the faces of the model turn green after applying dimensions and geometric tolerances.

16. Save and close the file.

TUTORIAL 3 (Using the MBD Dimensions Annotations in drawings)

1. Open the Tutorial 2 part file.
2. On the Quick Access Toolbar, click **New > Make Drawing from Part/Assembly**.
3. Select **A3(ANSI) Landscape** from the **Sheet Format/Size** dialog and click **OK**.
4. On the **View Palette** located at the right side of the window, check the **Import Annotations** and **DimXpert Annotations** options.

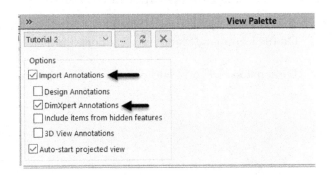

5. Drag the Front view from the **View Palette** onto the drawing sheet.

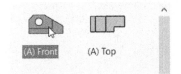

6. Click **Close Dialog** on the **Projected View** PropertyManager.

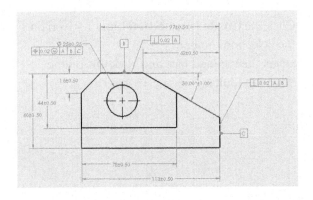

7. Likewise, drag the Right and Isometric views.

8. Adjust the dimensions by dragging them.

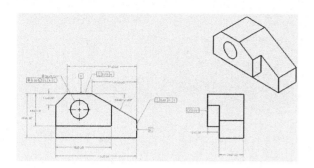

9. Save and close the drawing file.

TUTORIAL 4 (Pattern Feature)

1. Open the Tutorial 4 part file.
2. On the CommandManager, click **MBD Dimensions > Pattern Feature**.
3. On the PropertyManager, select **Linked Patterns**.
4. Select anyone of the holes of the curve pattern.

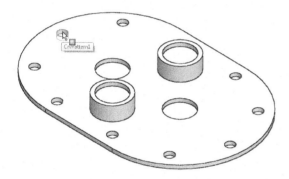

5. Click **OK** and notice the Hole Pattern in the DimXpertManager.

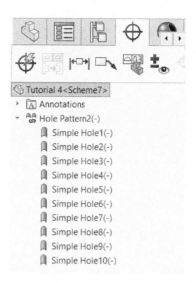

6. Change the instant count of the curve pattern to 10. Notice that the Hole Pattern in the DimXpertManager is also updated.
7. Activate the **Pattern Feature** command and select anyone of the large holes.

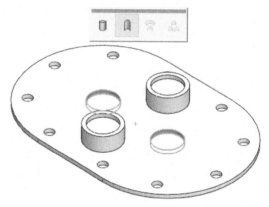

8. The other hole of the same size is selected, automatically. In addition, the **Manual Patterns** option is active as the holes are created as two separate instances. The **Find all same face** option selects all the features of same size.
9. Click **OK**. The Hole Pattern appears in the DimXpertManager Tree.
10. Activate the **Pattern Feature** command and select **Collection**.
11. Select the side faces of the geometry.

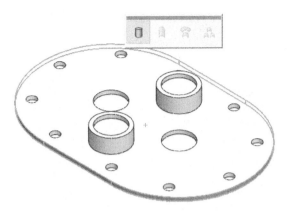

12. Click **OK** on the PropertyManager
13. The **Collection** feature appears in the DimXpertManager Tree. All the faces inside the **Collection** feature appear as a single DimXpert feature. You can add a single annotation to all the faces of the collection feature at a time.

TUTORIAL 5 (DimXpert Options)

1. Start a new Part document.
2. On the Quick Access Toolbar, click **Options** to the **System Options** dialog.
3. Click the **Document Properties** tab and select **Drafting Standard** from the tree.
4. Set the **Overall drafting standard** to **ISO**.
5. Click **DimXpert** in the tree.

The **Methods** is set to **General Tolerance**. This type of tolerance is commonly used with ISO standard. You can define the **Tolerance class** as Fine, Medium, Coarse, or Very Coarse in the **General Tolerance** section located at the bottom on the dialog.

The **Block Tolerance** method can be used, if you are using the ANSI drafting standard. You can define the decimal values for the length and angle dimensions in the **Block tolerance** section.

6. Click **DimXpert > Size Dimension** in the tree.

On this page, you can define the default tolerance values to be added to the DimXpert size dimensions. You can specify three types of the tolerances (Symmetric, Bilateral, and General) for various types

285

of features. The tolerances can be specified separately for each feature.

7. Click **DimXpert > Location Dimension** in the tree.

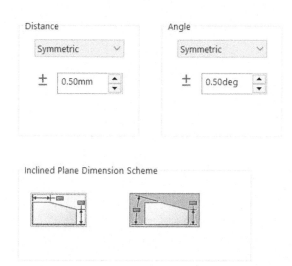

On this page, you can define the default tolerance values for the location dimensions. In addition, you can set the type of the dimensions to be added to inclined planes using the **Auto Dimension Scheme**.

8. Click **DimXpert > Chain Dimension** in the tree.

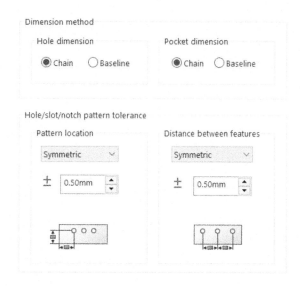

On this page, you can define the dimensioning method for holes and pockets using the **Auto**

Dimension Scheme. In addition, you can define the tolerances for patterns.

9. Click **DimXpert > Geometric Tolerance** in the tree.

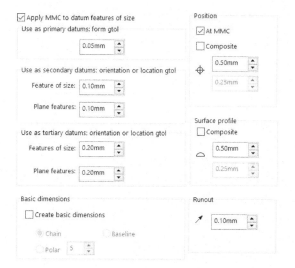

This page allows you to set the default options for geometric tolerances to be added using the **Auto Dimension Scheme**.

Likewise, you can set the default width and tolerance settings on the **Chamfer Control** page.

10. Click **Display Options** on the tree.

286

SOLIDWORKS 2019 Learn by Doing

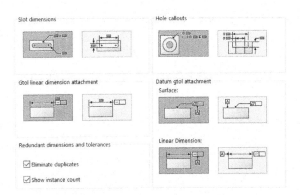

This page allows you to control the way the dimensions and tolerances are displayed using the **Auto Dimension Scheme**. In addition, you can control the redundant dimensions and tolerances using **Eliminate duplicates** and **Show instance count** options.

11. Click **OK** to close the dialog.

SOLIDWORKS 2019 Learn by Doing

Chapter 14: Appearances and Rendering

In this chapter, you will:

- Add Appearances and Textures to the model
- Apply Backgrounds and Scenes to the model
- Render Images
- Add Cameras and Lights
- Create Walkthroughs
- Add Decals

TUTORIAL 1 (Adding Appearances to the Complete Part)

1. Download the Appearances and Rendering part files from the Companion website and open the Tutorial 1 file.
2. On the View Toolbar, click the **Edit Appearance** icon.

You can also right click on the part in the FeatureManager Design Tree and select **Appearances > Tutorial 1**.

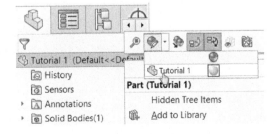

3. Click the **Basic** tab on the PropertyManager. Notice that Tutorial 1.SLDPRT is listed in the **Selected Geometry** section. You can use the **Select Part**, **Select Faces**, **Select Surfaces**, **Select Bodies**, and **Select Features** icons to select different types of geometry.
4. Leave the entire part as **Selected Geometry** in the PropertyManager.
5. Click the **Appearances, Scenes, and Decals** tab on the Task pane located on the right side of the graphics window.
6. On the Task pane, click **Appearances (color) > Metal > Aluminum**. Notice the various types of Aluminum listed on the lower portion of the Task pane.

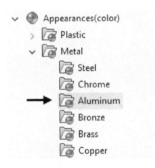

7. Select **blue anodized aluminum** from the Task pane.

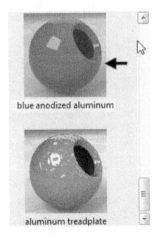

8. Click **OK** on the PropertyManager to apply the selected material to whole part.

289

9. Click the **DisplayManager** tab and notice that the material is added to the **Appearances** tree.
10. Expand **blue anodized aluminum** and notice that the material is attached to the entire part geometry.

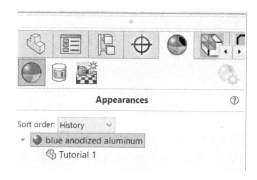

Also, notice the brushed copper on the **DisplayManager**.

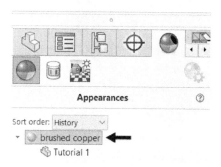

11. Right click on the appearance and select **Edit Appearance**.
12. On the Task pane, click **Appearances (color) > Metal > Copper**. Notice the various types of Copper listed on the lower portion of the Task pane.
13. Select **brushed copper** from the Task pane and click **OK** ✓.

14. Right click on **brushed copper** and select **Remove Appearance** (or) select the appearance and press Delete (or) right click on the appearance and select **Edit Appearance**, and then click **Remove Appearance** on the **Selected Geometry** section.
15. Click **OK**.

The appearance is removed from the geometry.

TUTORIAL 2 (Adding Appearances to Faces, Surfaces, and Features)

SOLIDWORKS allows you to apply different appearances to a single part. For example, you can display some faces of the geometry differently from others. To add different appearances to the part geometry, you need to understand the hierarchy in which the appearances are added. For example, if you add an appearance to the entire part, and then add a different appearance to a part feature, the feature appearance will be added on top of the part appearance. If you add a new appearance to a face of the feature, the face appearance will be added on top of the feature appearance.

1. Open the Tutorial 2 part file.

Now, you need to add appearance to the Boss-Extrude feature, as shown.

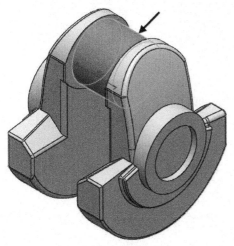

2. Click on the **Boss-Extrude** feature and select **Appearances > Boss-Extrude**.

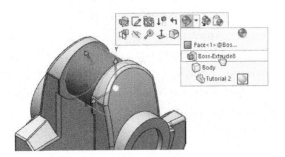

Notice the Boss-Extrude feature in the **Selected Geometry** section.

16. On the Task pane, click **Appearances (color) > Metal > Bronze**. Notice the various types of Bronze listed on the lower portion of the Task pane.

17. Select **cast bronze** from the Task pane and click **OK** ✓.

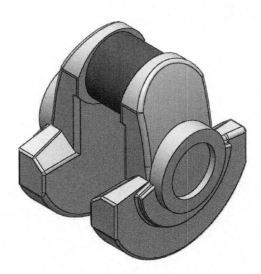

Notice the **cast bronze** on the **DisplayManager**. It is attached to the Boss-Extrude feature

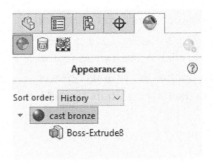

18. Press the Ctrl key and select the faces of the geometry, as shown.

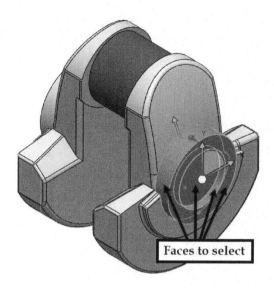

You can also use the Copy and Paste options to apply appearance to multiple features/faces of the geometry.

19. On the DisplayManager, right click on the **cast bronze** appearance and select **Attach To Selection**. The appearance is attached to the selected faces.

20. Click on anyone of the faces with the **cast bronze** appearance, and select **Copy Appearance** (or) right click on the **cast bronze** appearance and select **Copy Appearance**.
21. Select the face as shown and click **Paste Appearance**.

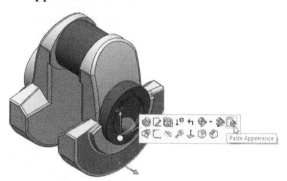

The **Appearance Target Palette** appears on the screen. Place the pointer on the icons of this palette and notice the appearance of the part.

22. Click the Boss-Extrude icon on the **Appearance Target Palette**. The **cast bronze** appearance is pasted on the extruded boss.

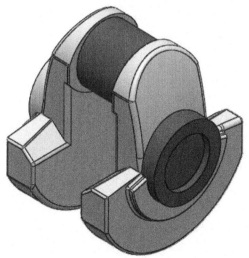

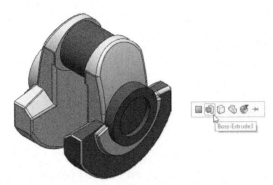

TUTORIAL 3 (Adding Textures)

Textures are two-dimensional images that are wrapped around a 3D model. The process of adding textures to the 3D model involves selecting an image and mapping it onto the 3D model. As you add a texture, SOLIDWORKS increases or reduces the image size, rotates, and patterns it to completely cover the part geometry.

1. Open the Tutorial 1 file.
2. On the View Toolbar, click the **Edit Appearance** icon.

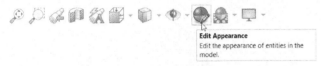

3. Select **texture** from the Task pane.

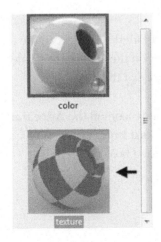

4. On the PropertyManager, under the **Image** section, click the **Browse** button.

5. Go to *C:\Program Files\SOLIDWORKS Corp\SOLIDWORKS\data\Images\textures\metal\rough*.
6. Select **cast** and click **Open**.

7. On the PropertyManager, click the **Mapping** tab.

The **Mapping** tab has options to select the geometry, and set mapping style and size.

8. On the **Mapping Controls** section, click on different Mapping styles and notice the appearance on the geometry. Each of the mapping style affects the appearance on the geometry. You can select the Mapping style based on the shape of the geometry.

9. Click on different **Mapping sizes** and notice the difference.
10. Leave the default options and click **OK** ✓.

TUTORIAL 4 (Texture Mapping options)

1. Start a new part file.
2. Create a box, sphere and cylinder.
3. Select the box from the graphics window.
4. Select **Boss-Extrude-1** from the top left corner.

5. On the View Heads Up toolbar, click the **Edit Appearance** .
6. Select **texture** from the Task pane.

texture

7. Click the Browse button on the PropertyManager and go to the location: C:\Program Files\SOLIDWORKS Corp\SOLIDWORKS\data\Images\textures\fabric\loop.jpg
8. Double-click on the loop.jpg file and click **OK** ✓.
9. Likewise, apply the loop texture separately to the other features.

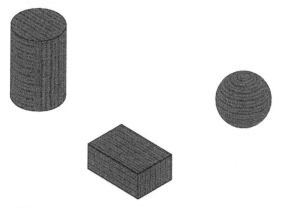

10. Click on the box and select **Edit Appearance > Boss-Extrude**.

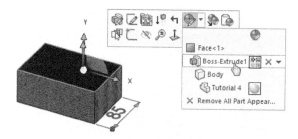

11. On the PropertyManager, click the **Advanced** tab, and then click the **Mapping** tab. Notice that the options found in the **Mapping** section are same as the Mapping style options in the **Basic** tab.
12. On the **Mapping** tab, select **Mapping > Surface**. This mapping style arranges the image to fit the surfaces of the geometry.
13. On the **Mapping** section, drag the **Horizontal Location** and **Vertical Location** draggers. Notice that the position of the texture image changes horizontally and vertically.

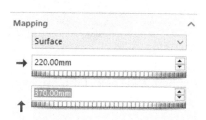

14. Select **Mapping > Projection** and set the **Projection direction** to XY. The texture image is projected onto the feature in the XY direction.

15. Set the **Projection direction** to **Current View**.
16. Rotate the model and click the **Update to Current** button. The texture is projected based on the current orientation of the model.

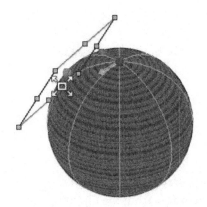

17. Set the **Projection direction** to **Selected Reference** and select the vertical edge of the box. The image is project along the selected edge.

You can also use the **Size/Orientation** options to modify the texture image size and orientation.

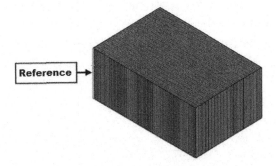

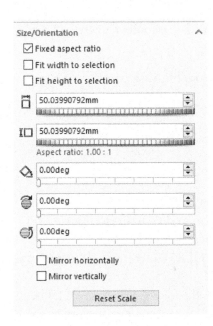

18. Click **OK** ✓ on the PropertyManager.
19. Click on the sphere and select **Edit Appearance > Revolve**.

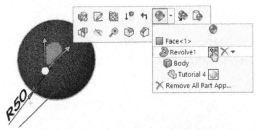

20. On the PropertyManager, click the **Advanced** tab, and then click the **Mapping** tab.
21. On the **Mapping** tab, select **Mapping > Spherical**. This mapping style arranges the image to fit the surface of a sphere.
22. Drag the **Offset Latitude** and **Offset Longitude** draggers on the **Mapping** section. The position of the rectangle changes.
23. Drag the dotted handles of the rectangle to increase/decrease the size of the texture image.

The **Fixed aspect ratio** option locks the aspect ratio of the image.

The **Fit width to selection** locks the image width to its current size. You can change only the height of the image.

The **Fit height to selection** locks the image height allowing you to change only its width.

24. Drag the **Rotation** ⬦ dragger and notice that the image is rotated about the current position of longitude and latitude.

295

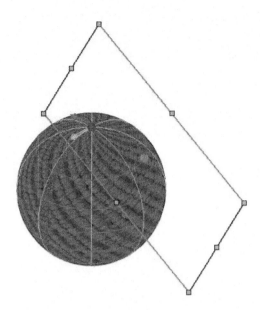

25. Drag the **Axis direction 1** dragger to change its orientation.

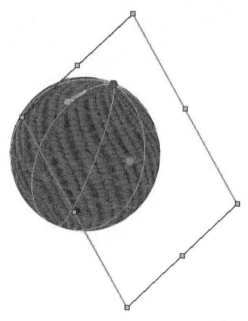

26. Likewise, drag the **Axis direction 2** dragger to change its orientation.

You can use the **Mirror horizontally** or **Mirror vertically** options to mirror the image.

27. Click the **Reset Scale** button to reset image scale to its default value.
28. Click **OK** on the PropertyManager.

29. Click on the cylinder and select **Edit Appearance > Boss-Extrude2**.

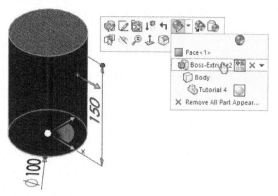

30. Click the **Advanced** tab on the PropertyManager.
31. On the **Mapping** tab, select **Mapping > Cylindrical**. This mapping style arranges the image to fit the surface of a cylinder.
32. Set the **Axis direction** to XY and drag the **About Axis** and **Along Axis** draggers.

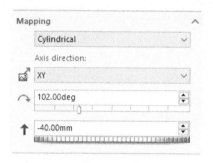

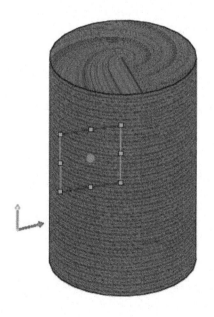

33. Click **OK** on the PropertyManager.

TUTORIAL 5 (Surface Finish)

1. Open the Tutorial 5 file.
2. Apply the **knurl2** texture to the cylindrical face of the geometry. The location of the texture image is C:\Program Files\SOLIDWORKS Corp\SOLIDWORKS\data\Images\textures\metal\machined\knurl2.jpg
3. Click the **Basic** tab on the PropertyManager.
4. On the **Mapping** section, set the **Mapping Style** to **Surface mapping** and **Mapping Size** to **Big mapping size**.

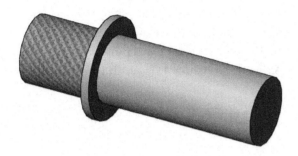

34. Click the **Advanced** tab, and then click the **Surface Finish** tab.
35. Select the **Knurled** option from the **Surface Finish** drop-down. You can also select the **From file** option and specify an image file to define the surface finish.
36. Check the **Dynamic help** option.
37. Place the pointer on the **Knurl angle** and **Knurl height cap** boxes, and notice the descriptions.
38. Set the **Knurl angle** and **Knurl height cap** to 90 and 1, respectively.
39. Click **OK**. The knurled surface finish will be visible in the rendered image. SOLIDWORKS will process the bright areas of the texture image as height and the dark areas as depths.

TUTORIAL 6 (Illumination)

1. Open the Tutorial 5 file.
2. Click on anyone of the face of the geometry and select **Edit Appearance > Revolve**.
3. On the Task Pane, select **Appearance > Metal > Steel**.
4. Select **machined steel** from the lower portion of the Task pane.
5. Click the **Advanced** tab on the PropertyManager.
6. Click the **Illumination** tab and check the **Dynamic help** option. The options on the **Illumination** tab control the illumination of the geometry.
7. Place the pointer on the edit boxes, and notice the descriptions.
8. Modify the values on the **Illumination** tab and notice the change in the graphics window.
9. Click **OK**.

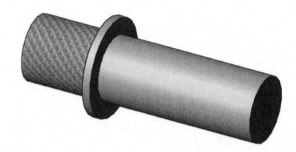

Tutorial 7 (Scenes)

After adding Appearances, a Scene is an important part of the rendering process. An appearance is added to the geometry, whereas a scene is added to the SOLIDWORKS environment. A scene creates a realistic environment in which the model is placed. For example, you can add a road scene to a car model.

1. Open the Tutorial 7 file.

2. Click the DisplayManager tab, right click on Scene, and select **Edit Scene**.
3. Click **Yes** on the **Background Display Setting** dialog.
4. On the Task pane, expand **Scenes** and notice the folders below it.
5. Click on the **Basic Scenes** folder and notice the thumbnails displayed in the browser. The basic scenes have plain or gradient environments and background.

3 Point Beige

3 Point Blue

3 Point Faded

3 Point Green

3 Point Orange

Backdrop - Ambient White

Backdrop - Black with Fill Lights

Backdrop - Grey with Overhead Light

Backdrop - Lightbox Studio

SOLIDWORKS 2019 Learn by Doing

6. Select **3 Point Beige** scene from the browser.
7. Click the middle mouse button and drag the mouse. Notice that the viewpoint changes as you rotate the part.
8. Click the **Studio Scenes** folder in the Task pane. Most of the studio scenes have static backgrounds.

Reflective Floor Black

Reflective Floor Checkered

Factory Floor

Dusty Antique

Misty Blue Slate

Strip Lighting

Light Cards

Grill Lighting

Traffic Lights

9. Select **Reflective Floor Black** from the browser.
10. Rotate the model and notice that the background remains static.
11. Click the **Presentation Scenes** folder and select **Factory Background**.

Factory Background

12. Rotate the model and notice that the environment is sphere shaped and encloses the part completely. You can set the viewpoint at the angle.
13. Click the **Basic Scenes** folder and select **Plain White**. Notice that the background is changed to plain white. However, you can change the background to suit your requirements.
14. On the PropertyManager, select **Background > Color**.
15. Click on the **Dominant color** box available in the **Background** section.
16. On the **Color** dialog, select the Yellow color and click **OK**. The background is changed to yellow.

17. On the PropertyManager, select **Background > Gradient**.
18. Click in the **Bottom gradient color** box, select the blue color, and click **OK**. The bottom gradient is changed to blue.

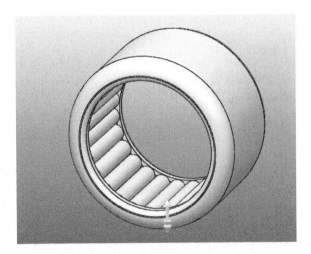

19. On the PropertyManager, select **Background > Image**.
20. Select the Background.jpg and click **Open** (Download the Background.jpg file from the companion website).
21. Position the model, as shown.

22. On the PropertyManager, select **Background > Use Environment**. The default environment appears, as shown.

An environment is a spherical shaped enclosure. The image used in the environment is specially designed and looks similar to the one shown next. The image file types that are commonly used for environments are HDR files and panoramically designed JPEG files.

You can click the **Browse** button and select an image for the environment background.

23. Click **OK** on the PropertyManager.

TUTORIAL 8 (Rendering using PhotoView 360)

PhotoView 360 is a SOLIDWORKS Add-In, which allows you to create photo-realistic images.

1. Open the Tutorial 8 file.

2. On the Quick Access Toolbar, click **Options > Add-Ins**.
3. On the **Add-Ins** dialog, check the **PhotoView 360** option and click **OK** (or) click the **PhotoView 360** icon on the **SOLIDWORKS Add-Ins** tab of the CommandManager. The

Render Tools tab is added to the CommandManager.

4. On the CommandManager, click **Render Tools > Edit Appearance** .
5. On the Task pane, select **Appearances > Metal > Aluminum**, and select **polished Aluminum** from the browser.
6. On the PropertyManager, under the **Color** section, click in the **Dominant Color** box and select the light grey color from the **Color** dialog. Click **OK**.
7. Click in the **Secondary Color** box and select white from the **Color** dialog. Click **OK**.

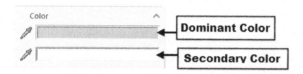

8. Click **OK** on the PropertyManager.
9. On the CommandManager, click **Render Tools > Edit Scene** .
10. On the Task pane, select **Scenes > Presentation Scenes**, and select **Kitchen Background** from the browser.
11. Rotate, zoom, and pan the model to position it, as shown.

12. On the **View Heads Up** Toolbar, click the **View Orientation** drop-down and deselect the **View Selector** icon.
13. Click the **New View** icon on the **View Orientation** drop-down.

14. Type **Render1** on the **Named View** dialog and click **OK**.
15. Rotate the model to the different orientation.
16. On the **View Heads Up** Toolbar, click the **View Orientation** drop-down and select **Render1**.

If you are working in the Assembly environment, the **Take snapshot** tool can be used to capture the different view orientations of the model.

17. Click **OK** on the PropertyManager.

Adding Cameras

1. Click the DisplayManager tab on the left pane, and then click **View Scene, Lights, and Cameras** .
2. Right click on the **Camera** folder and select **Add Camera**.

The PropertyManager appears and it has options to set the camera type, target point, camera position, camera rotation, field of view, and depth of field.

In addition, the graphics window is split in two. You can adjust the camera position in the left window and preview the camera perspective in the right window.

3. On the PropertyManager, set the **Camera Type** to **Aimed at target**. The camera will always show the selected target point regardless of the camera position. The Floating camera type changes the site as you change the camera position and orientation.
4. Zoom out in the left window and notice a camera.

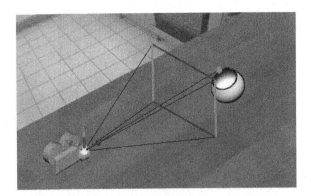

5. Click and drag the red dot attached to the camera. Notice that the target changes as you drag the red dot.
6. Select the outer face of the model to define the target point.
7. Click and drag the yellow dot to change the position of the camera. You can also use the axes of the triad attached to the change the camera position.

Notice that the camera focuses on the target point regardless of its position.

8. Expand the **Camera Rotation** section and drag the **Roll(Twist)** dragger to rotate the camera.
9. Set the **Roll(Twist)** angle to 0 degrees.
10. In the **Field of View** section, select different options from the **Standard lens presets** drop-down and notice the area captured by the camera. You can also drag the **View angle**, **Distance to view rectangle**, and **Height of view rectangle** draggers to adjust the field of view.
11. Check the **Drag Aspect Ratio** option and drag the corner of the view box. The aspect ratio of the field changes dynamically.

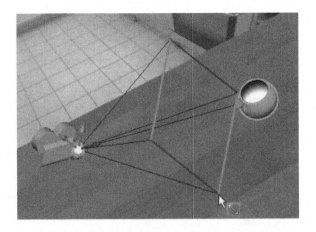

12. Set the **Aspect ratio (width: height)** to **1:1**.
13. Position the camera in such a way that the preview is displayed, as shown.

18. Click **OK** on the PropertyManager.
19. In the DisplayManager tree, expand the **Camera** right click on the **Camera1** and select **Camera View**. The view is locked to the camera.

PhotoView 360 Options

1. On the CommandManager, click **Render Tools > Options**. On the PropertyManager, you can modify the width and height of the image.
2. Check the **Use background aspect ratio** option to avoid the image to be stretched or distorted.
3. Set the **Image Format** to **JPEG**.
4. In the **Render Quality** section, set the **Preview render quality** and **Final render quality** to **Good** and **Best**, respectively. Note that the

303

processing time will increase as you increase the image quality.
5. Leave the other default options and click **OK** ✓.
6. On the CommandManager, click **Render Tools > Preview Window**. Notice the preview of the rendering.

7. On the CommandManager, click **Render Tools > Edit Scene**.
8. On the PropertyManager, click the **PhotoView 360 Lighting** tab.

On this tab, you can adjust the **Background brightness**, **Rendering brightness**, and **Scene reflexivity**. You can also rotate the environment using the **Environment Rotation** dragger.

9. Leave the default settings on the PropertyManager and click **OK**.
10. Click the **Final Render** icon on the **Render Tools** tab. The **Final Render** window appears and rendering is processed. You can click the **Abort** button on the Final Render window, if you want to stop the rendering process.
11. Click the **Statistics** tab to view various statistics of the rendering such as processing time, elapsed time and so on.

After the image is rendered, you can switch between the **Final Color Output** and **Alpha Output** using the **Output** drop-down.

12. Wait until the image is rendered.
13. Click the **Image Processing** tab, and then click the **Advanced Image Processing** button. Notice various image editing options on this tab that are similar to other image processing softwares. You can modify the image using these options.
14. Click the **Compare and Options** tab and notice the options to compare two rendered images.
15. Press and hold the left mouse button on the **Save Image** button, and select **Save Layered Image**.

16. Save the image as Tutorial8.psd file and close the **Final Render** window.

You can use the **Recall Last Render** tool on the **Render Tools** tab to open the last render.

17. Save and close the part file.

TUTORIAL 9 (Lights)

Lights are very important in rendering a photorealistic image. They can enhance the image to look more realistic by highlighting some portions and creating shadows. You can access the lights on the DisplayManager tree. Click the **DisplayManager** tab, and then click **View Scene, Lights, and Cameras**. Expand the **Lights** folder and notice the default lights available in the SOLIDWORKS environment. Expand the **PhotoView 360 Lights** folder and notice the lights available in PhotoView 360. You can turn ON/OFF lights in PhotoView 360 by right clicking on them and selecting **On in PhotoView 360**.

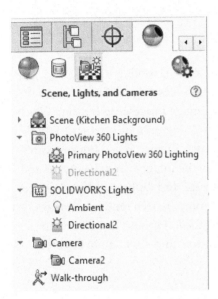

Editing the Ambient Light

By default, the Ambient light is created in the SOLIDWORKS environment, automatically. The Ambient light falls on the model from all directions.

1. Open the Tutorial 9 file.
2. Click the **DisplayManager** tab on the left pane.
3. In the **View Scene, Lights, and Cameras** tree, expand the **SOLIDWORKS Lights** folder, and double click on **Ambient**.
4. On the PropertyManager, click the **Edit Color** button, select the red color from the **Color** dialog, and click **OK**. Notice that the red light falls on the model.
5. Drag the **Ambient** dragger to change the intensity of the light (or) type-in a value between 0 and 1 in the **Ambient** box.

6. On the PropertyManager, uncheck the **On in SOLIDWORKS** option and notice the difference in the graphics window.
7. Check the **On in SOLIDWORKS** option to turn ON the ambient light.
8. Click **OK** to apply changes to the model.

TUTORIAL 10 (Working with Directional Lights)

SOLIDWORKS adds a Directional Light to the model, automatically. It is used to highlight a portion of the geometry and display shadows. You can add, delete, move, or adjust the Directional Light.

1. In the **View Scene, Lights, and Cameras** tree, right click on the **SOLIDWORKS Lights** folder, and select **Show Lights**. The directional lights appear, as shown.

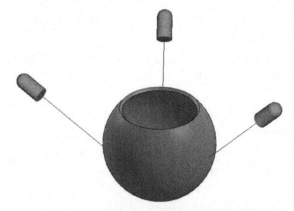

2. Under the **SOLIDWORKS Lights** folder, right click on the **Directional1 light** and select the **Off in SOLIDWORKS** option. The directional light is turned OFF.
3. Likewise, turn of the other two directional lights.

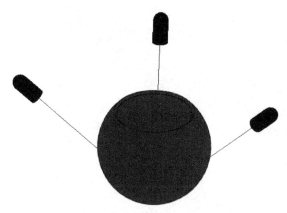

In addition, the directional lights change depending on the type of scene.

4. On the CommandManager, click **Render Tools > Edit Scene**.
5. On the Task pane, click **Scenes > Studio Scenes**, and select the **Reflective Floor Checkered** scene from the browser. Notice two directional lights related to the selected scene.

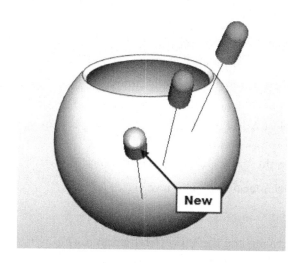

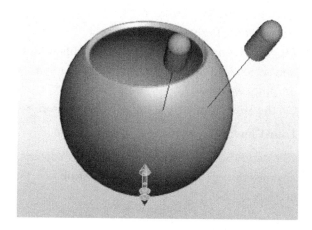

6. Click **OK** on the PropertyManager.
7. On the DisplayManager tree, right click on the **SOLIDWORKS Lights** folder and select **Add Directional Light**. A new directional light appears in the graphics window. The PropertyManager has three tabs: **Basic**, **SOLIDWORKS**, and **PhotoView 360**.

8. On the **Basic** tab, check the **Keep light when scene changes** option to retain the light for all the scenes.
9. In the **Light Position** section, drag the **Longitude** and **Latitude** draggers to change the position of the light (or) click and drag the light to define its position.
10. Uncheck the **Lock to model** option and rotate the model. Notice that the light is fixed as the model is rotated.
11. Check the **Lock to model** option and rotated the model. Notice that the light rotates along with the model.
12. Click the **SOLIDWORKS** tab on the PropertyManager. You can turn ON/OFF the light by checking the **On in SOLIDWORKS** option. You can also change the **Ambient**, **Brightness**, and **Specularity** of the light using **SOLIDWORKS Lighting** options.
13. Click the **PhotView 360** tab. You can turn ON/OFF the light while rendering by checking the **On in PhotoView 360** option.
14. Check the **Dynamic help** option and review the options on the **PhotoView 360** tab.
15. Click **OK** on the PropertyManager.

TUTORIAL 11 (Working with Point Lights)

A point light radiates lights in all directions. It can be used to add lightening effect to models such as torch lights.

1. Open the Tutorial 11 file.
2. Click the **DisplayManager** tab, and then click **View Scene, Lights, and Cameras**.
3. Right click on **SOLIDWORKS Lights** folder and select **Add Point Light**. A red dot appears in graphics window.
4. On the **View Heads Up** toolbar, click **View Orientation > Four View**.
5. Make sure that the **Link Views** icon is activated on the **View Orientation** drop-down.
6. Click and drag the red dot as shown. You can also use the options in the **Light Position** section.

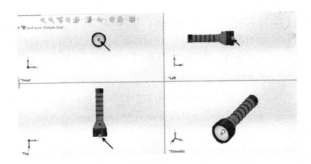

7. On the **Basic** tab, check the **Keep light when scene changes** option.
8. Click the **SOLIDWORKS** tab and adjust the Ambient, Brightness, and Specularity.
9. Click the **PhotoView 360** tab and check the **On in PhotoView 360** option.
10. Adjust the brightness, shadows.
11. Check the **Fog** option and adjust the **Fog radius** and **Fog quality**.
12. Click **OK** on the PropertyManager.
13. On the **View** toolbar, click **View Orientation > Single View**.
14. Render the image as shown.

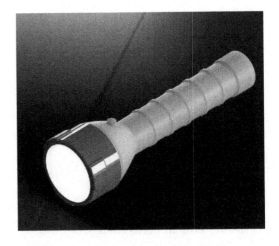

15. Save and close the file.

TUTORIAL 12 (Working with Spot Lights)

Spot lights are similar to the directional lights. However, they create brighter and sharp lights targeting a specific area.

1. Open the Tutorial 12 file.
2. Click the **DisplayManager** tab, and then click **View Scene, Lights, and Cameras**.
3. Right click on the **SOLIDWORKS Lights** folder and select **Add Spot Light**. A cone appears in graphics window.
4. On the **View** toolbar, click **View Orientation > Four View**.
5. Click and drag the red arrow as shown. You can also use the options in the **Light Position** section.

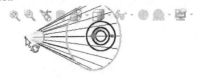

6. Drag the green circle of the cone to reduce its size.

SOLIDWORKS 2019 Learn by Doing

7. Drag the red dot to set the target point of the spot light.

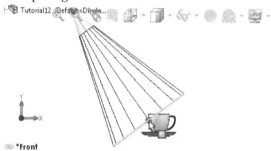

8. Check the **Keep light when scene changes** option.
9. Click the **PhotoView 360** tab and check the **On in PhotoView 360** option.
10. Increase the **Shadow quality** to 70 and click **OK** .
11. On the **View** toolbar, click **View Orientation > Single View**.
12. Change the **View Orientation** to **Trimetric**.
13. On the Task pane, click **Appearances, Scenes, and Decals** tab.
14. Click **Scenes > Basic Scenes**, and then drag the **Pitch Black** scene into the graphics window.
15. Render the image, as shown.

16. Save and close the file.

TUTORIAL 13 (Working with Sun Lights)

Sunlight in SOLIDWORKS represents the real-world sunlight and is controlled by the geographic location that you specify.

1. Open the Tutorial 13 file.
2. Click the **DisplayManager** tab, and then click **View Scene, Lights, and Cameras**.
3. Right click on **SOLIDWORKS Lights** folder and select **Add Sunlight**. The sun appears along with a compass.

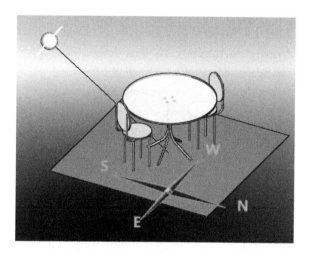

4. Select the right edge of the floor to define the north direction. You can also use a real compass to determine the north direction at your location, and then define it in SOLIDWORKS.

SOLIDWORKS 2019 Learn by Doing

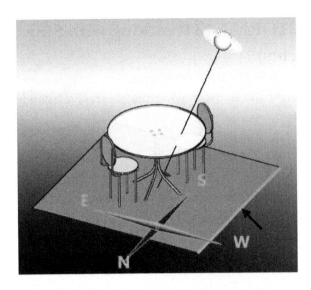

5. Click the **Reverse direction** button next to the **North direction** box. The position of the sun is changed, accordingly.
6. Select different locations from the **Location** drop-down and notice the position of the sun. In addition, the Time Zone is updated in the **Time zone from GMT** drop-down.
7. Under the **Location, Time, and Date** section, select **Location > Specify Location**.
8. Drag the **North Latitude** and **East Longitude** draggers to define the location. You can use a map as the reference, and enter values in the **North Latitude** and **East Longitude** boxes.
9. Select New York from City, NY from the **Location** drop-down.
10. Set the Date to 07-02-2019.
11. Set **Time of day** to 12:00. Notice that the **Information** section displays all the data related to the location. You can save this information in a file using the **Save Information to file** icon located at the bottom.
12. Click the **Advanced** tab and examine all the options with the **Dynamic help** option selected.
13. Click **OK** on the PropertyManager.
14. Click **Preview window** on the **Render Tools** tab and notice the shadows.

15. Close the Preview window.
16. In the DisplayManager tree, right click on **Sunlight** and select **Edit Sunlight**.
17. On the PropertyManager, change the **Location** to **Sydney**, and click **OK**.
18. Click **Preview window** on the **Render Tools** tab and notice the shadows.

19. Close the **Preview** window and file.

TUTORIAL 14 (Walk-through)

SOLIDWORKS Walk-through allows you to visually navigate through the design, and then create a video for the presentation purpose.

1. Open the Tutorial 14 file.
2. Click the **DisplayManager** tab, and then click **View Scene, Lights, and Cameras**.
3. Right click on **Walk-through** folder and select **Add Walk-through**. The PropertyManager appears.

Now, select a plane to define the vertical direction.

4. Make sure that the Top plane is selected. The vertical direction is defined normal to the selected plane/face.
5. Under the **Viewport Settings** section, set the **Viewing height** to 900. The viewing height is offset from the Top plane.
6. Expand the **Motion Constraints** section and select the spline, as shown. The motion path is defined.

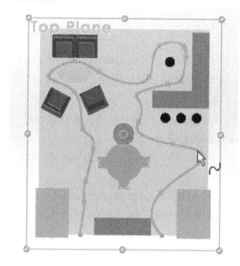

7. Make sure that the **Turn avatar to follow paths** option is checked.
8. Click the **Start Walk-through** button on the PropertyManager.
9. Notice the **Walk-through Quick Start Instructions** and click **OK**.
10. Click the **Show/Hide Map** icon on the Panel. The **Map View** window appears showing the position of the avatar.
11. Click the **Toggle Constraints** icon on the Panel.
12. Select the spline sketch from the **Lock to Constraint** drop-down on the Panel. The avatar is locked to the path.
13. Click the **Set Home** on the left side of the Panel. The start point of the path is set as home.

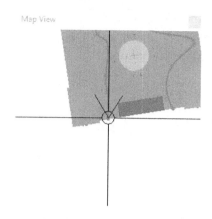

14. Press and hold the **Move Forward** arrow on the Panel. The avatar moves forward along the path. You can increase or decrease the avatar speed using the Rabbit and Turtle icons.

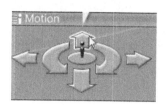

15. Click the **Go Home** icon after reaching the endpoint of the path. The avatar is positioned at the start point.
16. Click the **Toggle Record** icon on the Panel. The **Record** section appears.
17. Click the **Record** icon in the **Record** section and navigate through the model.
18. Click **OK** on the Panel after reaching the end of the path.
19. On the PropertyManager, click **Play Recording** icon.
20. Close the **Record** panel after the avatar reaches the path end. If the video looks good, then proceed further to generate the video.
21. On the PropertyManager, **Generate Video** icon, type-in the name, specify the file type and location.
22. Set the **Renderer** type.
23. Specify the settings in the **Image Size and Aspect Ratio** and **Frame Information** sections, and then click **Save**.

24. Specify the **Compressor** type on the **Video Compression** dialog, and then click **OK**.
25. Click **OK** on the PropertyManager.

TUTORIAL 15 (Decals)

SOLIDWORKS allows you to add images such as logos to your model by using the Decals option. Adding decals makes the rendered model look more realistic.

Adding the default Decals to the Model

1. Open the Tutorial 15 part file.
2. Click the DisplayManager tab, click the **View Decals** icon, and then click the **Open Decal Library** button. You can also click the **Appearances, Scenes, and Decals** tab on the Task pane and select the **Decals** folder.
3. Click and drag the **Recycling** decal from the Task pane onto the model.

4. Click and drag the corner of the rectangle to change the size of the decal.
5. Click **OK** on the PropertyManager.

6. On the DisplayManager tab, expand the **Decals** tree, right click on **recycle**, and select **Delete**.

Creating your own Decals

1. Download the globe.jpg from the companion website.
2. On the CommandManager, click **Render Tools > Edit Decal**.
3. On the PropertyManager, click the **Browse** button.
4. Go to the location of the globe.jpg file and double-click on it.
5. On the PropertyManager, click the **Save Decal** button.
6. Click **Save** and SOLIDWORKS creates the *.p2d file.
7. On the SOLIDWORKS message, click **Yes** to add the location of the decal file to the Task Pane.
8. Click **OK**.
9. On the Task Pane, click the **Appearances, Scenes, and Decals** tab and expand the **Decals** folder. Notice the new folder added to the **Decals** folder.
10. Click on the new folder and notice the Decal in the lower portion of the Task Pane.
11. Select the globe decal from the Task Pane.
12. Drag the globe decal from the Task Pane and place it on the outer surface of the model.

13. Click the **Mapping** tab on the PropertyManager. The options available on this tab are similar to that available on the **Mapping** tab of the texture PropertyManager.
14. Set the **Mapping** type to **Label**.
15. In the **Size/Orientation** section, change the **Rotation** value to **90** degrees.
16. Set the **Width** value to 50.
17. Use the Horizontal Location and Vertical Location draggers to position the decal properly.

18. Click the **Illumination** tab and check the **Use underlying appearance** option.
19. Click the **Image** tab on the PropertyManager.
20. Under the **Mask Image** section, select the **Selective color mask** option.
21. Click the **Pick color** icon.
22. Go to the **Decal Preview** section and select the white color from the preview image. The color is displayed in the **Selected colors** section and removed from the decal. You can remove it from the **Selected colors** section by selecting and clicking the **Remove color** button.

23. Click **OK** on the PropertyManager.

Made in the USA
Las Vegas, NV
22 April 2021